ROUTLEDGE LIBRARY EDITIONS: 17TH CENTURY PHILOSOPHY

Volume 7

IDEAS OF CONTRACT IN ENGLISH POLITICAL THOUGHT IN THE AGE OF JOHN LOCKE

IDEAS OF CONTRACT IN ENGLISH POLITICAL THOUGHT IN THE AGE OF JOHN LOCKE

MARTYN P. THOMPSON

LONDON AND NEW YORK

First published in 1987 by Garland

This edition first published in 2020
by Routledge
2 Park Square, Milton Park, Abingdon, Oxon OX14 4RN

and by Routledge
52 Vanderbilt Avenue, New York, NY 10017

Routledge is an imprint of the Taylor & Francis Group, an informa business

© 1987 Martyn P. Thompson

All rights reserved. No part of this book may be reprinted or reproduced or utilised in any form or by any electronic, mechanical, or other means, now known or hereafter invented, including photocopying and recording, or in any information storage or retrieval system, without permission in writing from the publishers.

Trademark notice: Product or corporate names may be trademarks or registered trademarks, and are used only for identification and explanation without intent to infringe.

British Library Cataloguing in Publication Data
A catalogue record for this book is available from the British Library

ISBN: 978-0-367-27875-5 (Set)
ISBN: 978-0-429-29844-8 (Set) (ebk)
ISBN: 978-0-367-27925-7 (Volume 7) (hbk)
ISBN: 978-0-367-33108-5 (Volume 7) (pbk)
ISBN: 978-0-429-29877-6 (Volume 7) (ebk)

Publisher's Note
The publisher has gone to great lengths to ensure the quality of this reprint but points out that some imperfections in the original copies may be apparent.

Disclaimer
The publisher has made every effort to trace copyright holders and would welcome correspondence from those they have been unable to trace.

IDEAS OF CONTRACT IN ENGLISH POLITICAL THOUGHT IN THE AGE OF JOHN LOCKE

Martyn P. Thompson

Garland Publishing, Inc., New York & London
1987

Copyright © 1987 by Martyn P. Thompson
All rights reserved

Library of Congress Cataloging-in-Publication Data
Thompson, Martyn P.
Ideas of contract in English political thought in
the age of John Locke.

(Political theory and political philosophy)
Includes index.
1. Social contract—History. 2. Political science—
Great Britian—History. I. Title. II. Series.
JC336.T48   1987   320.1'01   86-26982
ISBN 0-8240-0830-8

All volumes in this series are printed
on acid-free, 250-year-life paper.

Printed in the United States of America

IDEAS OF CONTRACT IN ENGLISH POLITICAL THOUGHT IN THE

AGE OF JOHN LOCKE

MARTYN P. THOMPSON

Privatdozent, Englisches Seminar
University of Tübingen

CONTENTS

	Preface	page
	Part I	
1	Introduction	7
2	Appeals to Contract in the Controversies over the Revolution	18
	Part II	
3	Constitutional Contract	48
4	William Atwood	75
5	Robert Ferguson	104
	Part III	
6	Philosophical Contract	126
7	John Locke	150
	Part IV	
8	Integrated Contract	185
9	Algernon Sidney	197
10	James Tyrrell	226
	Part V	
11	Conclusion	254
	Notes	263
	Index	314

PREFACE

This book took shape over a decade ago and its author would like to think that he has grown wiser in the intervening years. Had it been written yesterday, it would, no doubt, have looked somewhat different. Both the subject discussed and the period covered have attracted considerable attention from some of the most sensitive and learned historians that the English-speaking world has ever produced and that attention continues to grow. It is especially gratifying that much of this subsequent research has tended to support rather than to undermine the suggestions for historical revision that are made here. I have, nevertheless, taken the opportunity to rewrite a number of passages where I believed the originals were utterly inadequate. And I have indicated in the footnotes where scholars working in the field have disagreed with my views and where, often quite independently, their research has tended to lend support. But the book remains in all essentials as it originally was.

I have suggested that both our standard histories of social contract theory and the particular histories of English political thought during the late seventeenth and early eighteenth centuries have misrepresented the meaning of the term contract as a key term in political argument. My reading of the primary sources reveals that there was no such thing as **the** social contract theory to which various writers made more or less adequate appeal. Still less was there a social contract theory which was held in ideological monopoly by one side in the political and constitutional controversies of the late seventeenth and early eighteenth centuries. Reading the political literature of Restoration and Revolutionary England in search of what the term contract denoted to writers and readers reveals a near hopeless variety. But reading that same literature in search of the connotations of the term and the coherence of arguments invoking an idea of contract reveals a clear, distinctive and significant division of contractarian argument. I have attempted to show that there were in fact three different types of contract theory, three different patterns of contractualist argument, during the period in question. And my own research subsequent to this book leads me to believe that those patterns are evident in early modern European political thought generally. My conclusions, then, extend well beyond the narrow temporal and geographical confines of Britain at the turn of the eighteenth century. I have called the three patterns "constitutional," "philosophical," and "integrated" contractarianisms. In the following pages, I attempt to portray the characteristics of each, their distinctiveness and interrelationships, and in doing so I endeavour to provide a more adequate understanding of what contract meant in political debate during the age of Locke than anything else so far available.

My debts have been considerable. The example and encouragement of Professors Michael Oakeshott, Elie Kedourie and Maurice Cranston have been invaluable to me, much more so than they could possibly know. For many useful criticisms, I am very grateful to Professor M.M. Goldsmith. It would take far too long to list the many other contemporary scholars whose work has greatly influenced my own. Several have turned, in the intervening years since this book was written, from being distinguished names only to being distinguished names, who are also friends and colleagues. I hope my acknowledgements in the text and footnotes are not too insufficient a testimony here. One debt stands out above all others. Without the encouragement, detailed criticism, incisive comments, kindness, example and friendship of Professor K.R. Minogue, this work could never have been produced.

Finally, I should also like to thank Frau Ursula Schröter who has endured without complaint my tiresome rewrites and produced with great speed and accuracy the final copy of my manuscript. The book is dedicated to Penny and Daniel.

PART ONE

CHAPTER 1

INTRODUCTION

My concern in the following work is to analyse what Englishmen understood by the term contract in political discussions during the late seventeenth and early eighteenth centuries. The period I have chosen to consider is fairly short in terms of our standard histories of social contract theory but it is crucial. Gough referred to the seventeenth and eighteenth centuries as the "heyday" of contract theory and what I term the age of Locke - the period roughly between the death of Hobbes in 1679 and the first decade or so of the eighteenth century - is itself central to that period. Concentration upon this relatively narrow but crucial age in the history of appeals to contract in political argument allows a much more detailed consideration of the contemporary meanings of contract than can easily be accommodated in a general survey. It encourages a consideration of contract as a political term appearing in the whole spectrum of works ranging from the philosophical treatise to the sermon, tract and polemical pamphlet. It enables us, in short, to gain an appreciation of how the literate public of the age understood references to contract in political debate. And since it was this public which the writers of the Great Texts of seventeenth century contract theory (like Hobbes, Pufendorf and Locke) were intending to address, a consideration of how their audiences understood references to the term provides important evidence for understanding the texts themselves.[1] Thus my detailed concern with English political thought during the late seventeenth and early eighteenth centuries will not only provide evidence for

INTRODUCTION

reconsidering conventional accounts of the relationships between political ideas, groups and practices of the period, but it will also provide evidence for re-examining the general history of modern European contract theory.

Indeed, one of the principal beliefs behind the current work is that our standard histories of European contractarian thought have been distorted by the assumptions and organizing ideas of the established classics in the field. These ideas and assumptions are all to be found in J.W. Gough's **The Social Contract**, the work which has dominated this area of scholarship in the English-speaking world since its publication in 1936. According to Gough, there is only one fully-fledged contract theory and this theory has appeared in a number of more or less incomplete forms throughout history. The theory acquired its distinctiveness from the self-conscious application of a legal analogy to the understanding of social and political affairs. In its fullest development, the theory contains two contracts or, at least, two stages of contracting. The first contract, the contract of society, appears as the agreement of previously independent individuals to constitute themselves into a society; the second contract, the contract of government, is the subsequent agreement of those individuals to form a government to rule their society, to choose governors and to define the extent and ends of political power. The purposes of the theory, still according to Gough, are first, to provide an historical account of the origins of government, the state or society, and secondly, to provide an account of the nature and limits of political obligation. Possessed of these ideas, Gough proceeded to depict the history of post-medieval contract theory as a development from concerns almost exclusively with the contract of government, to concerns with the fully developed theory of a contract of society and a contract of government (during the "heyday" of the seventeenth and eighteenth centuries), to eventually (in the Europe of Rousseau and beyond) an almost exclusive concern with the contract of society.[2]

INTRODUCTION

For all the occasional, major disagreements in our standard accounts of the history of contract theory, they share an unquestioned adherence to the basic assumptions and organizing ideas which are so transparent in Gough's work. Thus from Gierke, Ritchie and Atger to Barker and Patrick Riley, the prevailing assumption seems to be that it is appropriate to discuss a model contract theory. The model is generally taken to comprise the two component parts of a social and a governmental contract. The parts are supposed to be logically connected rather than contingently related and the theory itself is supposed to be essentially individualistic and liberal, designed to establish limited government with individual rights of resistance.[3] The historian's central task, on this view, is to trace the emergence of the first, proper articulation of the model, to outline its fate until its eventual demise, and to assess individual thinkers and pieces of contractarian writing in terms of the "juristic sharpness" or otherwise with which the model was given expression. As Professor J.G.A. Pocock and Quentin Skinner have recently insisted, however, there is something thoroughly unsatisfactory from an historical point of view in organizing historical research around the supposed careers of model theories, ideologies or unit-ideas.[4] The main problem requires brief restatement. Implicit within it is a defence of an alternative approach to historical evidence, an approach which has been adopted in the present study.

The attractiveness of models for students of intellectual history is clear. Common sense would seem to require that we must first possess a model of the basic elements of a theory, ideology, or complex idea before we can set about writing its history. Hence the very decision to write such a history appears to presuppose models as organizing ideas. But for all the gains in simplicity and clarity that might possibly result from interpreting evidence in terms of models, the cost is enormous. For such models lead to a loss of sensitivity to context and to the particular and specific. The historian's attention is directed away from the historically specific (what particular writers were endea-

INTRODUCTION

vouring to do; what questions they were asking themselves; what evidence they appealed to in the course of their enquiries and arguments; what specific ideas they associated with the vocabulary central to the supposed model) and toward the predeterminated and prestructured patterns of thought which are contained in the model. Models, in short, interpose a highly structured set of expectations between the historian and his evidence, expectations which may bear little or no relationship to the intended meanings and actual patterns of thought contained in the historical evidence itself. They are a recipe for historical misunderstanding.[5]

As an alternative approach, appropriate for the recovery of historical meanings, Pocock and Skinner have suggested concentration upon past languages or vocabularies. A history of contract construed according to this suggestion will be based on those political writings whose central contentions were made by recourse to the term contract or one of its synonyms. The decision to adopt contract terminology and the uses made of it will be explained by the purposes of the user. But what actually happened in particular instances when contractual language was employed, what questions were being asked, and how contract was used to answer them must in each case be recovered by historical enquiry alone. The organizing idea of a language of contract has the virtue of not prejudging the issue. Patterns of argument and strategies of usages will emerge. A language is, after all, a common property. But the patterns will change as the language changes and usages once found persuasive will cease to be so. New patterns will emerge and so on. Yet the historical actors will remain individuals writing and speaking, not theories or ideas growing, developing, or whatever, according to the laws of some supposed inner logic. They will be patterns which emerge from historical enquiry rather than patterns imposed on historical evidence.[6] This is the approach which I have pursued. Distinctive patterns of contractualist argument and thought emerge and none of them bear much relationship to the model theory used as an organizing idea by Gough and the rest.

INTRODUCTION

My concern, then, is with the deployment of contractualist vocabulary in political argument rather than the fortunes and misfortunes of an historically fictitious entity called **the** social contract. The patterns of thought and argumentative strategy which emerge will provide a new basis for rewriting the history of contractualist theories (in the plural) in the modern world. But my concern is not solely with patterns of contractualist argument. The detailed study of the use of contractualist vocabulary will also provide grounds for reworking conventional, historical generalizations about the relationships between political argument and politically significant groups in late seventeenth and early eighteenth century England. Just as Gough's work provides a brilliantly clear example of those assumptions and organizing ideas which have led to the largely false and historically insensitive accounts of contractualism contained in our standard histories, so it rehearses the equally false generalizations about English political thought in the age of Locke which are still to be found in many modern text-books.[7] Gough's chapter devoted to "Locke and the English Revolution" is crucial here.

During the Revolution period, Gough writes, English political thought "was divided between two main schools - the Anglican Royalists who believed in the divine hereditary right of kingship, and their Whig opponents, who maintained the cause of popular rights and a limited monarchy." The contract of government was a "cardinal principle for the Whigs."[8] An equally common remark appears later in Gough's chapter. Locke, he asserts, "summed up, and published in an easy, readable style, the accepted commonplaces of the political thought of his generation."[9] For all the important new work by Dunn, Kenyon, Franklin and Pocock, this last point is still widely available in the secondary literature. The common assertions, for example, that Locke's **Second Treatise** contains an admirable summing up of the principles of law which triumphed at the Revolution,[10] and that "Locke's general theory of government had its counterpart in most exclusion pamphlets,"[11] both imply that Locke's work was representative for his time. But these

INTRODUCTION

views, as I shall argue, are wrong. They arise largely from inadequate attention being paid to the variety of arguments employing contract terminology and the particularities of English political theory during the late seventeenth and early eighteenth centuries.

As might perfectly well be expected, the political literature of late seventeenth century England contains an enormous number of references to contracts. But even a fairly superficial acquaintance with such references gives rise to the suspicion that the meaning of the term was by no means always the same. One of the most famous appeals to contract, for example, was contained in the Convention Parliament's resolution attempting to clarify the legal state of the nation after James II's fall. On 7 February 1688-89, the Convention accepted the resolution that:

> King James the Second, having endeavoured to subvert the Constitution of the Kingdom, by breaking the original Contract between King and People, and by the Advice of Jesuits and other wicked Persons, having violated the fundamental Laws, and having withdrawn Himself out of this Kingdom, has abdicated the Government; and that the Throne is thereby vacant.[12]

The contract referred to here, as Gough and others have remarked, was certainly not the same as that which appeared in the other most famous source of late seventeenth century English contractarianism: Locke's **Second Treatise** (1690). The Convention Parliament, that is to say, was not referring to "an agreement between individuals to form a civil society and 'submit to the determination of the majority'."[13]

A closer inspection of the political pamphlets, tracts and treatises that were published between 1679 and 1714 can only reinforce the suspicion that conventional accounts of the history of appeals to contract have not done justice to all the evidence. The order which has come to be imposed on references to contract evaporates as we encounter more and more different

INTRODUCTION

meanings of the term, different synonyms used for it, and different occasions upon which it was invoked. All sorts of writers - philosophers, lawyers, politicians, historians, divines, journalists and propagandists - refer to contracts in their political writings. But they only rarely appear either aware or concerned that they are employing a traditional political concept. They were mainly concerned to advance a specific cause, or to defend the activities of a particular group, or to offer an explanation of some particular problem or event. The fact that arguments from contract were arguments drawing upon a legal analogy was generally not their concern. The word contract frequently appeared in their works as a synonym for, or in conjunction with, other legal notions like trust, stipulation, capitulation, covenant, compact, and even coronation oath and law itself.[14] But equally often, when occasion appeared to suit, writers left the realm of law and legal analogy and considered the term much more loosely as a synonym for promises, bargains, compromises, barriers, or agreements.[15] Thus the use of the term contract is by no means evidence that a legal analogy was actually being employed.

The wide range of synonyms for contract is also evidence of the absence of any single, precise meaning of the word in the political literature of the period. And this impression is reinforced when we find not only very loose usages of the term but also many specifically different types of contract being spoken about and discussed. As we turn the pages of the sermons, speeches, pamphlets, tracts and treatises, we encounter not only government contracts and social contracts, but also "fundamental contracts," "constitutional contracts," "political contracts," "original contracts," "mutual contracts," "express Original and continuing" contracts, "implicit contracts," and even a "Popular Contract and rectoral Contract."[16]

Equally surprising, against the background of Gough's assumptions and generalizations, is the fact that there was no obvious correspondence between advancing contractualist arguments and upholding "the rights of the individual" or even being concerned "with

13

INTRODUCTION

consent as the basis of government, and with democratic, republican, or constitutional institutions."[17] Nor, in the period after 1688, was there any simple association between appealing to notions of contract and defending the William and Mary regime. Thus even so entrenched an idea as that English political opinion at the time of the 1688 Revolution was divided between two main schools of Royalist divine righters and Whig contractarians must be thoroughly reconsidered. For even some Jacobite pamphleteers, like Jeremy Collier, Charlwood Lawton and Robert Ferguson, were prepared to argue at least part of their case by reference to a contract embodied in the past or present English constitution. These Jacobite arguments, like their occasional Tory counterparts, cannot be accounted for in terms of a Hobbesian tradition of contractarian thought. For not only were these royalists concerned with different questions from those which engaged Hobbes' attention (theirs were arguments about the requirements of English constitutional law, rather than about the nature and necessity of civil society), but also, as Gough and Laslett have noted, there is not much evidence of any tradition of Hobbesian disciples or a sense of a valuable Hobbesian contribution to political speculation amongst practical political writers of the late seventeenth and early eighteenth centuries.[18] Certainly, **de facto** arguments similar to those employed earlier in the century in the Civil War Engagement Controversy are to be encountered. Frequently, such arguments were branded as "Hobbist." But they were not exclusive to Hobbes and their proponents never invoked Hobbes' name as an authority. The point seems rather that their opponents dismissed them as "Hobbist" and in doing so they revealed how disreputable Hobbes' name was currently felt to be.[19]

Jacobite and Tory appeals to contract in fact turn out to be frequently of a very similar kind to many Whig arguments. Indeed, in the writings of one of the most colourful characters of the period, Robert Ferguson "the Plotter," we find two very popular pamphlets, both apparently written in good faith, both employing arguments based on the idea that the English constitution embodied a contract between ruler and ruled, but one was a Whig

INTRODUCTION

tract written in defence of William of Orange and the other was a Jacobite tract written in defence of the deposed James II. The arguments were of exactly the same form. But the conclusions drawn were diametrically opposed.[20]

The numerous, varied, and confusing references to contracts that I have just noted serve to underline the doubts about the adequacy of any approach to the evidence through the medium of a preconceived model of what contract theory really is. Such models lead to excessive simplification and the neglect of intended meanings in favour of merely putative ones. But the variety which I have sketched by no means implies the opposite extreme. It does not invite the conclusion that contract was used merely randomly or that its usage was arbitrary and idiosyncratic. The term was far too prominant, far too significant, in the political literature of the age for that. When Englishmen talked or wrote about a contract they were addressing themselves to publics accustomed to hearing the term, with a view to persuading them of something. Those publics were familiar with at least some understandings of the word contract and it is these public understandings (which in the nature of the case must be relatively stable for otherwise public debate could not take place) that I shall outline and examine. A writer may very well misuse a term, or endeavour to modify an audience's understanding of it, but this can only be determined by considering specific, particular statements and usages in relation to the general uses and ideas evoked by the term.

We shall, then, misunderstand ideas of contract in political debate if we approach them in the belief that they represent employments of something called **the** theory of contract. We must admit a plurality of understandings, understandings expressed in a variety of particular usages of contractualist terminology at any given time. The recovery of those understandings must begin with the identification of the range of usages of the term contract in the political literature of the period in question. Tracing the appearance of the word soon reveals other key-terms in the contractualist

15

INTRODUCTION

vocabulary. The search after the meanings of these terms attains a structure from the conversations, arguments and enquiries that those who chose to employ contractualist vocabulary engaged in: the questions they asked; the evidence they appealed to; the opponents they were concerned to refute; and the arguments and practices which they proposed to further by reference to contract and related terms.

The period with which I am concerned was politically violent and unstable. It opened with the Popish Plot and Exclusion Crisis in the late 1670s - with political assassination and near civil war. It witnessed Monmouth's abortive rebellion (1685), the successful revolution of 1688, numerous treason trials, assassination attempts against all reigning monarchs and similar attempts against the lives of leading politicians and publicists. War was the keynote after the Revolution and the country was thrown into periodic panic at the threat of foreign invasions in 1691, 1696 and 1708. The age closed with the threat of renewed civil war and the actual Jacobite uprising in 1715.[21] The literature which both served and reflected upon this unstable political life was full of references to contracts. But the initial bewildering variety of particular appeals to contract and occasions upon which those appeals were made break down into a number of simple patterns, patterns which remained remarkably stable throughout the whole period. These patterns which emerge from the evidence of particular usages of contractualist vocabulary in changing political circumstances provide my study with its basic framework.

In Chapter 2, I shall examine the use of contractualist vocabulary within the context of the most significant of all the constitutional controversies in the age of Locke, the controversies which raged from 1688 to 1693. The three basic patterns of contractualist argument that emerge, patterns based on a dichotomy between historical and legal argument on the one hand and philosophical argument on the other, will occupy my attention in the rest of the work. Each pattern will be treated in a similar way: a general chapter discussing

INTRODUCTION

the character and theoretical assumptions associated with the pattern in question will be followed by detailed studies of writers whose major, contractualist writings appear to exemplify most clearly the uses to which the pattern was put. In identifying three such patterns and in endeavouring to exemplify how individual writers can best be interpreted as writing in terms of one or other of them, my concern will be to chip away constantly at the presuppositions and pre-judgments that have so far dominated studies of social contract theory in the history of political thought. In this sense, my study claims to be no more (and no less) than the result of working as an historical "underlabourer in clearing the ground a little" for a more adequate understanding of ideas of contract in the history of political thought.[22]

CHAPTER 2

APPEALS TO CONTRACTS IN THE CONTROVERSIES
OVER THE 1688 REVOLUTION

The dramatic events from James II's second Declaration of Indulgence (7 May 1688) to his eventual flight into France (22 December 1688) produced a deep crisis in the English political conscience. The myths of glory and peacefulness that became associated with the 1688 Revolution were not so apparent to the majority of Englishmen who were neither ardent Williamites nor endowed with the hindsight and critical apparatus of the "Whig interpreters of history."[1] It may be, as some historians have argued, that the Revolution secured the victory of parliamentary government over royal absolutism, that it presaged an era of increasing moral respectability and political stability, even that liberty had at length triumphed over authority and was paving the way for enlightenment.[2] But for most Englishmen educated into the Church of England's doctrines of passive obedience and non-resistance, and living amidst rumours of Irish massacres and French invasions, the Revolution meant none of these things. Doubt, confusion, conflict and guilt were here the most common reactions to James II's flight.

In recent decades, historians have come to recognise the wide disparity between Whiggish glorifications of the Revolution and its appearance to contemporaries. This disparity is exemplified in the difference between Macaulay's picture of the Revolution and that of one of its more recent historians. For Macaulay, the Revolution "averted" the "calamities" of arbitrary and despotic government. "It was a revolution strictly defensive," he tells us, "and had prescription and legitimacy on its side."[3] But if attention is focussed on the dilemmas of contemporary Englishmen (as has recently been done by R.A. Beddard and others) the Revolution appears radically different. To the Church of England man, who, if a member of the politically relevant classes,[4] was likely to have sworn oaths of allegiance to James, "the Revolution meant breaking faith with his lawful sovereign, the violation of sacred oaths, and nothing short of a national apostacy from the doctrines of passive obedience and non-resistance, a cherished legacy that had come down from the age of the apostles. It was impossible for him to acquiesce in usurpation without doing violence to his conscience."[5] The difference between these two views of the Revolution is crucial for an understanding of the relationship between political ideas and politically important groups during the principal crisis of the period. For the Whig interpretation of the Revolution originates in the propaganda of the time and contains the bias of the most convinced anti-Jacobites. And yet this interpretation did come to dominate Englishmen's understandings of the nature of the Revolution and contributed to the wide acceptance of those largely false generalisations about the political thought of the late seventeenth century which I noted in the previous chapter.

The Whig interpretation of English political thought at the time of the Revolution has come under the scrutiny and attack of much modern scholarship. Most notably here, J.R. Western has emphasised the confusion and instability of the Revolution period; W.H. Greenleaf has clarified the rationale and coherence of divine right theories; G.L. Cherry has defended the legal and philosophical views of the Jacobites; G. Schochet has examined the coherence of patriarchalist thought; and G.M. Straka has convincingly argued that it was a transition in divine right theory from "the divine right of kings" to the "divine right of Providence" that did most to reconcile Englishmen to the Revolutionary Settlement, and not the outright victory of secular contractarianism.[6] More recently still, J.P. Kenyon as gone a considerable way towards portraying the complexity of the interrelationship between ideas, attitudes and activities at the time of the Revolution.[7]

REVOLUTION CONTROVERSIES

A glance at the mass of political literature published during the period immediately following the decline in James II's fortunes (from 1688 to 1693) reveals the extent of this complexity. We find, for example, that beliefs in the divine right of kings were by no means confined to Tory or Jacobite writings; that contract ideas were held alike by Williamites, Jacobites, Tories, Whigs, Republicans - by defenders and opponents of the Revolutionary Settlement; and that there were not only fierce debates about the justification of the series of events which constituted the 1688 Revolution, but also acrimonious disputes about what really had happened and what should as a consequence be done. In the rest of this chapter, I shall outline the complexity of the issues and ideas involved in the Revolution debates. My main concern is with the role played by appeals to contract, but this can only be appreciated by examining them within their broader context.

The majority of literate Englishmen became reconciled to James II's fall in three closely related and roughly consecutive stages.[8] The first concerned interpreting the events culminating in James' flight; the second, suggesting what should be done as a result; and the third, explaining the status of the new regime. One oath had been broken, and now another had been sworn. What was its status? I shall first sketch the main views advanced in the first two stages of the debates and then consider in more detail the arguments of the crucial third stage.

The pamphlets and books that were published in response to the Revolution, together with the records of the Convention Parliament's deliberations, allow us to piece together several different contemporary explanations of what had actually happened to cause James' withdrawal. One legal idea canvassed was that James had abdicated the government and although this was vigorously contested in the Convention it was one of the views eventually accepted by Parliament.[9] Another view was that James had deserted the government, a view less legalistic than abdication and more acceptable to those unprepared to argue that James was no longer **de jure** king.[10] A third idea suggested was that William had conquered England, forcing James to retire, although this was often qualified, because of associations between conquest and slavery, into the view that William had conquered James but not England.[11] A fourth interpretation offered was that James had been forced to leave by a successful rebellion and that therefore the Revolution was illegal and allegiance was still due to the king now in forced exile.[12] A fifth idea was that James had knowingly broken England's fundamental constitutional laws and had withdrawn, leaving the throne vacant, rather than suffer the reprimand of an outraged parliament.[13] A sixth view, in many ways the most widely accepted of all, was that King James had simply suffered the judgment of Providence for his misgovernment.[14] Further, it was also suggested that James had broken the original contract and that therefore he had either ceased to be king or been forced to leave. And finally, somewhat more simply, it was argued that these two consequences followed from James having broken his coronation oath or trust.[15]

The suggestions offered about what should be done in the absence of a **de facto** monarch were similarly varied. Some suggested the immediate unconditional recall of James,[16] others his reinstatement upon additional guarantees or limitations of the prerogative power,[17] whilst a Regency,[18] the crowning of Mary,[19] the crowning of William and Mary together,[20] or a republican remodelling of the government were further serious suggestions canvassed during the interregnum.[21]

Many of these different views of the Revolution were, of course, mutually compatible. The argument from Providence, for example, could and frequently did feature alongside practically all the other views. Similarly, although interpretations of what had happened affected judgments of what should be done in response, there was no simple relationship between them. To modern ears most of the debate sounds so rarefied that we are tempted to dismiss impatiently the seemingly small and excessively fine distinctions. But to do so is inevitably to miss the point of the debates and therefore the significance of the Revolution for its contemporaries. For it is only from these debates that the contemporary understandings of the Revolution can be properly assessed.

The debates about the status of the William and Mary regime were similarly marked by fine and sometimes rather tortuous distinctions. C.F. Mullett has attempted to characterize these debates by noting that they bear a closer resemblance to scholastic disputes than to modern political argument. The reason for this, he explains, is that during the late seventeenth century political questions were still considered as, in essence, a branch of religious enquiry: that the content and language of political discourse were closer to medieval than to modern styles.[22] In one sense Mullett's observations are correct: the literature with which he was concerned was written, in general, by far from first-rate minds, and focussed on issues of oaths, revolution and conscience, matters in which the Church of England could fairly claim to be an important and authoritative guide. But greater and more perceptive minds were engaged by problems far removed from those of medieval political life. Religious ideals and life were undergoing considerable modification under the impact of enquiries inspired by rationalist, scientific and empiricist thought.[23] This modification had affected the practical political debates of the late seventeenth century. Arguments from scripture were no longer sufficient to resolve disputes, if indeed they ever had been, and accepted doctrines of the Church were scrutinised and changed in order to appear 'rational.' The apparent conservatism of political arguments, the constant appeal to scripture and the concern with Church dogma that almost all of the pamphlets portray, should not be accepted unquestioningly as evidence of medieval style. The fact that it was only in sermons that exclusively religious arguments were used in reference to political affairs, and that most printed polemics appealed to the separate tenets of reason, religion, history and law, is indicative of this change. Religion appears as a vital authority, but as one amongst others and itself open to interpretation and change.[24]

The new oaths of allegiance imposed a positive, sacred and public act of approbation upon the literate public, and thus a coherent and persuasive justification of the Revolution became of considerable practical importance. The oaths of allegiance to James had been broken and although James' unpopular actions had alienated practically all sections of opinion from him (including the established Church), still most Englishmen recognised a deep gulf between their interest in getting rid of James and their duty to continue obeying him because of their oaths. This conflict between interest and conscience became a dominant theme of the debates during the third stage of the Revolution controversies.

The defenders of the Revolution were concerned to portray the new regime as the necessary and, more important, the lawful successor to James' government. If these could be proved, particularly the second, then the new oaths of allegiance could be taken with a clear conscience and the stability of the new regime would be the greater. Arguments from necessity seemed to carry the least conviction. Despite James' unpopularity and the fears he had created about the immediate prospects of popery and arbitrary power, it does not seem to have been felt satisfactory simply to argue that resistance had been necessary to safeguard the supposed constitutional liberties of the citizens. For this avoided the three principal problems which made the debate of such intense and important practical concern: the problems of moral right, legal right and the stability of government.

At least since the Reformation, it was claimed, the Church of England had officially preached the doctrine of passive obedience and non-resistance; a doctrine which taught, as Abednego Seller reminded Englishmen in 1689, "That it is the duty of every Christian, in things lawful, **actively** to obey his Superior; in things unlawful, to **suffer** rather than obey, and in any case, or upon any pretence whatsoever not to resist, because, whoever does so, **shall receive to themselves Damnation.**"[25] The established Church, then, adjudged resistance to be morally wrong and the problems of the moral status of the new regime were made all the more intractable to those who had taken oaths of allegiance to James II. But to the problem of moral right was added that of the positive law. Statute laws, for example the Corporation Act of 1661 and the Militia Acts of 1661 and 1662, undoubtedly part of the continuing law of the land, declared that "it is not lawful upon any pretence whatsoever to take arms against the King ... or against those that are commissioned by him."[26] Any comprehensive defence of the Revolution, then, needed to take account of these unequivocal statute laws which declared the enterprise illegal. Attempts to overcome the legal difficulties, however, would have to avoid a further problem. This was, given the widespread belief, as one writer quoting Hooker put it, that "the Law is the very soul that animates the Body Politick,"[27] that arguments overriding one law did not threaten "to loosen the Bond of due Subjection" and thus threaten the stability of any regime.[28]

The arguments, then, in defence of the Revolution from the position that "Necessity in exceptional circumstances overruled Human Laws"[29] were seen as inadequate when confronted with the problems of moral right, legal right and the stability of government. As one defender of the Revolution remarked, necessity might explain and in certain circumstances excuse action, but it did not justify it.[30] Arguments from necessity in fact play only a very minor role in the disputes over the Revolution and their shortcomings help explain why most of the defenders of the new regime attempted far more ambitious arguments. The Revolution, it was more often claimed, was certainly necessary, but much more importantly, it was lawful.

Justifications of the lawfulness of the new regime took many different forms. Not only were there a number of different activities to be proven lawful - armed resistance, transferring allegiance from a living monarch, calling a Convention, breaking or modifying the hereditary succession, by-passing statute laws - but there were also a number of different standards of law to which appeal could be made - divine law, natural law, the law of nations and positive law. Appeals to the higher laws of nature and God were the easier to uphold because they involved more general matters than the intricate and specific positive law. But just because they were more general, they were more easily open to dispute. Arguments from divine law and the will of God were, of course, some of the principal means whereby the legitimacy of the Revolution was defended. The well-known controversy which followed William Sherlock's decision to take the new oaths of allegiance highlights the strengths and weaknesses involved in arguments from Providence.[31]

Sherlock initially refused to take the oaths not because he wanted James II's return, nor because he distrusted William and Mary, but simply, so he claimed, "out of pure Principles of Conscience."[32] Allegiance had been sworn to James and was therefore due to him for as long as he remained king. And no action which disregarded the Church's doctrine of passive obedience could ever rightfully dismiss a king. On these grounds Sherlock had refused the oaths and was prepared, along with the rest of the non-juring clergy, to be deprived of his benefices.

But Sherlock recanted on the eve of losing his livelihood, took the oaths and was promoted to the deanery of St. Paul's. He justified this change by referring to a doctrine in Bishop Overall's **Convocation Book** of 1606. This strongly royalist book had been republished in the early 1680s as part of James II's defence. But in one passage relating to the **de facto** authority of the revolutionary government of the United Provinces, Sherlock claimed to have found a Church authority to justify swearing allegiance to William and Mary.[33] In his **The Case of Allegiance Due to Sovereign Powers** (1691), Sherlock argued that the controversies over the rightfulness of the new oaths had become hopelessly confused. Many writers, he noted, had been arguing that legal rights were the only grounds for paying obedience, and thus it had become necessary to justify the Revolution on positive law grounds. "But ... to judge truly of this," he claimed, "requires such perfect skills in Law and History, and the Constitution of the **English** Government, that few men are capable of making so plain and certain a judgement of it, as to be a clear and safe Rule of Conscience."[34] Claiming Overall's **Convocation Book** as authority, Sherlock declared that the dispute over positive law right was unnecessary. The Divine Will was the surest guide and the strongest bind of conscience. Allegiance was due, he asserted, "to those Princes whom God hath placed and settled in the Throne, whatever Disputes there may be about their legal Right."[35] Precisely this the **Convocation Book** had affirmed through the following two propositions:

> 1. That those Princes, who have no legal right to their Thrones, may yet have God's Authority.
> 2. That when they are thoroughly settled in their Thrones, they are invested with God's Authority, and must be reverenced and obeyed by all.[36]

The only question, then, in reference to 1688 should be whether the new regime were thoroughly settled, and, if it were, allegiance ought to be sworn to it. Sherlock insisted that the "distinction between a King **de jure**, and a King **de facto**, relates only to Human Laws, which bind Subjects, but are not the necessary Rules and Measures of the Divine Providence."[37] His argument was simply that it did not matter whether William and Mary could be shown to have a legal right to the English throne, it was sufficient that they enjoyed a quiet possession. A rightful monarch, that is to say, need only be **de facto** and sufficiently secure in his position to be able plausibly to maintain that he had God's blessing.

Sherlock's arguments provoked a vast number of replies. Many of these were purely personal, accusing him of succumbing to his wife's materialism and so on. But of those which considered his views seriously, exception was taken by both defenders and opponents of the Revolutionary Settlement. Jeremy Collier, from the more extreme wing of the non-juring clergy, criticised Sherlock for asserting that "Legal Right must always give place to Unjust Power."[38] Since the English constitution was clearly monarchical and not republican, he insisted, then James, or at the very last his new-born son, should be king. Sherlock was in fact nothing less than a "**Hobbist**" in arguing as he had.[39]

The concern shown by Collier for legal rights was apparent in most of the other critics of Sherlock and the derogatory label of "Hobbist" was freely used.[40] Samuel Johnson, for example, accused Sherlock of setting up "Two Kings, one of **Right**, the other **by Providence**,"[41] and of implying that the new regime was "an unjust Usurpation, and the Revolution illegal."[42] And Robert Jenkin reaffirmed the need for justifications from positive law when he declared, against Sherlock, that "the Laws of that Constitution of Government under which we live, ... are to determine when the Authority of Sovereigns ceases, and the Allegiance of Subjects; and we are not to think their Power and Authority transferred, unless it be transferred legally."[43]

Sherlock's arguments from the divine right of Providence, then, met with considerable opposition. There was a widespread desire to go further and to support or oppose William and Mary according to their titles as **de jure** monarchs. Nonetheless, the sort of defence that Sherlock presented for taking the new oaths was of considerable importance. By arguing that it was God's hand that had expelled James and established William and Mary in his stead, Sherlock provided one way in which Englishmen's consciences could be reconciled to the Revolution. Indeed, as G.M. Straka has argued, it was precisely this transition in Anglican political theory (of which Sherlock's ideas represent the finished product) from the "Stuart concept of divine hereditary right" to the post-Revolution theory of "the divine right of providence" that in fact persuaded most Englishmen to accept the new regime.[44] And it certainly is the case that arguments from Providence formed a crucial part of the juring Church's self-justification. Bishops Tillotson, Tenison, Burnet, Sharp and Lloyd of St. Asaph all made considerable use of such arguments. Laymen, too, like William Atwood, Samuel Johnson, Sir George Eyres and even Edmund Bohun (who was Filmer's editor in 1685) attempted to persuade their readers that the Revolution was a "miracle" of Providence.[45] William, it was claimed, was a king by divine right as surely as any English king before him - he was king by the divine right of Providence and therefore, as Samuel Johnson claimed, "the Rightfullest King that ever sat upon the English Throne."[46]

Thus when Sherlock asserted that William and Mary were monarchs by divine right he was arguing a very widely accepted point. It was rather his insistence that to be rightful monarchs they need only be **de facto** which created most antagonism. Defenders of the new regime affirmed that the new monarchs were **de jure**, whilst opponents insisted that allegiance should be paid to James, the king **de jure** who was now in forced exile. Sherlock, as it happens, was frequently misrepresented, since he never denied that William and Mary were **de jure** monarchs. His point was rather that this was irrelevant to the question of obligation. But in the furore of polemical dispute misrepresentation is far from unusual.

As an argument to uphold a **de facto** prince's right to the allegiance of his subjects, however, Sherlock's writings were open to an obvious line of criticism. If it were possible to dispute whether God actually directed the outcome of the Revolution, then Sherlock's divine right could be made to appear little more than a justification of successful force. Without direct evidence of God's participation in the Revolution, Sherlock's sort of arguments might equally well be used to justify Cromwell while he had been successful. And even the most determined Williamites and anti-Jacobites ardently denied any parallel between the Civil War and the Revolution. The anonymous author of **Providence and Precept: Or, The Case of Doing Evil that Good may come of it** (1691) made precisely these criticisms of Sherlock. By resting his defence of William solely on an unproven intervention by God, Sherlock had reduced William's right to 'success.' And, in that case, the author continued, "if Strength and Force be the only determination of Right and Wrong, Religion and Laws will quickly become useless."[47]

When interpreted in this way, Sherlock's arguments appeared little different from another very popular, but short-lived, justification of the lawfulness of the Revolution. This was the idea that the new regime had been established by a just conquest in a just war. Charles Blount, the author of **King William and Queen Mary Conquerors** (1693), produced one of the most forthright statements of the conquest case. It has been argued that Blount wrote the work as an elaborate practical joke but there is very little evidence to support this.[48] Blount himself claimed that he wrote the work because he found "that several, who are not yet satisfied with any thing that hath been hitherto offered, do declare, That if it could be made appear that their present Majesties have on their side all the Right of Conquest, they would entirely submit to the Government, and take the Oath."[49]

Conquest arguments justifying 1688, however, enjoyed only a short-lived acceptability. In late January 1693, Parliament ordered that **King William and Queen Mary Conquerors** and Bishop Gilbert Burnet's **Pastoral Letter** (1689) should be burned publicly by the common hangman. A pamphlet by William Lloyd, Bishop of St. Asaph, would probably also have joined them had not the managers of the case misread the relevant passage.[50] The error of all three books, it was argued, lay in asserting that William and Mary were king and queen by right of conquest over James. The books deserved their fate, according to parliament, because such an assertion "was highly injurious to their majesties' rightful title to the crown of this realm, and inconsistent with the principles on which this government is founded, and tending to the subversion of the rights of the people".[51] The Licenser of the Press, Edmund Bohun, excused his authorising publication of the works because he believed the argument to be "innocent" since "many

Treatises had been published higher on this point" and nothing had as yet been done against them. In this Bohun was undoubtedly correct.[52]

Nonetheless, it was also true that very few defenders of the new regime were prepared to justify the Revolution solely upon the grounds of conquest. The legitimacy of a conqueror seems to have been too questionable for that. Many felt, with Locke, that the consent of the governed was in some way necessary for the legitimate foundation of a government.[53] The strength of this feeling goes some way to explaining the revival of an earlier Engagement Controversy argument which to modern eyes looks like an extraordinary piece of mental gymnastics. Some of the proponents of the conquest case attempted to reconcile conquest with consent. William Sherlock, for example, in his **A Vindication of the Case of Allegiance due to Sovereign Powers** (1691), argued that since a conquest destroys the previous government it forces the ex-citizens to consent to the conqueror's regime in self-defence. And consent, he triumphantly asserted, is universally accepted as the lawful medium by which rights may be transferred.[54] Timothy Wilson, in a pamphlet entitled **God, the King, and the Countrey, United in the Justification of this Present Revolution** (1691), produced a variation of Sherlock's argument which was to have far-reaching consequences. Wilson here argued that since the purpose of government was the protection of its citizens - a common enough supposition in the seventeenth century - when a country is conquered the citizens may swear allegiance to the new government without sin or illegality because only an effective government can fulfil the role of securely protecting the lives, liberties or estates of the citizen body.[55] This sort of argument, as Quentin Skinner has suggested, provided one of the main avenues through which the idea of conquest was assimilated into Whig thought.[56]

Most defenders of the William and Mary government, however, were not prepared to rest their case on appeals to the general laws of God and Nature or on the Divine Will alone. They wanted instead to establish an even stronger legal proof of the legitimacy of the new regime. Gilbert Burnet, in one of his most popular pamphlets, stated clearly the issues involved in effecting such a proof. He argued that the problem with the Divine Will argument was that it was uncertain and tended to justify all successful usurpers. Thus, instead of referring simply to God's will as the determinant of political obligations, citizens should look to positive laws. In brief, his argument was that "the degrees of all civil authority are to be taken from express laws, immemorial customs, or from particular oaths." This view of the grounds determining political obligation was widely accepted. But as Burnet recognized, there was one "main and great difficulty" in the way of justifying the legality of 1688: the existence of such statute laws as that of 13 Charles II st, 2c which I have already quoted. Burnet's solution to the dilemma involved asserting a number of doubtful propositions about the nature of law. The propositions all derive from a widely-held view that it was not so much what a law said that mattered, but what its makers might reasonably be expected to have intended to say. The imputation of intention, however, was not a matter for lawyers. Burnet was a bishop and no trained lawyer. But on his account of law, the written word might be totally rejected by appeal to a "supposed ... tacit exception and reserve" if the consequences would otherwise be unfortunate. And yet still the law could not be said to have been broken.[58]

Burnet's argument, offering a reinterpretation of the English constitution and the rules for legal exegesis, was purely a *pièce d'occasion* - a political argument masquerading as legal orthodoxy intended to justify the extremely questionable legality of the events leading to the crowning of William and Mary. Lest his defence of the Revolution from positive law should fail, however, Burnet covered himself by asserting the "principle, that in all the disputes between power and liberty, power must always be proved, but liberty proves itself; the one being founded only upon a positive law, and the other upon the Law of Nature."[59] Thus if the legality of the Revolution could not be maintained from positive law, Burnet was declaring, it could certainly be maintained according to natural law.

The desire to defend William and Mary as **de jure** monarchs was reflected in many pamphlets adopting arguments similar to Burnet's. One writer, Samuel Johnson, emphasised the importance attached to these arguments. The Revolution Settlement, he affirmed, was "founded upon Legal Principles" and William and Mary were thus **de jure** monarchs. The consequence of denying this, as for example Sherlock had, was to maintain: "That all Kings are absolute, and have Authority from God to trample upon our Religion, Liberties, and Laws, at their sovereign Will and Pleasure;" that the Revolution was illegal and that obedience was still due to James; and that a counter-revolution was the only righful course for Englishmen.[60]

Johnson's supposedly legal arguments in defence of the Revolution were based on the assertions that the English constitution was "Hereditary as to Family, elective as to Persons;" that it was "limited, and founded in Contract: that a King, who Acts without regard to the Fundamental Contract, is not a Legal King;"[61] and that civil rights were rights at positive law and therefore any defence of them must be by reference to positive laws.[62] But, Johnson insisted, it was only **inferior** magistrates who could legally be resisted according to the law of the English constitution.[63]

A vast number of pamphlets appeared during the five years from 1688 to 1693 containing arguments upholding the legality of the Revolution. In addition to the sort of arguments of Burnet and Johnson, reference was made to a variety of **dicta** and authorities, to defend this view. For example, it was sometimes asserted that the design of the law should be the overriding consideration in interpreting particular laws. The design of the law was usually said to be either the protection of the citizens or the well-being of the community. In either case, the point was that general considerations could be used to modify radically or overrule entirely particular laws. Some pamphleteers also argued that the Convention Parliament had resolved the problem of legality and that it, as the legally competent and representative body of the nation (a hotly-disputed point), should be followed in the conclusion that William and Mary were lawfully king and queen.[64] Others again referred to Henry VII's Statute of Treasons and to Coke's judgment that English law required obedience to be sworn to a **de facto** monarch.[65] Reference was also made to the notion of the dissolution of government. James II, it was maintained, had destroyed the laws by his misconduct and the government was dissolved. Thus anything citizens might do for their own safety could be accounted lawful.[66] And finally reference was made to the legendary ancient constitution, which, it was supposed, James had subverted and William restored.[67]

Now in all of these arguments ideas of contract featured prominently. In the previous chapter I noted one of the most famous references to contract in justifying the Revolution: the notion referred to in the Convention Parliament's resolution concerning the state of the nation as a result of James II's flight. James, it was claimed, was no longer king because he had broken "the original Contract between King and People," because he had "violated the fundamental Laws," and because he had "abdicated the Government."[68] Although this appeal to contract featured as only one of three explanations of James' fall, still several writers, amongst them Peter Allix, considered that breaking the original contract was the "foundation" of the case against James.[69] Even if this were an accurate assessment of the complicated arguments that I have just outlined, the evidence still shows enormous variety in the terminology and use of contract ideas in the Revolution literature. Practically all the legal arguments for and against the Revolution were at some time or another defended by reference to a contract. Appeals were frequently made to an original contract which supposedly began the English constitution, to a contract that was supposedly **embodied within** English constitutional law, and to a contract supposedly **presupposed** in any legitimate government. But there was certainly no general agreement about the specific provisions of these contracts. Nor, indeed, was there any connection between arguing from England's original contract and supporting the 1688 Revolution. Those few records of the Convention Parliament debates which are readily available make this abundantly clear. Transferring allegiance from James II was both defended and attacked on contractualist grounds.

The Bishop of Ely and the Earl of Pembroke, one might note, were leading exponents of the contractualist case **against** William's right to the throne. Pembroke, for example, argued:

> The laws made are certainly part of the **original contract**; and by the laws made, which established the oaths of allegiance and supremacy, we are tied up to keep in the hereditary line <of succession to the throne> ... There (I take it) lies the reason why we cannot (of ourselves) without breaking that contract, break the succession, Which is settled by law, and cannot be altered but by another, which we ourselves cannot make.[70]

This contractualist argument occurred in a debate which contained much more familiar references to contract. Sir Thomas Lee, for example, upheld a popular right to alter law by appealing to the contract of government:

> But, my Lords, I would ask this question, Whether upon the **Original Contract** there were not a power preserved in the nation, to provide for its self in such exigencies?
> That contract was to settle the constitution as to the Legislature ... so we take it to be: And it is true, that it is a part of the contract, the making of laws, and that those laws should oblige all sides when made; but yet so, as not to exclude this original constitution in all governments that commence by compact, that there should be a power in the states to make provision in all times, and upon all occasions, for extraordinary cases and necessities, such as ours now is.[71]

Only one of the members of the Convention - the

REVOLUTION CONTROVERSIES

Earl of Clarendon - is recorded as rejecting the idea of an original contract altogether. He did so, he claimed, because "this breaking the original contract is a language that hath not long been used in this place; nor known in any of our law books, or publick records. It is sprung up, but as taken from some late authors, and those none of the best received."[72] But his critique of the legal status of the original contract did not prevent the acceptance of the idea by the Convention as justification for replacing James by William and Mary. Clarendon's objections failed in this respect partly because they had already been anticipated and rejected by a strong body of legal opinion.

When the Convention Lords first considered the resolution which claimed that James had broken "the original Contract between King and People" they suggested that a Committee of the whole House be instructed by "the learned counsel of the law ... of what the original contract is, and whether there be any such or not." Nine experts were called to give their views and, although the records of what they said are far from complete, it is clear that in general they were agreed that something like an original contract was at the root of English law. Sir Robert Atkyns, for example, is recorded as arguing in the following way:

> I believe none of us have it <the original contract> in our books or cases; not anything that touches on it. Thinks it must refer to the first original of government. Thinks the King never took any government, but there was an agreement between King and people. It is a limited monarchy and a body politic, and the King head of it. If there were an original contract, yet it is subject to variations as the times. Mr. Hooker says all public government is by agreement. James I, himself admits in 1609 that there is a paction between prince and people. "Every just King," he says, "in a settled kingdom is bound to obey the paction made to his people by his laws." Reads preamble to the Act concerning Peter's Pence, &c., giving rules by which the prince shall govern and

35

the people obey. This shows what the contract is, the laws of the kingdom. All public regiment seems to have arisen by contract between men and princes. Grotius de Bello, fol. 51. David who was made King by God, called all Israel together at Hebron, and made a convenant with them.[73]

Sir Edward Montagu, following Atkyns, agreed that the law books were silent, but thought, both "as a lawyer and in reason, ⟨that⟩ ... government is made up of a contract **ut ante.**" Dolben believed "In reason" that there was "some such thing ... originally" and Sir Edward Nevill insisted that it "must of necessity be implied by the nature of Government." Bradbury and Lord Chief Justice Holt were also firmly convinced that the English government was by contract and Bradbury even asserted that the "body of the Common Law must be taken to be that original contract." The remaining experts, Levinz, Whitelocke and William Petyt, seemed less obviously convinced that there was an original contract. Levinz was content to note that "this contract is government according to the king on the one side and the people on the other. You may call it an original contract, though you know not when it began, because there are oaths on both sides, king and people, one to govern, the other to obey." Whitelocke accepted that the term was appropriate - at least he was prepared to use it - for although there was nothing about it "printed in book cases," at least "there is no book case to the contrary." And Petyt, despite apparently not making use of the word contract, still asserted that there "was always an agreement in the Saxons' times, and so it continues."[74]

An authoritative group of lawyers, then, was prepared to argue that the notion of an original contract was something known to, or at least consistent with, English law. And the Convention Parliament further underlined the legal status of the idea by accepting the clause in the resolution concerning James' breaking "the original Contract between King and People" with a vote of 54 to 43. Thus references to the contract in political debate during the late seventeenth century could claim to be references not so much to a legal analogy as to legal fact. The judgments of the Convention did not go unchallenged, but at least some legal opinion could be appealed to as evidence of the fact of an English original contract.

But this was not the only context in which appeals were made to an original contract. In the disputes which focussed on the Revolution, ideas of contract were introduced into a variety of sorts of argument. Appeal was certainly made to the supposed legal fact of an original English contract but frequently, too, the term contract featured as little more than a rhetorical device with which to label a set of political proposals. Yet it also featured as a descriptive term, descriptive of the activity which the Convention Parliament was principally engaged in during the interregnum. It was, for example, invoked by a rather luke-warm republican as a means to gain a hearing for his proposals. The Convention, he suggested, was about to make a new contract now that the old one had been dissolved and he offered his proposals as a basis for that new contract. In the 1690's, Sir James Montgomery and Robert Ferguson went further along the same lines, and attacked William for, as Montgomery insisted, his "manifest infractions of that original contract which we made with him, upon the maintaining and preserving of which our allegiance was expressly founded." Timothy Wilson argued from the new contract of 1689 that Englishmen were bound to obey William and Mary and a Jacobite pamphleteer criticised the whole revolutionary settlement as being "a government built upon the most destructive principles to the peace and tranquillity of the nation, ... viz. the original contract with the people."[75] Often, indeed, the appeal to contract was more than simply a rhetorical weapon. Sometimes an argument from contract was accompanied by a fairly systematic examination of the theoretical presuppositions involved in adopting such a position. But at least as often contract arguments accompanied many other types of arguments (appealing to reason or authority, to law, necessity, religion and history) arranged as a loosely-knit catalogue of supposed reasons for accepting an author's political opinions.

REVOLUTION CONTROVERSIES

The loose way in which contract ideas were used indicates both the extent to which they had become commonplace and the variety of meanings that had become associated with them. Jeremy Collier went so far as to record that "most Men believe the pretended Breach of that which they call **The Original Contract**, was designed for no more than a popular Flourish."[76] But this appears to have been more the fancy of a convinced Jacobite than the serious reflection of an impartial critic. Collier himself was prepared to accept that some constitutions embodied an original contract. Arguments from contract, then, feature in the political writings of Williamites, Jacobites, pro-Revolutionaries and anti-Revolutionaries, clerics and laymen alike. This only appears surprising because we have become accustomed to identify appeals to contract in the late seventeenth century with the ideas and arguments of Locke's **Two Treatises** and with opposition to royal power. In fact, however, an appeal to contract implied neither rejecting divine right arguments, nor denying the patriarchal origins of states, nor necessarily upholding a popular right of resistance.

Indeed, even some of the most ardent defenders of royal power and of James II's continuing right to the English throne accepted that a contract was the basis or origin of some governments. Jeremy Collier, for example, as I have just suggested, accepted that the constitutions of Flanders, Poland and Hungary were founded upon an explicit contract between ruler and ruled. He only denied that England had such a constitution and insisted that "the Silence of our Laws and History as to any such **Compact**, is a sufficient disproof of it."[77] Collier's acknowledgement that contract could be a legitimate origin of government reflected some of the results of historical enquiries which were being conducted in the late seventeenth century. Sweden, Denmark, Germany, Poland, Hungary, France, Spain, Aragon, England and Scotland - in short, all the supposed "Gothic Kingdoms" - sported historians during this period who endeavoured to portray each original constitution as a limited monarchy founded by contract.[78]

As well as being consistent with some royalist historical argument, upholding a contractual origin of government by no means implied rejecting the divine origin of royal power. Robert Ferguson, for example, drawing upon an argument common enough in sixteenth century French **monarchmachi** literature, argued that all government was ordained by God. But, he insisted, this was for the purpose of the public well-being only. Thus rulers, he claimed, were "under Pact and Confinement" to God to rule in the public interest and this constituted a sort of higher contract which no human laws could alter. Human contracts, then, simply "prescribe and define what shall be the measures and boundaries of the publick Good, and unto what Rules and Standards the Magistrate shall be restrained."[79] The distinction between God's ordaining government in general and human freedom to establish particular forms was widely affirmed and it permitted the linking of contract arguments with divine right in a way that only seems unusual because of entrenched, but thoroughly misleading, beliefs that the political thought of the period consisted of Royalist divine righters combatting Whig contractarians.

Just as contract arguments were consistent with some notions of divine right, so they might also be consistent with some patriarchalist arguments. Most writers did not enter those definitional controversies above power which were of such concern to Locke, Tyrrell and Sidney. The distinction between a father's economic power and a magistrate's political power by means of which Locke and the others sought to dispose of Filmer's patriarchalism hardly featured at all in the debates about the Revolution. Contractarians seemed prepared to argue (if the need arose) that the first government in the world was a "Genarcha," or a patriarchal government, but that this government was transformed into a contractual government either "insensibly" or when the original patriarchs died or were overpowered, or when men stopped living for hundreds of years at a time.[80] And when they talked of the contracting parties, it was more often in terms of fathers and masters of families than of free, equal and independent individuals.[81]

Whether or not the English government was founded by a contract was subject to fiercer dispute than whether any government could be legitimately so founded. But even here there was no simple relationship between adopting contractarian political principles and defending the deposition of James II. A Jacobite pamphleteer, one Charlwood Lawton, for example, argued in 1691 that "our oaths, and the original contract of our law-books, bind us to restore the King."[82] And in his **Letter formerly sent to Dr. Tillotson, and for Want of an Answer made publick** (1690?), he outlined the terms of that original contract as establishing that the English monarchy was hereditary, that the king could do no wrong, and that he was not accountable to the people.[83] Another Jacobite, Robert Jenkin, argued to a similar point by means of an analogy between the contract of government and a marriage contract. The original contract, he argued, is a contract made before God and thus it is eternally binding. Like a marriage contract it is sealed with the command **"whom God hath joyned together, no Man may put assunder."** And although Jenkin was prepared to allow the possibility of divorce through mutual consent, or a "mutual Relaxation," his point in reference to 1688 was that even "If the People did set up Kings by Consent and Compact, this is no argument that they may depose them."[84]

All of these varied references to contract both supporting and opposing the 1688 Revolution that I have so far noted did have one important point in common. They all pretended, in one way or another, to be explications of English constitutional law. Even Robert Jenkin's account of the eternally binding contract was intended to describe the actual constitutional relations between the people of England and their sovereign. But these understandings of contract in terms of constitutional law were certainly not the only ideas of contract discussed in the Revolution debates. This emerges very clearly from the pages of James Tyrrell's compendium of contemporary political argument, the **Bibliotheca Politica**, which he began in 1692. In sorting out the arguments for and against a right of resistance,

Tyrrell argued, it was necessary to approach matters from three distinct and quite separate angles. It was necessary, in short, to argue as a moralist, as a divine, and as a lawyer. And Tyrrell, accordingly, devoted three separate sections of his work to a consideration of each of these.[85]

The arguments of the moralist involved essentially an appeal to notions of natural law and natural right. Those of the divine were concerned with scriptural exegesis and the doctrines of the Church of England. Those of the lawyer concerned only "the History and Laws of this Nation." But in each section notions of contract and covenant were prominent. The supposedly legal arguments were by far the longest and the notions of contract discussed there were similar to those which preoccupied the Convention Parliament. The divine, too, had his own scriptural contracts, not the least of which was the covenant with Saul establishing or confirming a monarchy in Israel, as recounted in the First Book of Samuel, chapter 11. But it was the moralist, drawing on Grotius, Pufendorf and Locke, who discussed contractualist theories of resistance in terms most familiar from the point of view of our standard histories of contract theory. Here questions of historical fact and constitutional propriety were hardly in evidence at all. Instead, discussion was focussed on questions of moral right and in this context the original contract appeared, as in Locke's **Second Treatise**, as the agreement of independent and equal individuals in a state of nature to form a civil society and be governed by the majority of the community.[86]

The moralist, then, was concerned with natural right, natural law, and the transition from a state of nature to civil society. And all this was without doubt different from the discussions of English constitutional law and history which characterized debates in the Convention Parliament and elsewhere about England's constitutional contracts and fundamental laws. It was also very different from the divine's attempts to untangle the moral and political significance of God's having directed Samuel to anoint Saul as king before the tribes of Israel "chose" him as such. But it is the moralist's contract that has seemed to subsequent generations as the most interesting and, indeed, most plausible. And this has led to a remarkable reversal of history. For it has been assumed that since Lockean contract theory appeared subsequently as the most interesting and persuasive, so the participants in the post-Revolution debates must have thought the same thing. But all the evidence suggests that nothing could be farther from the historical truth.

The point is important. Certainly, Locke's **Two Treatises of Government** were published as a contribution to the debates over the status of the William and Mary regime. In his preface, Locke expressed the hope that his arguments would be "sufficient to establish the Throne of our Great restorer, Our present King William."[87] Yet the hope proved vain. Locke's work was not an immediate success and in the late seventeenth and early eighteenth centuries the name of Locke did not feature prominently amongst the authorities of pro-Revolution writers. One of the main reasons for Locke's relative lack of success was precisely that **Two Treatises** were untypical of the rest of the political literature of the day. They were not designed to describe or defend the particular provisions of the English constitution and their arguments were pitched at a much higher level of generality than that to be found in the vast majority of pro-Revolution books and pamphlets.[88] Locke's arguments, of course, were not **sui generis**. Something very similar is to be encountered in works by Pufendorf, Sidney and Tyrrell and, indeed, several pamphleteers prefaced their remarks about English constitutional contracts with brief excursions into much more general matters concerning the original, extent and end of civil society. Some even, like T.H. in **Political aphorisms**, lifted whole chunks from Locke.[89] But the fact remains that Lockean contract theory was untypical of late seventeenth century usages of contractualist vocabulary and the arguments of **Two Treatises** were quite extraordinary in containing hardly a reference to the fierce controversies over the historic rights and liberties of Englishmen which engaged so much of the attention of Sidney, Tyrrell and, indeed, practically every other political writer of the time.[90]

The fact that **Two Treatises** were untypical is, in itself, hardly surprizing. We might expect nothing less of a work that has so obviously escaped the circumstances of its creation and which has acquired a secure place in the canon of Great Texts of political theory. But the way in which the **Treatises** were untypical requires close consideration. For the differences between Locke's understanding of contract and, say, the constitutional law contracts of his contemporaries cannot be explained, as J.W. Gough has attempted to argue, in terms of the differences between a social contract and a contract of government.[91] Locke's questions were different from those of the constitutional controversialists. Where Locke pursued an enquiry into the natural rights of man, the controversialists enquired into the particular rights of Englishmen; where Locke sought to explain the origin and nature of legitimate government, they set out to explain the origin of the English constitution; where Locke enquired into the nature and necessity of political power, they debated the legal limits to the powers of the English monarch and parliament; where Locke discussed a natural right of resistance, they debated whether Englishmen had a legal warrant to rid themselves of James II. Certainly, Locke was concerned to explain the origin of society and the controversialists were not. And certainly, too, Locke did not write of a contract of government. Government, for Locke, was a trust. But it would have been quite consistent, given the kind of enquiry in which Locke was engaged, for such a notion to have appeared. After all, Pufendorf had discussed government as a contract and Pufendorf, on Locke's own testimony, had written the best work so far in the same genre as **Two Treatises**.[92] Thus the differences between Locke's understanding of contract and that of the constitutional controversialists cannot be explained by means of a simplistic and mechanical division between writers interested in a social contract and those interested in a contract of government. Any such mechanical division inevitably overlooks the crucial differences between types of question asked and the level of generality of answers given that I have just noted.

A failure to appreciate these differences also mars one of the most recent attempts to make sense of contractualist language at the time of the 1688 Revolution. Thomas P. Slaughter has suggested that all of the varied usages of the term contract can be fitted within a framework of either a Lockean or a "Hobbesian type" of contract and although these were very different, they were not necessarily incompatible. What Slaughter had in mind, here, emerges most clearly from his analysis of the role of contract in the Convention Parliament debates, an analysis which he summarized as follows:

> The Lords believed that James broke the original contract by subverting the constitution **and** by deserting the throne. In the former case they spoke of a Lockean type of contract. By deserting the throne and thus ceasing to provide protection for his subjects James had also broken a Hobbesian type of bond between sovereign and subject ... The Commons stressed James's subversion of their rights and liberties under an original contract. The Lords emphasized James's dereliction in leaving his subjects unprotected. Both Lords and Commons acknowledged that James was subject to deposition for either form of contract breaking.[93]

For all Slaughter's ingenuity in forcing the Convention debates into a Lockean-Hobbesian mould, his arguments are vulnerable to the charge of his having misread his evidence. After all, Locke did not conceive of the relations between government and governed as those of contract, but of trust. And Hobbes never considered the relations between sovereign and subjects as those of covenant.[94] Slaughter seems, in fact, to have fallen victim to the unhistorical view that I mentioned a moment ago. He seems to have assumed that since the most interesting and persuasive contract theories of the late seventeenth century appear to be those of Hobbes and Locke, then Locke's contemporaries must have thought the same. The fact that those contemporaries wrote in a very different vein from Hobbes or Locke; the fact that they show every appearance of having addressed themselves to different questions and to have sought their answers by appealing to very different sources of evidence; all this does not excape Slaughter's attention entirely. But he renders the differences insignificant by the simple and far too hasty remark that "we should not expect to find pure versions of any theory in the parliamentary debates. Politicians are not philosophers."[95] Unobjectionable as this observation might seem, it serves in Slaughter's case to divert attention away from what the constitutional controversialists were actually doing with the vocabulary of contract by assuming that they must have been struggling along in the shadows cast by the great Hobbes and the great Locke. In fact, as I shall attempt to show, what the controversialists were doing is perfectly capable of explanation without recourse to the theories of either of the two, towering figures that hindsight has created for us.

So far, then, we have encountered a considerable number of different uses of the word contract in the political discourse of the late seventeenth century. This variety of uses highlights the inadequacy of conventional accounts of the history of contract thinking. Yet our attempt to understand what Englishmen during this period meant when they referred to contract in their political writings cannot end with this apparent confusion. It is precisely the looseness and variety of understandings in wide-ranging types of political utterance that adds point to pursuing our enquiry. Englishmen in the late seventeenth century clearly felt that political capital could be made by introducing a notion of contract into their political writings. They knew that they were addressing an audience accustomed to the terminology and ideas associated with that notion. Thus any endeavour to portray late seventeenth century understandings of the notion must elucidate the associations of ideas which an appeal to contract might have been expected to evoke and to outline the context of argument which made that appeal and its associations plausible. If we concentrate exclusively on what contract **denoted** in political argument, then we are faced by bewildering variety. Significant and interesting patterns of meanings, however, do emerge if we concentrate on the various **connotations** of the term.

I have emphasised that appeals to contract in **constitutional debate** occurred in arguments intended to establish utterly conflicting conclusions. But despite the conflicting intentions of their authors, the references to contract shared one obvious characteristic: the contract originated or was embodied in a particular constitution and continued to enjoy the status of positive constitutional law. I have noted also that references to contracts occur in works of constitutional history, both sacred and profane. These contracts, too, supposedly began a particular constitution and supposedly established fundamental rights and duties which continued as the legal birthright of the citizens of the country concerned. And finally I have noted that an idea of contract was invoked in a very different sort of argument from the constitutional: a seemingly **philosophical argument** into the nature, necessity and limits of society, government and political power.

In the rest of this work I shall argue that there were, indeed, two very different understandings of the word contract. The one understanding of contract - the "constitutional contract" as I shall call it - formed part of a legalistic view of politics. References to it were particularly identifiable by the complex of words and ideas associated with it: the vocabulary, that is to say, of fundamental law, fundamental rights, fundamental or original contract and ancient constitution. The other understanding of contract - the "philosophical contract" - belonged to a more philosophical view of the nature of politics. It, too, was easily identifiable in terms of the distinctive complex of terms and ideas associated with it: but this time it was the vocabulary of state of nature, natural law, natural rights, original and social contract. But although these two understandings of contract were distinct from one another, and although each had its own theoretical framework, they still shared certain common features. The recognition of these common features helps to explain the appearance of a third type of contractualist argument evident in the political literature of the late seventeenth century. The understanding of contract exhibited in this third type of argument was distinguished by the attempt to integrate the ideas and arguments associated with the other two languages of contract. By doing this, the third type of contractualist argument - the "integrated contract" as I shall call it - effected to reconcile the requirements of English law with what were believed to be the dictates of reason, morals and religion.

There most certainly was not, then, a single contract theory subscribed to by political writers in the late seventeenth century. Nor was there a single, or two-part idea of contract. Nor was contractualist argument conducted within a framework established by Hobbes and Locke. Understandings of contract during the period were much more complex than this. But precisely what these understandings were will become clear only after we have examined the uses, arguments and theoretical underpinnings associated with references to the "constitutional contract," the "philosophical contract" and the "integrated contract." I shall begin by examining constitutional contractarianism.

PART II

CHAPTER 3

CONSTITUTIONAL CONTRACTARIANISM

There was, of course, nothing new in appealing to ideas of contract in political and constitutional controversies. Such appeals already had a long history by the late seventeenth century. More than mere casual references to a **pactum, foedus, compact, contract**, and so on, first begin to appear as key terms in Huguenot legitimations of resistance in the years following the St. Bartholomew's Night massacre in 1572.[1] The Huguenots here, and subsequently some members of the Catholic **Ligue** (when the tables were turned), appear to have been drawing upon the very common practice in Reformation Europe of referring to intra-polity settlements of disputes as contracts, **pacta**, and the like.[2] The disadvantaged parties in the French Wars of Religion, as in the conflicts between Castile and Aragon,[3] and in the disagreements between prominent **Landsherren** and the Reichstag, all sought to rectify their grievances by renegotiating or reforming the terms of their 'contracted' constitutional arrangements.[4]

Writers in the late seventeenth century were certainly aware of this considerable body of past writings appealing to real or supposed contractual obligations in practical, legal and quasi-legal contexts. They engaged in heated discussions about the lineage of contractualist ideas and a number of famous contractualist treatises of the past, like the **Vindiciae Contra Tyrannos** (1579), Buchanan's **De Jure Regni apud Scotos** (1579/80), and Parsons' **A Conference about the next Succession to** the *Crown of England* (1593), were republished during the 1680s and 1690s as contributions to contemporary discussions. Yet although these works contained arguments about legal and constitutional arrangements that centred around ideas of contract, they were arguments of a somewhat different kind from those to be encountered in the Revolution period. Similarly, Civil War treatises containing apparently legalistic arguments from contract by authors like Philip Hunton and John Milton were also republished at the end of the century. But again, even these English works were not quite the same as the later productions of Atwood, Cooke, Ferguson, Petyt, and a host of still minor pamphleteers. The difference is largely to be explained in that the late seventeenth century writers grafted their notions of constitutional contracts onto a highly articulated theory of fundamental law and the ancient English constitution, something which earlier writers rarely, if ever, attempted.

The circumstances in which this was done were peculiar to England of the late seventeenth century. The implications for understandings of contract in constitutional argument were quite specific, though in the nature of the case, once the associations of constitutional contract with ancient constitution and fundamental law had been established there was no legislating for the kind of practical political purposes that might be furthered by appeal to the language of constitutional contractarianism. I shall begin my account of this kind of contractarianism by outlining the views of the constitutional lawyer and historian William Atwood. Atwood's writings provide one of the clearest expositions of a doctrine which had far reaching consequences in the late seventeenth century. My account will be very general since Atwood's and Ferguson's manipulations of constitutional contractarianism will receive closer attention in the next chapters. For present purposes, Atwood's views will set the scene for an account of a transition in Whig constitutional thought that has been neglected by historians of the period but which is crucial for an understanding of talk about contracts at the time.

CONSTITUTIONAL CONTRACT

According to Atwood, questions about the requirements of the English constitution should be settled by reference to constitutional law alone. This assertion, which seems far from astonishing, was a pointed remark in terms of contemporary disputes. It was aimed at the contributions both divines and laymen were making with supposedly constitutional arguments drawn from natural or divine law. Throughout his career Atwood was thoroughly sceptical about the practical political usefulness of natural law arguments and he shared this scepticism with several other constitutional writers of his day. His contract theory, then, contained no significant references to natural law, natural rights or states of nature. Instead, it purported to be a legally and historically valid account of the English constitution. In summary, his theory was the following:

At some time in the distant past, or to be precise, at the time of the Saxon Heptarchy, our Saxon ancestors contracted together and set up fundamental laws to secure their liberty and property. They agreed to establish a monarchy and to choose the monarch. The monarch agreed to maintain the fundamental laws and any subsequent laws made by King, Lords and Commons assembled in parliament. The prospective king was made to swear in his coronation oath that he would only act according to law, and the people promised to obey him if he kept within the law. Thus, Atwood argued "The King's Oath is the real Contract on his side, and his accepting the Government as a Legal King the virtual one; and so it is **vice versa**, in relation to the Allegiance due from the subject."[5] This ancient constitution Atwood called "Gothic." The Saxons were descended from the Goths - a freedom-loving people who, in the earliest times, had spread across the whole of Europe and Scandinavia setting up the only constitution consistent with liberty, a mixed or limited monarchy. The Saxons, then, transplanted their Gothic mixed monarchy into post-Roman Britain and this was the ancient English constitution. Post-Saxon constitutional history was interpreted in the light of this belief and considerable effort was spent in attempting to show that no substantial constitutional change had occurred for some eleven centuries. More specifically, this effort was spent on the issues of the Norman Conquest and the origin of the House of Commons. The Norman Conquest was no conquest at all. And the House of Commons was a distinct part, though possibly not as a separate institution, in the original Saxon constitution. The ancient English constitution, then, was established by contract and followed the Gothic model. The coronation oath embodied the original contract, or at least it was a representation of it.

Atwood's interpretation of the original contract gave rise to, and provided coherence for, several interesting arguments. It provided a way of relating the ancient constitution to the contemporary, seventeenth century constitution, since all monarchs were required by their oaths to swear to keep the laws of their predecessors, and so on back to the original laws. Here was one reason, but by no means the only one as we shall see, why historical enquiries into Saxon and feudal law were of considerable practical importance in late seventeenth century political argument. Furthermore, the original contract became of much greater general significance than it could have been had it simply referred to the past events which created the ancient constitution. The original contract did not simply refer to events of the distant past. Rather, and much more importantly, it was also the "express Original and continuing Contract,"[6] whereby the consent of the governed was made a constant legal requirement for legitimate governmental action. The theory also allowed considerable flexibility in interpreting what the fundamental laws enjoined. In the absence of any historical records concerning a constitutional question, or as an aid to interpreting the supposed true meaning of any such records, it was relevant and acceptable on this theory to argue from the supposed intentions of the rational and freedom-loving original contractors.

The fundamental laws designed by our Saxon ancestors defined and guaranteed their fundamental rights and liberties. According to Atwood, the whole body of these laws and liberties, together with such subsequent ones as were created in furtherance of the intentions of the original contractors, constituted the fundamental constitution. The most interesting thing about this fundamental constitution was not so much the particular provisions that it was supposed to have contained, it was rather its barely concealed rationalism. The theory provided an extraordinary legal principle of constitutional interpretation. Since the fundamental constitution of England was designed by our ancestors, and since our ancestors were rational men, it followed, Atwood argued, that they would never have designed anything that could be harmful to themselves or their descendants. He admitted that the original framers of the constitution would not have been able to foresee the several turns of state that occurred in later ages, but he argued that they did make constitutional provision for dealing with them. Again, they must have done this, he felt, since they were rational men. They neither insisted that all the laws they made should be accounted fundamental laws, nor that all fundamental laws should remain unalterable. He thought it certainly true that "They that lay the first foundation of a Commonwealth, have Authority to make Laws that cannot be altered by Posterity, ... For Foundations cannot be removed without the Ruin and Subversion of the whole Building."[7] But this restraint on constitutional change only applied, in the last resort, to what he called the "Chief Fundamental Law," the law that **salus populi suprema lex esto**.[8] This law, the most important of all the fundamental laws, the "Foundation" of the original contract as Atwood called it, was **"the scope and end of all other Laws, and of Government itself."**[9] It was the test through which all laws and public actions had to pass before they could be accepted as constitutionally valid.

This, indeed, was an extraordinary principle of constitutional interpretation. In fact, it was not constitutional at all. Law books, records, history, all were ultimately subordinate to the fundamental law of **salus populi**. We need do no more than note the paradox in this theory of English constitutional law. Atwood insisted that he wrote in accordance with the constitutional law of the land. He insisted that he could justify the various causes he believed in by reference to historical and legal testimony alone. But he ended by asserting that it was only by being in accord with the vague criterion of the public well-being that a rule or action could properly be described as constitutional.

Not only did Atwood believe that his contract theory was legally valid, however, he also believed it was based on sound historical evidence. Countless critics have ridiculed contractarians for holding this second belief. But contract theorists of the late seventeenth century thought they had at least one piece of irrefutable historical evidence of the English original contract: the document known as **The Mirror of Justices**. This document was first noted in 1550 by Plowden who believed it had been written before the Norman Conquest. It was circulated quite widely in manuscript form and Coke drew many arguments from it. He, too, believed that it was mainly pre-Conquest in origin but thought that one Andrew Horn had added to it at the time of Edward I. The document was first printed in 1642 and was translated into English in 1648. It was, however, a fake. According to Maitland, it was probably written at the end of the thirteenth century by Andrew Horn from old manuscripts and his own imagination. Nonetheless, the document gained considerable reputation as an original and authoritative source of Saxon constitutional history and law.[10]

The chapter of the **Mirror of Justices** entitled "Of the Coming of the English" recorded an event which was often interpreted as the English original contract. One passage referred to the early English Saxons as follows:

> Of which folk there were as many as forty sovereigns, who all aided each other as follows, They first called this land England, which theretofore was called Britannia Major. And they, after great wars and tribulations and pains long time suffered, chose from among themselves a king to rule over them and to govern the people of God and to maintain, and defend their persons and goods by the rules of right. And at his coming they made him swear that he would maintain the Christian

faith with all his power, and would guide his people by law without respect of any person, and would submit to justice and would suffer right like any other of his people. And after this the Kingdom became heritable. [11]

We shall meet these sentences again in the writings of Atwood, Tyrrell and Allix, where they appear as historical evidence for the English original contract. We shall also encounter references to the Saxon contract and the **Mirror** in several other contemporary pamphlets. But it is interesting to note here just how informal this late seventeenth century understanding of the original contract might be. The passage from the **Mirror** indicates that there was nothing very original about the original contract and that the contract itself was not a very democratic affair. Government was not originated by the Saxon contract since forty sovereigns already existed. All that was achieved was the constitutional unification of Saxon England. It was not the body of the Saxon people which contracted with the king - only the forty sovereigns were involved. This undemocratic feature of the original contract, however, did not affect its radical implications. The insistence that the king submit to justice and suffer right like any other of his people was certainly no less repugnant to a divine right monarch for all that. Indeed, most contractarians of the late seventeenth century seem to have restricted their views of who the original contractors were to a section of the population only. To Atwood, Tyrrell and Pufendorf, the contractors were "the fathers and masters of families," or the "proprietors, especially of land;"[12] to Sir Robert Atkyns and Daniel Defoe the term 'the people' referred most often to "The Freeholders" who were the "true Proprietors of the Nation and the Land;"[13] and many of Locke's arguments have been interpreted as presupposing a similarly limited understanding of the term "the People" to that of Atwood.[14]

Here, then, in outline, is Atwood's version of constitutional contract theory. It is apparent that the theory combined elements of three distinguishable traditions of seventeenth century constitutional thought: the traditions of the ancient constitution, of Gothicism and of a kind of contractualist talk in politics. Speculation within the first of these traditions has been brilliantly examined by J.G.A. Pocock in his study of the peculiarities of constitutional historiography in seventeenth century England.[15] One of the principal modes of constitutional argument during the century was historical. Within this field of historical study and argument, two main schools arose in opposition to one another. On the one side were the common lawyers who believed that the English constitution was immemorial; on the other side was a much smaller group of legal writers (like Spelman and Brady) who believed that the constitution had been at least considerably modified by the Norman Conquest and the introduction of feudal law. The common law view of the English constitution saw constitutional law as customary law and custom as immemorial and unchanging. In these terms, Pocock relates the history of seventeenth century constitutional historiography from two connected standpoints. The one is the rise of an increasingly historical consciousness, centring around the issue of the Norman Conquest as a break in the continuity of unchanging custom. The other is the creation of a polemical situation through partisan use of historical enquiry. The notion of immemorial custom was retained and used by the advocates of limited monarchy. Their arguments were of the form: the rights and duties of citizens vis-a-vis the monarch have existed "time out of mind," they are immemorial custom and therefore bind the present. The notion of discontinuity was utilized by the advocates of strong monarchy with arguments of the form: all laws and thus legal rights are the products of the king's will, they are the grants and concessions of a conqueror and are therefore revocable at pleasure.

By the time of the Exclusion Crisis these debates had firmly crystallized around the critical issues of the Norman Conquest and the position of the House of Commons in the pre-1066 period. A Tory group, championed by Dr. Robert Brady, was asserting that William I had really conquered England and had introduced the system of feudal law that radically broke with traditional

Saxon law. The House of Commons, this group claimed, was no more ancient than the reigns of Henry III or Edward I. In the face of these assertions, a Whig group championed by William Petyt sought to reaffirm that William neither conquered England nor altered the legal system. William I had a claim to the throne made good by trial of arms, they insisted. He was elected by acclamation and swore to maintain the ancient laws in his coronation oath. Some of his actions contradicted his oath and were therefore illegal but the damage was rectified by Henry I. The House of Commons, they also insisted, did not owe its being either to rebellion against, or to the concessions of, a king ruling by right of conquest. It had existed, although perhaps not as a separate body, "time out of mind." The pecularities of the historical arguments employed in these debates will engage our attention at several subsequent points in our examination of late seventeenth century contractarianism. At the moment the general contours of the ancient constitution argument will suffice to identify one of the main traditions from which late seventeenth century constitutional contractarianism drew its inspiration.

A much more amorphous tradition of constitutional speculation located the origin of the ancient constitution in the Gothic past. The specific provisions of the Gothic constitution might be precisely the same as the immemorial customary law of the common lawyers but the origin was different. Instead of being an indigenous growth, the Gothic constitution was invented by the Goths and transplanted into England by the Saxons who were the descendants of the ancient Goths. According to this tradition, the whole of Europe had been over-run by Gothic peoples as the Empire declined and thus the first post-Roman constitutions had all been similar. Frequently, as we shall see, this sort of Gothic history was connected to biblical accounts of the peopling of Europe after the Flood. The Goths were here regarded as the direct descendants of the sons of Japhet, Noah's son, and thus Gothic political arrangements were regarded as the earliest of any still existing. The post-Roman spread of Gothicism was thus a restoration of the original European constitutions.[16]

CONSTITUTIONAL CONTRACT

By the late seventeenth century the term Gothic constitution was widely used to describe a good, orderly and just form of government which operated by balancing elements of monarchy, aristocracy and democracy. Gothic constitution, mixed monarchy, limited monarchy and balanced government were thus largely interchangeable terms. References to the English constitution as Gothic appear in a variety of polemical and historical writings intermingled with arguments from contract and immemorial custom. In short, by the late seventeenth century Gothic thought appears to have lost that distinctiveness that led Professor Pocock to insist on its earlier difference from common law thought.[17]

The third tradition of constitutional speculation which contributed to the development of constitutional contract theory was that of contractualist argument itself. The writers of the late seventeenth century most certainly did not invent the notion that governments embodied or were originated by contracts. The republication in the 1680s and 1690s of much earlier works containing these sorts of ideas served as a constant reminder of this. But what was most obviously different about the majority of arguments from contract in the constitutional debates of the late seventeenth century was that they took place within the context of the ancient constitution controversies. It appears that around 1680 the interpretation of the ancient constitution as based on immemorial custom was superseded by a view of the ancient constitution as originated by, and continuing to embody, an original contract. The critical points in the ancient constitution debate concerning the Norman Conquest and the origin of the House of Commons remained as contentious as ever. But the supposed provisions of the ancient constitution were significantly modified. The common law view of the ancient constitution had maintained that the monarch alone was not sovereign. Supreme power was shared by King, Lords and Commons. The law guaranteeing this partnership was immemorial customary law. None of these institutions could lay claim to being "author" of this law and thus none of them derived their being from the will of any other. In the original contract view of the ancient constitution, on the other hand, it could be claimed that all the institutions of King, Lords and Commons depended upon the will of the citizens. The constitution had been designed by its citizens and could be changed by them.

The evidence of this transition in Whig constitutional thought from the immemorial ancient constitution to the original contract ancient constitution, as well as the reasons behind it, can be found in the political conflicts that occurred between the Exclusion Crisis (1679-81) and the 1688 Revolution. In 1684, for example, Robert Brady was still describing his opponents as divided into two separate groups. As it turns out, these corresponded to original contract theorists on the one hand and immemorial ancient constitution theorists on the other:

> Two sorts of Turbulent Men there are in the World, who under **plausible Pretences** have appeared for the Liberty of the People...
> One of these sort of Men preach to the **People**, That the Origin of all Power and **Government is from Them; That Kings or Magistrates derive their Authority from them; That they have none, nor more than what they give them** ... These Men are Pretenders to **Platonic** and **Eutopian** Governments, such as never had a **Real Existence** in any part of the World, nor never can be practicable amongst any People, or in any Nation whatsoever ...
> The other sort are such as hold forth to the People, **Ancient Rights** and **Privileges**, which they have found out in **Records**, and **Histories**, in **Charters**, and other **Monuments of Antiquity**; by these Men the People are **taught** to prescribe against the Government for many Things they miscal Fundamental Rights.[18]

Brady was one of the most influential writers on the royalist side and it is significant that he should have divided the opposition into these clearly defined types. He was particularly concerned to refute the arguments of the second type and the opponents he singled out were William Atwood, William Petyt and Edward Cooke.[19] All three had published works defending parliament against what they believed were the illegal encroachments of an increasingly powerful monarch. The arguments they had used were initially very much in the style of Brady's second category. But, as I have suggested, Atwood was soon to start framing arguments in the language of constitutional contractarianism - a style of argument which combined notions drawn from both of Brady's types. Edward Cooke's views, especially in his **Argumentum Anti-Normannicum** (1682), were mainly of the fundamental rights kind but they also contained interesting references to the contractual origin of the English government and to English kings deriving their authority from the English people. And William Petyt, Atwood's tutor in the Inner Temple, portrays in his manuscripts an increasing concern throughout the 1680s with questions about the origin of government and expresses a preference for Hooker's explanation of these matters.[20]

Three main factors seem relevant in accounting for these changes in defences of parliamentary rights and in the increasing reliance on arguments from original contract rather than immemorial custom: first, a serious attack upon the notion of immemorial custom; second, the challenge to parliamentary rights which centred around the republication of Filmer's writings in the Exclusion Crisis period; and third, the modification of the claims of parliamentarians in the 1680s from a demand for the restoration of the balanced constitution to a demand for the legal sovereignty of parliament.[21]

In the ancient constitution debate the notion of custom as immemorial and unchanging came to be savagely attacked. William Petyt noted the attack and attempted a counter argument in two drafted, but unpublished, replies to Robert Brady during the late 1680s. Petyt quoted Brady's argument as being:

> What: were the Commons of England, as now Represented by Knights, Citizens and Burgesses, Ever an

Essential Constituent Part of the Parliament,
1. From Eternity?
2. Before Man was Created?
3. Or have they been so Ever since Adam?
4. Or Ever since England was Peopled?
5. Or ever since the Britains, Romans and Saxons inhabited this Island;
6. Certainly there was a time when they began to be soe represented.[22]

Petyt was prepared to accept that there must have been a time when the House of Commons originated. But he refused to allow Brady that this was in "Anno 49.H.3" (1265 A.D.). The Commons themselves, Petyt argued, regarded their presence in parliament as dating from time immemorial and that was good enough testimony for him.[23]

This rather weak reply did not simply mean, as C.C. Western has suggested, that Petyt was concerned to date the Commons' participation in parliament from before the coronation of Richard I (3rd September 1189) - "the date at the common law when legal memory began."[24] "Immemorial" meant far more to Petyt and the other participants in the ancient constitution debates than simply pre-1189. Petyt was intensely interested in the constitutional arrangements of Norman and Saxon England and in proving that the Norman Conquest had not altered the ancient constitution. Where necessary he was prepared to conjecture about the actual origins of that constitution "from some footsteps remaining in historyes and Records."[25] But had he simply been concerned to locate the origin of the Commons in the pre-1189 constitution then the great debate about the Norman Conquest and the legal continuity of the Saxon and Norman governments would have become irrelevant.[26] It did not.

But the substitution of an original contract for immemorial customary law as either the conjectured or historically provable origin of the English constitution did avoid the main problem that Brady had emphasised in his critique of Petyt. The idea that the Commons had always been a part of parliament was replaced by the notion that parliament had been set up at a definite time in English history with the Commons as an indispensable part of it. Thus the force of Brady's assertion that parliament and the Commons must have originated at some time could be recognized, whilst at the same time his further argument that the Commons must owe their rights solely to the will of the monarch could be denied. In the constitution begun by contract, neither King, nor Lords, nor Commons owed their right to participate in government to any of the others, but all owed their existence and right to the will of the people.

William Atwood thoroughly modified his account of the English constitution along these lines during the 1680s. William Petyt, however, did not go so far. The terms contract and compact hardly ever occur in his writings, nor do their common synonyms. But during the 1680s, Petyt increasingly concerned himself with conjectures about the origin of government. He adopted arguments clearly drawn from Hooker to justify what he believed the most plausible conjecture that government originated in consent. And references to the Germanic or Gothic origin of the English constitution appear more and more often in his work. Both these notions, as we have seen, had become associated with contractualist ideas by the late seventeenth century.[27] Further than that, however, Petyt did not go.

Reference to an original contract, then, could overcome some of the more immediate difficulties involved in arguing from an ancient constitution composed of immemorial customary law. The existence of some historical and legal testimony (like that contained in the **Mirror of Justices**) made the change all the more acceptable. These considerations go some way in accounting for the popularity of the idea of an original contract to writers like Atwood, Cooke, Hunt, Atkyns, Allix and Tyrrell - all of whom had at least some legal training and had engaged in legalistic justifications of the House of Commons in the 1680s. Nevertheless, many of the historical difficulties involved in the common law view of the ancient constitution could not be overcome simply by replacing the original contract for immemorial custom. The principal of these was the issue of the

CONSTITUTIONAL CONTRACT

Norman Conquest.

If England had actually been conquered in 1066, as Brady and a mounting body of evidence insisted, then two important consequences seemed to follow. First, there appeared no alternative to the view that the constitution depended solely upon the will of a conqueror and that it was therefore an absolute monarchy in which the rights of parliament and subjects could be ultimately revoked by the monarch. Secondly, there could be no practical point in discussing the pre-Norman constitution (that is, the constitution that was claimed to be based on contract) because William I had secured a total change in government. Constitutional contractarian arguments were employed in the denial of both these consequences and this involved denying that the Norman Conquest was a conquest at all. At first sight it seems strange that so much effort should have been invested in attempting to prove that the Saxon constitution had survived the coming of the Normans. Given the cavalier approach to historical evidence that characterized most of the discussions here it is surprising that no attempt was made to locate the original contract in the post-1066 period and thus avoid the difficulties of the Norman Conquest question altogether. Indeed, three possible locations featured prominently in the historical debates of the time. The first was the earliest date when the Bradyite historians would allow the House of Commons to have existed (1265 A.D.). The second was Magna Carta, recognized by all sides as a crucial document in English constitutional history. And the third was the Norman Conquest itself since, once again, all sides agreed that some change had occurred in 1066 although they disputed the proper significance of it.[28]

There were, however, good reasons for not adopting any of these alternatives and in noting these we might gain a clearer appreciation of some of the common implications of constitutional contractarian arguments. First, the constitution would become that much more modern and thus its strength, thought to be derived from having stood the test of time, would be correspondingly reduced. Secondly, to have dropped the Norman controversy would have involved either repudiating those arguments which had hitherto formed the basis of legal justifications of the House of Commons or relegating them to insignificance. In both cases, constitutional contractarians could hardly have disguised their loss of one constitutional argument and their consequent (or apparently consequent) shift of grounds. Thirdly, the alternative dates to the Saxon contract could not offer the same seemingly unequivocal evidence of a contract as that contained in the **Mirror of Justices**. But perhaps most important of all was the fact that if any of these other events were taken by the defenders of the House of Commons as major turning-points in English government, then the legitimacy of that government itself was open to question. For all these events were preceded by, or involved, armed struggles: struggles in defence of the ancient constitution the champions of the Commons claimed, struggles for innovation according to their opponents. William Atwood made the general point here when defending Petyt's ancient constitution against Brady's criticisms:

> <Dr. Brady> seems to trample on the best Constitution, our Government itself, under Colour of its being New in the 49th. of Hen.3 when it arose out of the indigested Matter of Tumults and Rebellion; and so not having a legitimate Birth, as not born in Wedlock between the King and his People; it may be turn'd out of Doors, by the help of that Maxim.
> Quod initio non valet, tractu temporis non convalescit.29

We have seen that as the basis of a constitutional theory, the replacement of immemorial custom by contract did overcome some historical problems encountered in the common law view of the ancient constitution. But problems of historical criticism are not in themselves sufficient to explain the timing of the transition. In order to provide a fuller explanation, attention must be paid to two further aspects of political debate during the 1680s.

CONSTITUTIONAL CONTRACT

The first concerns the republication of Filmer's works in 1679-80. Appearing at the height of the Exclusion Crisis, the new edition of Filmer's writings added a deeper dimension to political debate and exacerbated the conflict. The Tory case became openly an attack on the position of parliament. Filmer's works seemed to prove that from the very nature of society political power was monarchical, that parliaments were the gifts of kings, and that, in the event of a conflict between king and parliament or king and law, the monarch must be supreme. Monarchy and hierarchical society were natural. The natural was ordained by God. Thus whoever denied the legitimacy of either unfettered monarchy or hierarchical society was guilty of denying God's will.

These arguments presented the protagonists of parliamentary rights against the monarch with serious theoretical opposition. A rethinking, or at least a reiteration, of more basic political principles was necessary. If government had always been, then given the almost universal belief in the validity of biblical history, there seemed no alternative but to concede a fundamental point to Filmer - Adam's authority was of a political nature. Thus monarchy was both the first form of government and directly created by God. But if this were conceded then most of what Filmer had built upon it would also have to be admitted. Government could no longer be held to rest on consent and could only be legitimate if it were an absolute monarchy. Filmer's conclusions would be almost inescapable because all participants in the debate shared a number of fundamental beliefs.

All sides agreed, it seems, that what government was like at its origin should be the standard against which governments in the present should be judged. If the first form of a government were markedly different from its present form, then the present constitution was illegitimate. This was how practically all arguments about legitimacy were formulated. Everyone acknowledged also that if God had revealed his will regarding the form of government necessary for earthly society, then that will had to be obeyed. But Filmer's arguments purported to show that the first government in the world had been an absolute monarchy tempered only by Adam's paternal care, and this was God's will. Thus all should concede that present day governments, including the English, ought to be absolute monarchies. An obvious theoretical escape from this chain of reasoning lay in denying first that government had always been, and secondly that God had revealed a preference for monarchy. Current ideas about the contractual origin of government could serve as the basis from which to reject Filmerian ideas that Adam's authority was political and that God had therefore authorized absolute monarchy.

The republication of Filmer's works, then, by adding a deeper dimension to he constitutional controversies of the Exclusion Crisis and by forcing the pro-Exclusionists in particular to re-examine the basis of their arguments, provided a further impetus for the adoption of constitutional contract arguments. But the republication of Filmer was associated with a second aspect of the political debates of the 1680s which helps to explain the increasing attraction of notions of constitutional contract. This was the increasingly radical demands that were made by the upholders of parliamentary rights against the king. The timing of the republication of Filmer's political writings was not fortuitous. The works appeared at the height of the Exclusion controversy when the House of Commons seemed on the verge of successfully barring Charles II's Catholic brother James from his constitutional right to succeed the throne. Filmer's literary resurrection was a deliberate act of policy intended to bolster the royalist case. The work carried royal approval and the official journal, the **London Gazette**, strongly recommended it.[30] By adopting Filmer as their champion, the royalists committed themselves to attacking parliamentary rights as coordinate in legislative matters to those of the king. Brady's argument in defence of the English monarch could certainly lead to the denial of parliamentary rights to participate in the exercise of legal sovereignty. But Filmer's arguments were explicitly this.[31] Brady's arguments did not necessarily involve the rejection of the idea that the seventeenth century English constitution was effectively, in its day-to-day workings, a mixed monarchy.[32] But to Filmer the idea of a limited or mixed monarchy was a contradiction in terms.[33]

The common law view of the ancient constitution was employed to combat royalist claims for the legislative supremacy of the monarch but it could not easily accommodate arguments for parliamentary supremacy. Yet parliamentary opposition to the king during the 1680s approached closer and closer to this demand. As the royalist case for the hereditary monarch became openly an attack upon the legislative authority of parliament (or was understood so to be), so the Whig Exclusionists and the more determined of their heirs retaliated by asserting something very close to the legislative supremacy of the House of Commons. The experience of the royalist reaction after the dissolution of the Oxford parliament - most notably in connection with the Rye House Plot (1683), Monmouth's rebellion (1685), the accession of James II, the attack on the boroughs and counties, and the Declaration of Indulgence (1687) - served to deepen the divisions within English political opinion that had appeared at the time of the Exclusion parliaments and to alienate many of moderate views from their loyalty to the person of the monarch. The trial of the Seven Bishops in 1687 even divided the loyalist Church of England. With the Church divided, moderate opinion becoming indifferent towards the fortunes of James II, hostile groups at home and a colony of exiled antimonarchical groups in Holland, the stage was set for the 1688 Revolution.

But if resistance were to be justified, and if parliament were to claim legislative sovereignty then reference had to be made to some other constitutional theory than that involved in the common law interpretation of the ancient constitution. For according to this latter theory both king and parliament had existed time out of mind and thus neither could claim supremacy over the other since neither depended upon (owed their existence to) the will of the other. The original contract ancient constitution provided just such a theory capable of upholding both parliamentary sovereignty and a right of resistance. For the original contract view of the ancient constitution claimed that the English constitution had been set up by the English people for a purpose specified in the contract with their monarch. The constitution depended upon the will of the people of England. It was a short step from this principle, although one beset with many difficulties, to the assertion that supreme power in the constitution must lie with the political public, or at least their representatives in parliament. If this were the case, whenever the king acted against the wishes of parliament he could justifiably be resisted. In the circumstances of the late 1680s, then, appeal to something like a constitutional contract rather than immemorial customary law became imperative for the radical constitutionalist case against James II.

Considerations of these kinds, concerned with the controversies over constitutional theory and practice during the 1680s, help explain the rise and attractiveness of constitutional contract theories. The extent of appeals to contractualist language in constitutional controversy, however, is another matter. To be sure, it was mainly in Whig writings of the 1680s that recourse was made to notions of constitutional contract. But after James II's departure, the language of constitutional contractarianism achieved a much wider currency.[34] Indeed, it seems that the idea of constitutional contracts caught hold of the English political imagination and there was no telling what arguments and causes might be furthered by reference to them. No doubt, one reason for the spread of contractualist talk after the 1688 Revolution was the quasi-official status that the notion of James II's having broken his original contract gained from the Commons' resolution of February 1689.[35] No doubt, too, the Jacobites and Tories who employed contractualist language frequently did so in order merely to embarrass their Whig opponents. But it seems that a more general feature of the intellectual life of the late seventeenth century was also involved here - a set of beliefs, arguments and assumptions, widely, though far from universally, shared which seem to lend plausibility and coherence to any appeal to contract in political argument. F.A. Hayek has called these beliefs "rationalist constructivism."[36]

In brief, rationalist constructivism derived from the view that all human institutions were or ought to be creations of conscious human reason. This involved a certain conception of man, society and history which had important implications for the study of politics. To arrive at a true view of politics and society, according to rationalist constructivism, the initial confusing complex of political society must be reduced to its essential elements - rational men. Then, by examining the characteristics of rational men, the complex whole should be rebuilt as a chain of necessary consequences. The recomposed complex need not bear much resemblance to how the original complex (which it explains) first appeared. Political explanation, then, was largely concerned with the elucidation of origins. But the origin of political institutions was by definition the conscious design of rational men. The history of those institutions consequently focussed on their original design. Changes over time could only properly be explained by reference to the conscious design of similarly rational men. But since what appeared reasonable to men in the seventeenth century was invariably assumed to be the same as what would have appeared reasonable to men in earliest times, and since reasonableness was accorded the status of the rational, historical change in institutions was generally looked upon with considerable suspicion. Ideally, the constitutional history of any particular country would exhibit no, or very little, change. The intentions of the founders of political institutions were supposedly the same, in essence, as the intentions of their descendents. Only those modifications of institutions which could be shown to be in accord with the designs of the founders could be accounted legitimate.

The prevalence of these rationalist constructivist beliefs helps explain why appeals to original contracts cut across the political divisions of the late seventeenth century. Origins, design and rational agreements were thrust into the centre of any political explanation. But it is nonetheless true, that references to contract appear much more frequently in the writings of proponents of resistance during the 1680s and amongst the defenders of the Revolution after 1688 than in the writings of their opponents. Part of the reason for this, aside from the continued popularity that arguments from divine right and patriarchalism still enjoyed in certain Tory and Jacobite circles,[37] arose from the burden of associations that the tradition of contractualist talk carried with it and which, in the circumstances of the time, practically every proponent of contractualist arguments felt obliged to disavow. Two of these sets of associations deserve closer attention: the connection of contract language with the writings of Catholics in the sixteenth and early seventeenth centuries; and an association with regicide arguments in the period of the Civil Wars and Commonwealth.

The Whig Exclusionists had objected to the Duke of York because he was a Catholic. Those who championed resistance argued for its necessity if England were to be secure from papal domination and if Protestantism were to survive. It was thus of considerable embarrassment to these writers when it was pointed out that their contractualist arguments had been anticipated in, and were possibly even derived from, Jesuit writers like Bellarmine, Mariana, Molina and Robert Parsons. Indeed, it seems that Parson's major work, **A Conference About the Next Succession to the Crown of England** (1593), was deliberately republished by royalists in 1681 so as to emphasise the Catholic derivation of contract arguments that were currently being deployed by the Exclusionists. In fact, the publication history of Parson's work is one of the most interesting of all contractarian treatises. Robert Brady, Abednego Seller, Sir Thomas Craig's editor, and the author of **The Royal Apology** (1684), all emphasised its extraordinary history, making political capital from it. According to Brady, for example, the first part of Parson's book contained "the very **Principles of Sedition and Rebellion.**" It had been republished in 1648, he claimed, "as a **Preparative** to the **Deposition** and **Murther of King Charles the First.**" It was Parsons who provided the Puritans during the Civil

Wars "with **Arguments, Reasons, Examples** and **Pretences for their Seditious Practices.**" An abridged version of the **Conference** had been published in 1655 possibly, according to Brady, "to set up a **Foreign Title**, or make way for **Oliver Cromwell's** Kingship."[38] And Milton, Lord John Somers, Algernon Sidney and even Thomas Hobbes were all accused by various writers of having raided Parsons for their arguments.[39] Thus the defenders of parliament's rights against the king, presenting themselves as the champions of Protestantism, were constantly taunted by claims that "the Popish DOLEMAN <Parsons' pseudonym> is the Oracle of the TRUE-PROTESTANT Party."[40] For all their declarations that the lineage of their ideas was irrelevant to their truth, for all their catalogues of previous Protestant contractarians, and for all their attempts to persuade James' Catholic supporters to accept their arguments precisely because of their popish lineage, the issue arose again and again in the pamphlet literature.[41]

But it was not only contractarian writers who suffered because of this intermingling of religion and politics. The Church of England itself was deeply divided. As Thomas Hunt emphasised in 1682, the Church was being pulled in two opposed directions. On the one side, adherence to the traditional Church doctrine of passive obedience led to support for, or acquiescence in, a Catholic monarchy and a Catholic succession. On the other side, opposition to Catholicism severely tested adherence to passive obedience.[42] Eventually, the second of these pulls proved the stronger. But in the process many prominent churchmen experienced an almost total turn-about in their political opinions. A comparison of two statements from the pen of Gilbert Burnet gives some indication of the extent of this change. In the early 1680s, Burnet was an ardent champion of passive obedience. In this role he declared that "Of all the **Maxims** in the World, there is none more hurtful to the **Government** ... than the saying, that the **King's Promises** and the **Peoples Fidelity** ought to be reciprocal; and that a Failure in the one, cuts off the other."[43] But in 1689 Burnet is to be found advancing precisely the maxim that he denies. His **Enquiry into the Present State Of Affairs** opens with the assertion: "It is certain, That the Reciprocal Duties in Civil Societies are Protection and Allegiance; and wheresoever the one fails wholly, the other falls with it."[44] In Burnet's opinion a justification of the Revolution depended on the validity of the maxim and from the time of the Revolution onwards he subscribed to the view that all legitimate constitutions were formed by, and embodied, a contract.

In the decade before the Revolution, then, references to contracts began to appear more and more in Whig writings about the ancient constitution and fundamental law. Despite the troublesome associations that such references carried with them, appeals to constitutional contracts were obviously considered to be persuasive. After the Revolution, contractualist language appeared in a much broader spread of political literature - both defences and attacks on the Revolutionary Settlement. To a degree, this broadening appeal of contractualist language in practical political argument can be detected in the classifications of contemporary political divisions that writers at the time of the Revolution advanced. Contemporaries tended to adopt a threefold classification of the principal groups in the Revolutionary debates. Burnet, for example, referred to three main groups during the interregnum. These, only very roughly corresponding to conventional divisions of Jacobite, Tory and Whig, were respectively those who advocated a regency (until such time as James could be conveniently restored); those who wanted Mary to succeed to the throne as next legitimate heir; and those who argued from an original contract to support William's right or William's and Mary's joint rights to the throne.[45] Thomas Long, too, adopted a threefold classification. But his division, more in line with our conventional historical generalizations, consisted of **jure divino** absolute monarchists; contractarian defenders of the people's right to resist monarchs when circumstances warranted; and the Church of England steering a middle course with the belief that monarchs were truly the ministers of God rather than the people, though their power was conveyed **"Medias Populo."**[46]

CONSTITUTIONAL CONTRACT

Whilst classifications such as these are useful as indications of how some contemporaries imposed order on the complex divisions of opinion they witnessed, they cannot be followed uncritically. For the complexity I have examined in the Revolutionary debates was also emphasised by many contemporary writers. Most notable amongst these were the two famous non-jurors, George Hickes and Jeremy Collier. Hickes insisted upon the "multiform variety" of reasons that the Revolution's supporters were giving to excuse their actions;[47] and Collier noted that although "the Gentlemen of the **Revolution** seem well satisfied with their new Allegiance, yet the Reasons (if not the Degrees) of their Compliance are very different."[48] Other writers emphasised the importance of appeals to contract in these debates and associated them with various specific causes or groups. The cause tended to be either a defence of the Revolution, as we have seen Peter Allix arguing, or else more generally a defence of the legitimacy of resistance. John Kettlewell, for example, insisted that "all the Power of the People ... is grounded by the Advocates for Resistance, on the **Original Contract**." The group identified with these appeals to contract varied from Whigs to "Dissenters" generally. But certainly, by the time of the Revolution, arguments from contract were gaining such wide appeal that one royalist noted with alarm the spread of contractualism, "as if the Doctrine were Apostolical."[50]

Whatever we might make of these contemporary thumbnail sketches of the role of ideas of contract in the Revolutionary debates, however, they were referring to arguments purporting to be based on English law, rather than natural or divine law. Indeed, the insistence that positive, rather than natural or divine law, was the proper authority for settling disputes about allegiance and resistance was a recurring theme in constitutional discussions of the 1680s and 1690s and was by no means confined to any one side in the disputes. Robert Brady, for example, rejected Edward Stillingfleet's arguments that appeal to the common good might legitimate political action and stressed that:

> The Legal Constitution by which the Kingdom hath flourisht, and been supported in great Reputation for some hundreds of years, is the best and safest Rule for all **sober Men** ... to proceed by. When Men go from he Law, and legal Establishment, they walk in the dark, and go they know not whither, and travel while they make themselves not only uneasie but miserable.[51]

Similarly, Robert Jenkin asserted that "the Laws of that Constitution of Government under which we live ... are to determin when the Authority of Soveraigns ceases, and the Allegiance of Subjects; and we are not to think their Power and Authority transferred, unless it be transferred legally."[52] Examples could be multiplied.[53]

A fairly clear distinction, it seems, was being made between ethical and legal right.[54] Indeed, the anonymous author of **A Disputation: Proving, That it is not convenient to grant unto Ministers secular jurisdiction** (1679) insisted on exactly this. The provinces of divine and civil law were separate:

> To be a right divine is to be a heavenly lawyer; but this a man may be, and be ignorant of a thousand ... matters in the laws and customs of England: they are so many, and so intricate, and so uncertain, and so out of the road of divinity, and the knowledge and study of universal right, that it would be against conscience and faithfulness, in a minister, to give himself to the study of them; and, without giving himself to the study of them, he cannot attain to the knowledge of them, competent for an English judge, and political magistrate.[55]

Several other writers of the period came to similar conclusions. Tyrrell and Sidney, for example, paid at least lip service to the distinction.[56] And Samuel Johnson, in 1689, argued:

> I grant that the Laws of God and Nature are more sacred and inviolable than the Laws of our Coun-

trey; but they give us no Civil Rights and Liberties, as the Laws of **England** have done. Every Leige-Subject of **England** has a Legal Property in his Life, Liberty, and Estate, in the free Exercise of the Protestant Religion established amongst us; and a Legal Possession may be Legally Defended.[57]

The significance of these distinctions for those who invoked constitutional contract ideas was twofold. First, they gave point to their concern to present a legally valid case according to the requirements of English constitutional law alone. And this concern was of enduring practical importance in view of the long-standing controversies over James II's legal title to the throne after the 1688 Revolution. Second, the distinctions served to emphasise an awareness of problems associated with attempting to defend particular activities by appeal to the general or universal laws of God and nature. Such appeals were to be found, on one reading at least, in the great social contract treatises of the time like Pufendorf's **De Jure Naturae et Gentium**, Hobbes' **Leviathan**, and Locke's **Second Treatise**. This awareness will engage our attention when considering the writings of Atwood. But at least one further reason for Locke's contemporaries to doubt the effectiveness of appeals exclusively to natural law in their constitutional controversies can be seen in Robert Ferguson's observation, in a theological treatise of 1673, that "Learned men do wonderfully differ, and some of them strangely prevaricate, in stating the Measure of natural law and in defining what Laws are natural."[58] Just what particular laws and practices accorded with natural law was certainly not at all clear. But where Ferguson believed the decalogue provided a key, William Atwood denied the possibility of ever being sure. Accordingly, Atwood sought to base all this arguments exclusively upon English positive law, interpreted and understood in the light of a theory of constitutional contract.

CHAPTER 4

WILLIAM ATWOOD

Historians of the late seventeenth and early eighteenth centuries have not devoted much attention to the writings of William Atwood. To be sure, Maurice Ashley and J.W. Gough implied that some of his work was significant, W.H. Greenleaf, Mark Goldie and J.G.A. Pocock have noted that he was a prominent "commonwealthman" or "radical Whig," Caroline Robbins was even prepared to bracket him with Petyt as a "learned lawyer," and one of the latest historians of the period, Julian H. Franklin, has asserted that he was "a particularly influential Whig apologist."[1] But generally his writings have been neglected, in part, no doubt, because according to Laslett he was "the worst of the Whig constitutional writers" and according to G.J. Schochet he was "among the least able of the Whig pamphleteers."[2] This neglect, however, has been both unwarranted and unfortunate.

Certainly, if Atwood's constitutional writings are assessed according to the standards of current historical and legal scholarship, they appear strange and inadequate. But one should hardly expect otherwise. The same would apply to the historical arguments (and the practical political inferences which were currently being drawn from them) of Petyt and Brady. Yet, as Professor Pocock's study has clearly shown, the neglect of 'bad history' itself led to the neglect of vital strands in the history of English political thought. In the same way, then, the dismissal of Atwood's historical writings as 'bad history' is of no help if we wish to understand the significance of his works for the audience that he was addressing. Atwood, quite as much as Petyt, was concerned to provide the opponents of strong monarchy with coherent legal and historical arguments.

The vehement attacks he encountered from Brady and others are indicative more of his success than of his failure in this task.[3] The judgments of fellow-travellers support this view. Petyt regarded him as an "**ingenious** Gentleman", Edward Cooke believed he was an "industrious and worthy Gentleman" and Henry Neville referred to "the learned discourses lately published by Mr. Petyt of the Temple, and Mr. Atwood of Grays-Inn; being gentlemen whom I do mention, **honoris causa**."[4] These testimonies alone warrant attention being paid to Atwood's works. And this attention is amply rewarded since Atwood's career highlights a significant transition in the constitutional theory of the late seventeenth century and his writings contain a coherent contract theory of an unexpected kind.

In his political works, Atwood's attention was constantly directed towards contemporary political affairs. His contractualist writings clearly reflected his concern with practice. They differed in several important respects from the works of Locke, Pufendorf, Sidney and Tyrrell. These differences are most immediately apparent in terms of the concepts Atwood neglected, or rather felt were unnecessary, for his theory. His contract theory is most remarkable for the absence of any reliance upon the notions of natural law, natural rights and states of nature that were so obviously of crucial importance to the theories of these other contractarians. Atwood was not in the least troubled by problems of the artificiality of contract society or of the relationship between natural law and positive law. He believed that the contract with which he was concerned was the actual, historically valid contract that founded the English constitution. It was crucial in his arguments, not only because it explained the otherwise inexplicable origin of government, but also because it provided him with constitutional laws which could **legalise** resistance to the monarch. Nevertheless, Atwood's idea of contract was less important for him as an explanation of the origin of the English constitution in the past than as a means of proving present constitutional law to be what he felt it ought to be. He understood the contract not so much as a past event but more as an "express and Continuing" process whereby the consent of the contractees was made a constant legal requirement for legitimate government.

As I noted in the previous chapter, however, Atwood began his career as a political pamphleteer writing in a tradition that did not require contractualist talk. He first started writing under the tutelage of William Petyt and Petyt was the principal advocate in the early 1680s of the limited ancient constitution based on immemorial custom.[5] Atwood's first four major political works closely followed his tutor's arguments.[6] The critical issues of the constitutional controversy, the Norman Conquest and the origin of the House of Commons, dominate these early works. In his **Ius Anglorum ab Antiquo** (1680), for example, Atwood declared that in Petyt's and his conflict with Brady:

> The Controversie between us, is of Right, whether or no, the **Commons**, such as now are represented by **Knights, Citizens,** and **Burgesses**, had Right to come to Parliament, any way, before the 49. of H.3 except, in the fancy'd way of being represented by such as they never chose, Tenants in **Capite**, by **Military Service.**[7]

Atwood was determined to prove that the Commons were truly represented in the constitution not only before the reign of Henry III but immemorially, that is, "beyond the account of Records or History."[8] The proof of this claim involved, as we have seen, a denial that the Normans conquered England and also an assertion that the constitution itself was based upon unchanging and immemorial custom. Thus the overall purpose of Atwood's early works was "to prove the continuance of the English Rights, or that William govern'd not as a Conqueror."[9]

It is interesting that by the 1680s the controversy between the royalist, feudal law interpretation of the constitution and the common lawyers' immemorial custom interpretation had become so exhaustively argued that Atwood could look upon these two problems as synonymous. If the Normans could be shown not to have conquered

England, then it was supposed to follow that English rights could be called continuous. Atwood does indicate the grounds for his assumption that English rights were the same in the eleventh century and earlier as they were in the seventeenth. These grounds were that the law of the constitution was customary law, and that custom itself was immemorial and unchanging. The assumption, he claimed, was shared by "the Great Fortescue."[10]

Atwood avowed purpose for delving into ancient records was to support "the admirable Constitution by King, Lords and Commons. Although, in general, it appears that he was more concerned to present a view of what the seventeenth century constitution ought to be, rather than to describe it as it was, he did not regard this as his intention. He made every effort to avoid accusations that he was presenting a novel interpretation of the constitution. He insisted that he was writing neither against the king nor on behalf of popular sovereignty. Thus he continued in his statement of purpose: "the Rights of the two last <Lords and Commons>, I have, according to my capacity, defended, being they have been controverted. But surely no man dares to be so presumptuous, to set himself against God's Vicegerent, by Divine Appointment, put over us, and that to our Great Happiness in all matters or Causes."[11]

No doubt, the compliment was merely rhetorical but the rhetoric was hardly that of a "radical Whig." And the extent of the distance between Atwood and the radical, plotting, Shaftesburyite Whigs of the early 1680s can be seen in **Lord Hollis His Remains** (1682). For here Atwood explicitly rejected notions of popular sovereignty and popular resistance. He claimed that the idea "that, notwithstanding any kind of Establishment, the dernier resort, and Supremacy of Power is always in the People" had to be rejected. For this was "a Notion that would unsettle all Governments, making them precarious. Whereas ... 'No Government can be legally, or by any lawful power chang'd but must remain for ever, once establish'd'."[12]

Atwood's early political works, then, purport to defend a view of the English constitution which avoided what he thought were the excesses of both monarchists and parliamentarians. The form that his defence took was historical. But to modern eyes, and indeed to the eyes of many contemporary Tory historians, it was a strange sort of history. His arguments involved asserting that the Norman Conquest had had no material impact upon the constitution, that constitutional law was essentially customary law, and that custom was immemorial and unchanging. He was searching, he claimed, for a "Foundation for our Government by King, Lords and Commons" and that foundation he felt had to be located in the past.[13] He was concerned with historical not rational foundations:

> As on Mr. **Petyt's** and my side the **design** can be no other than to show how deeply rooted the Parliamentary Rights are; So the Doctors <Brady> in opposition to ours, must be to show the contrary ... and 'tis a Question whether he yields these Rights to be more than **precarious**.[14]

Thus parliamentary rights were founded in history and grounded in immemorial and unchanging custom. But from the mid-1680s onwards, Atwood began to shift his position. His work continued to portray a concern with historical foundations but the justification of those foundations changed. The point of the enterprise became obvious in Atwood's post-Revolution writings. Atwood abandoned his opposition to notions of **dernier resort**. Much of his earlier concerns might remain unchanged but this crucial shift took its toll on the rest.

Thus in 1690, for example, after the accession of William and Mary, Atwood announced in very general and familiar terms what was to be his central concern throughout the rest of his career as a controversialist:

> as I am verily persuaded that our Government stands upon such a Rock as has been unmov'd for many Ages, and has no need of a Lie for its Support; I shall with the utmost Faithfulness

address myself to its Defence.[15]

This statement could, of course, be taken as the central theme of all his previous work. But by the 1690s a defence of the constitution on legal and historical grounds involved an additional problem, far more immediate than the Norman Conquest and Henry III's reign had been to defenders of the ancient constitution. James II had been forcefully driven from office and replaced by William and Mary, who, although members of the royal family, were not even next in line by proximity of blood. The constitution had been broken. Thus if the post-1688 constitution were to be proved to rest on "such a Rock as has been unmov'd for many Ages," not only did the Norman Conquest and the constitutional innovations of Henry III's reign still have to be denied, but also the Revolution itself had to be portrayed as completely constitutional.

Atwood's principal task in **The Fundamental Constitution of the English Government** (1690) was, indeed, to prove that "King **William** and Queen **Mary** are RIGHTFUL **King** and Queen, according to the ancient Constitution of the English Government." In order to do this, he informed his readers:

I shall shew;
1. That the People of **England** had a rightful Power lodg'd with them for the Preservation of the Constitution, in vertue of which they might declare king **William** and Queen **Mary** King and Queen of **England** and Ireland with all their Dependencies, tho J.2. was alive at the time of such Declaration.
2. That his rightful Power was duly exercis'd in the late Assembly of Lords and Commons, and afterwards regularly confirmed by the same Body in full Parliament.[16]

It was in proving these two points that Atwood introduced his notion of an original contract. But Atwood's idea of contract did not play a role within a complex set of notions of natural law, natural rights and state of nature. Indeed, throughout his career, Atwood was extremely sceptical about the use of these notions, even though they must have been very familiar to him from the writings of other contract theorists. In 1682, for example, he insisted that ideas of natural "**Rights** are thin and metaphysical Notions, which few are Masters or Judges of." Again, in 1698, he attacked one of Locke's admirers, William Molyneux, for his "wheadling Notions of the **inherent**, and unalienable Rights of Mankind." And in 1704, he reaffirmed his distaste for rhetorical "Flourishes about the Law of God, of Nature, and of Nations," by insisting that "nothing but the Law of **England** can settle Mens Judgements of the Nature of the **English Monarchy**."[17]

The problems which engaged Atwood's attention were constitutional and the answers he gave purported to be founded upon a correct interpretation of constitutional law:

> All the Opposers of our present Settlement, who pretend to talk Sense, when press'd home, grant that the Constitution of the English Government must be the Guide to their Consciences in this matter ... and thus Lawyers are **the best Directors of Conscience** in this case ...
> The great Unhappiness of this Nation is, that **Divines** not only set up for the greatest States-Men, but will pretend to be the best Lawyers and Casuists in these points.[18]

If a notion of contract were to be made part of constitutional law, it could not, on this view, be one idea in a complex of theoretical notions about the origin and nature of political power. Atwood's idea of contract definitely was not this. Instead, contract formed part of a complex of legal notions - fundamental law, fundamental rights, fundamental constitution, coronation oath - which were distinct from the philosophical.

The fundamental constitution that Atwood wished to defend was essentially quite simple. It consisted of a set of basic laws "on which ...**Regal Authority depended**, as well as <Parliament's> rights and Priviledges." The fundamental constitution then "may and doe's in **England** limit... Power **ab externo**."[19] The major powers of the constitution were, of course, King, Lords and Commons and, according to Atwood, their operation through "an Agreement between a **King**, with the **Lords**, and a full Representative of the **Commons of England** will bid fair<est> to being according to the **Original Constitution** of our Government." But the monarchy itself, Atwood asserted using a convenient medieval argument, was "fundamentally an **Elective Monarchy**, keeping within a Family, but not confin'd to the next of Blood."[20] At the centre of Atwood's view of the constitution seem to lie the notions of consent and property. As early as 1682, he wrote of "the Fundamental Constitution, which, as far as I could learn, was, and is, that every **Proprietor** (of **Land** especially) should in the **General Council** of the Kingdom, consent to the making those Laws under which they were to Live."[21] This view of the constitution, then, although intended to maintain limits upon the power of the king, was not particularly radical. Parliament's function was essentially only to channel the consent of the politically relevant subjects (the proprietors) to legislation. The consent of the governed was vital, according to Atwood, because without it a government would lose legitimacy. To make the point, he appealed to the authority of Hooker:

> Many have cited the Authority of the **Judicious Hooker** till it is thread-bare, to prove, that it is impossible there should be a lawful Kingly Power which is not mediately, or immediately, from the consent of the people where 'tis exercised.[22]

This idea of legitimacy underlies all Atwood's speculations about the English constitution. It was already of great significance in his early conflicts with Brady. If the constitution really were modified during Henry III's reign, he there argued, then that constitution was illegitimate. For Henry III's reign was marred by "Tumults and Rebellion" and any constitutional innovation arising from these could not be legitimate because it did not have "a legitimate Birth," it was "not born in Wedlock between the King and his People." And mere endurance, he insisted, in an argument anticipating the Sherlock Controversy, could not provide legitimacy since "Quod initio non valet, tractu temporis non convalescit." This idea that legitimacy was determined by "birth" remained one of Atwood's central principles throughout the whole of his career. But in the use he made of the principle, an even more fundamental notion becomes apparent. This, seemingly paradoxically, was that a maxim of reason could always count as a stronger argument than any historical evidence. For legitimacy, it turns out, was determined by **rational** births.

A legitimate government was a government founded in a particular way. The only way that legitimate government could be founded was by the peaceful, free cooperation of governors-to-be and the governed, of government and governed: either the continuous cooperation that had existed time out of mind of the immemorial constitution, or the explicit cooperation stipulated in contract of the contract constitution. Whichever way the cooperation was conceived, illegitimate government was identifiable by the absence of any signs of cooperation. Any constitution, then, that did not embody the cooperation of the government and the governed was illegitimate. But given this view, the criterion of legitimacy was a rational criterion, outside the realm of both positive law and historical argument. This, of course, it had to be, lest it become meaningless - all governments either powerful enough to rule, or that had ruled in the past, would otherwise be legitimate. But in Atwood's endeavours to prove the ancient English constitution to have been, and to have remained, the best and most legitimate of all governments at least since Saxon times, his history was constantly tailored to the requirements of his preconceived notion of legitimacy.[23]

The consent necessary for legitimate government, Atwood believed, would be based on rational self-interest. And it was this that supposedly proved government to be founded in contract:

> Indeed if we consider, it will appear, that never any Empire or other Civil Society was founded, but there was an Original Contract or Agreement among the people for the founding of it ...⟨for⟩ surely no People ever submitted to any ⟨authority⟩ without a prior Obligation, but where they had hopes or expectations of Advantages or Ease, the obtaining of which, if not made a Condition, was ever implied.[24]

This sort of argument about the origin and end of government was common of the basic presuppositions of rationalist constructivism. The insistence that "men would not have surrendered their natural liberty ... but for some special and great advantage" could be traced back at least to the **Vindiciae contra tyrannos** and other pamphlets of the French Religious Wars.[25] But for Atwood, the argument served as much more than just a hypothetical, explanatory device. It was also historically valid. Thus he described the historical origin of the English constitution by employing it as a premise:

> ⟨Men⟩ judge for themselves upon what Inducement 'tis fit to enter into ... a Society ... and therefore some Man eminent for Wisdom may have been made King, for having proposed such a Regulation of the way of Living together, that all happily Unite in promoting the **common Good**, by which Plenty and Prosperity is secured to every one in particular. These Regulations being **Universally agreed** to, became Laws, and hence the proposers of them have been esteemed Wise **Lawmakers** ...
> Hence arose the happy Constitution of the **English Monarchy**, which **Cicero** plainly saw in **Idea**, as the most perfect form of Government.[26]

Yet this supposed proof of the English contract was far from indisputable. More historical evidence was needed and here Atwood, like many others, turned to the **Mirror of Justices**. There at least, as we have seen, was an account of an event that could be interpreted as the

English original contract expressed in terms of a coronation oath. Atwood wrote: "The **Mirror**, at least, puts this Contract out of dispute; shewing the very Institution of the Monarchy, before a Right was vested in any single Family, or Person."[27]

Having located the original contract in English history, Atwood's next problem was to prove its relevance to the post-Norman constitution. He continued to deny that as a matter of historical fact the Normans had conquered England. But he no longer insisted that unchanging custom linked the pre-Norman to the post-Norman constitution. This link was now effected by equating the original contract with the coronation oath and thus viewing English constitutional history as a succession of reaffirmations of the original contract by each new monarch:

> If it to <sic> objected that the there might have been a Contract, with a Free People at the beginning, it ceas'd to be so from the time of the Conquest.
>   I answer;
> 1. Till there be a Consent and Agreement to some Terms of Government and Subjection, 'twill be difficult, if possible, to prove any Right in a Conqueror, but what may be cast off as soon as there is an opportunity...
> 2. Every Election of a King truly, so call'd, is an Evidence of a Compact; but Ancient Authors tell us, that W.I. was elected King, nay they are express that he was receiv'd upon a mutual Contract ...
>   The King's Oath is the real Contract on his side, and his accepting the Government as a Legal King the virtual one; and so it is **vice versa** in relation to the Allegiance due from the subject.[28]

Understood in this way the original contract defined and guaranteed the legitimacy of the English constitution. The constitution was legitimate because it arose from, and continued with, the free consent of contracting citizens. It consisted of fundamental laws set up in the distant past and it was thus both of considerable age and eminently reasonable. Its reasonableness was certain because our ancestors, being reasonable men like ourselves, must be presumed to have submitted themselves to a government for some good purpose. The original contract was still relevant to the seventeenth century constitution because it was represented not simply as a past event but rather as a series of events (the taking of coronation oaths by each monarch) reaffirming the essentials of the original agreement.

But in representing the coronation oath as the contract, Atwood encountered a problem about the fundamental laws consented to by each new monarch. Could they alter over time? If the answer to this question were no, then how could one account for the changes that had in fact occurred and which had been accepted as beneficial? If the answer were yes, then the whole point of the historical enquiries might be called into question. Atwood's concern, after all, was to explain the English constitution of the late seventeenth century. If the main constitutional laws, the fundamental laws, might change over time why not simply describe those which were currently accepted as law rather than examine the Saxon and Norman constitutions? Atwood's solution to these problems was a compromise: fundamental laws could change over time, but not so radically as to alter the limited nature of the government. There were, apparently, two levels of fundamental laws. For example, Atwood believed that in the early history of the English monarchy the people were protected against their king by powerful Tribune-like officials. These no longer existed in the seventeenth century and yet he was prepared to accept that it was "the Wisdom of this Government, to have the like Offices with us to be now only known in Story." The point of noting their past existence was, nonetheless, as evidence of what "English Liberties" **are.** Those liberties had not changed even though "the Subjects of the **Monarchy** have had greater Confidence in their Kings, than to insist upon having such setled Officers."[29]

The idea that constitutional law could change provided it did not do so fundamentally was inextricably connected to the notion of an original constitutional contract through the proposition, borrowed from a royalist divine, Robert Sheringham, but ultimately from Innocent Gentillet, that:

> They that lay the first foundation of a Commonwealth, have Authority to make Laws that cannot be altered by Posterity, in the Matters that concern the Rights both of a King and People, For Foundations cannot be removed without the Ruin and Subversion of the whole Building.[30]

If this were interpreted strictly it meant that not all laws were fundamental. Atwood did in fact adopt this position. The only law that could not be altered by posterity, it turns out, was the law of **salus populi**, for the public good itself was "the Foundation of the Agreement" to form the constitution.[31] It was this idea that enabled Atwood to argue that in all cases where the legality of an action was in question, that action could be accounted legal, irrespective of the dictates of all other laws, provided it contributed to the public wellbeing. In 1690, for example, Atwood defended the East India Company on these lines:

> But did not the Common and Statute Law of the Land, the Civil Law of the Romans, or other Maritime or Marshal Laws, afford sufficient Matter for an Apology <for the E.I.C.>, we might have Recourse to the Foundation of them all, and what upon Emergencies superseeds all, the **Salus Populi**: To which the Interest of both Prince and People must give way; whenever there is a Competition.[32]

But this notion of a foundation for all positive law brought Atwood close to the view that **salus populi suprema lex esto** because it accorded with natural law. He had consistently refused to make this kind of assertion in his analysis of the original contract and the fundamental law that it established. In one passage in **The Fundamental Constitution**, however, he did argue that "by the Law of Nature, Salus Populi **is both the Supream, and the first Law in Government: and the scope and end of all other Laws, and of Government it self.**"[33] Yet his understanding of the law of nature is a peculiar one. Natural law is not an immutable standard of right and wrong, good and evil - the standards that contemporary philosophers were arguing God had engraved on all men's minds. Instead it simply provided additional authority for existing and changeable positive law. Our knowledge of what accorded with the laws of God and nature was derived from existing positive law and thus natural and divine law could change as positive law did. Thus Atwood argued:

> I will not deny that <kings> enjoy the Crown according to **God's Law, Man's Law,** and the **Law of Nature:** For, as the great Fortescue has it. **All laws published by Men, have their Authority from God** ... Yet who can say but these ... **Ordinances of Men,** may be altered, as they were made?[34]

The sort of argument that Atwood based on this view of natural and divine law is often astonishing. When discussing James I's title to the English throne, for example, he insisted that James "having, upon an undoubted legal right, been recognised **King of England** ... thereby the Right became Divine."[35]

Salus populi, then, according to Atwood's constitutional contract theory, was the supreme fundamental law, but it was positive law for all that. It was essential for his purposes that it should be positive law because only by means of such a general notion as the public well-being could the events of 1688 be declared legal. He could not allow **salus populi** the status of a natural law since such things were "thin and metaphysical Notions, which few are Masters or Judges of." **Salus populi** was supreme because it was the foundation of the original contract. Atwood refused to believe that rational men could ever live freely under laws to which they had not specifically consented. Reason, then, was the test of law and if the law in any circumstances was to be found wanting it must give way. Yet Atwood's **salus**

populi would seem at most a principle of law and not the law itself. It might thus be a criterion for changing law but the act of change could only be called legal if it were carried out through recognized constitutional channels. Rebellion or force could never be such a recognized legal channel. When resort is taken to force the constitution, **ipso facto**, has broken down. Revolt might be necessary to restore or alter a constitution but it could never be legal according to the law of that constitution. The only standard by which rebellion might be called legal is the standard of natural or divine law. But the legality of an act according to natural law is a very different sort of legality from that which arises from constitutional law. Having refused to take this possible way out of his dilemma, Atwood had to try and reconcile his rational standard of the **salus populi** with existing constitutional law. Hence his appeal to an original constitutional contract.

The idea that the English constitution was in fact set up by a contract between rational men was an easily comprehensible way of uniting reason and history. It was far from entirely satisfactory, as Behrens has shown, but it did provide a fairly plausible basis upon which to defend the legality of the William and Mary regime.[36] The task of devising the best relationship between government and governed was thrust back upon the original framers of the constitution. Their decisions were enshrined in a set of constitutional laws which could all be modified in some degree by posterity, provided the essentials of the arrangements remained. Here lay a strength of the doctrine as far as Atwood was concerned. Any attempt to act in accordance with the **salus populi** could be interpreted as an act necessarily in accordance with the spirit if not the letter of the constitution. Thus any change of constitutional law, even if effected through extra-constitutional channels, could be interpreted as a defence of the original constitution rather than an innovation. It was a defence of the intentions of the original contractees.

Only constitutions founded by contract were legitimate. The English constitution was founded by contract, therefore it was legitimate. Contractual constitutions have as their supreme law the **salus populi** because this must be supposed the intention of all rational men in establishing governments in the first place. It followed from these propositions, Atwood's argument ran, that where government "is founded in Compact; the **Nobles** and **Commons** may join in the Defence of their **ancient and accustomed Liberty, Regiment and Laws; nor may they in such Cases well be accounted Rebels.**"37 The stigma of rebellion could thus be removed from the supporters of the 1688 Revolution.

The will of God revealed in the Bible did not provide evidence for refuting this deduction. Despite the arguments of divine righters from biblical sources, Atwood contended that Christianity did not "lay any Obligation upon the Subjects, beyond the Duty resulting from the particular Constitutions of the respective Governments." And here it had to be acknowledged "that the Laws ad <sic> customs of some Countries may allow of Resistance in some Cases." The English constitution he certainly supposed to allow this right. And so, he claimed, had the constitutions of Denmark, Sweden, Norway, and France, Venice and the German Empire, and even classical Rome, at some stage of their histories.38 The resistance that the English had shown to James II was, therefore, legal because Atwood believed it had been necessary. His argument was simply that "**the Oath of Allegiance ...is discharged or dispenced with, when Salus populi ... is concern'd, and in danger.**" And in such a case a change in the course of the succession "is so far from a Change of Constitution, that 'tis by vertue of the Chief Fundamental Law the **Salus Populi.**"39

This theory of an original constitutional contract combined elements of seventeenth century rationalism with legal history. The elements were held in uneasy balance. The former were the ultimate court of appeal in cases where the reasonable conflicted with the legal. This was so even though what was deemed to be reasonable was apparently a matter for the individual's judgment alone.40 The extent to which the requirements of reasonableness might override those of strict legality is evidenced in Atwood's solution to the problem of Charles II's statutes which outlawed resistance to the monarch. These statutes, as we have seen, were a major difficulty in the way of those who wished to argue that the Revolution had been perfectly constitutional. They were Acts of Parliament, indisputably part of the constitutional law of the land, and they declared unequivocally that armed resistance to the monarch was illegal. This was precisely the conclusion that Atwood wished to avoid and hence he insisted that it was "the common Fundamental Law" which was "in this case the Superior" and which was to "explain and limit the Sense of Acts of Parliament seeming to the contrary."[41] This common fundamental law was in essence the **salus populi**.

Atwood's supposed solution to the problem of Charles II's statutes is interesting not only because it rests on the idea of a **fundamental** fundamental law, but also because he chose to call that law the "common" fundamental law. By the end of the seventeenth century it had become commonplace amongst asssertors of parliamentary rights against the Crown that there existed a fundamental law guaranteeing those rights. The earliest theorists of fundamental law in England were mainly common lawyers like Coke and Hobart. They tended to argue that fundamental law was something like the "reason of the common law" - an abstract set of principles that were embodied in the history of common law. From this it was often argued that any Act of Parliament that contravened the reason of the common law was void, the strength of the argument resting on the superiority of common over statute law. And although this relationship was definitely changing, when Atwood described his fundamental law as the **common** fundamental law he was drawing on two sources of inspiration that helped to make his argument more persuasive to the less radically minded by concealing the ultimate rationalist basis upon which it rested.[41]

No doubt, the main characteristic of Atwood's fundamental law was its rationality but this was not derived from the historical experience of the common law. Instead, the fundamental law was rational because it had been designed by rational men who, in the distant past, had decided that government under a set of fundamental laws would be beneficial to them. Thus for Atwood to assert the superiority of fundamental over statute law was tantamount to asserting that reason should be the test of law. This was a perfectly plausible assertion but one that Atwood did not wish to make in such an unequivocal way. He wanted to argue his case upon the view that the only acceptable test of legality was positive law. Hence, when positive law definitely did contradict his argument, he appealed to the "common Fundamental Law" where reason was already linked to law through the accumulated wisdom supposedly embodied in the common law. But this, quite clearly, was a very different appeal to reason from that involved in making the **salus populi** the ultimate test of legality.

As far as Atwood was concerned, then, resistance to the monarch would not only be justified but also legal if **salus populi** were threatened. But two outstanding problems remained before his proof of the legality of resistance could be complete. These concerned first, who was to determine when **salus populi** was endangered, and second, what was the status of the constitution during the period when resistance was actually taking place?

Although Atwood's main point was to legalize resistance in some cases, he did not want "to go about to loosen the Bond of due Subjection to the Powers which are over us." Thus he donned the cloak of moderation.[43] Borrowing arguments that might be found in any number of pro-resistance tracts from the mid-sixteenth century onwards, he determined against an individual right of resistance. "If single Persons, or many together be injur'd by the **Prince**, they are oblig'd to suffer quietly, rather than disturb the Publick Peace."[44] For injuries caused to individuals by their government did not constitute breaking a contract. To justify this view, Atwood took over a similarly long-standing contractualist argument that can be traced back to Beza and the **Vindiciae contra tyrannos**:

> all the People collectively, or representatively,

were but **one Party in the Stipulation**, and therefore those Acts, by which a King must forfeit <his throne> are <only> such as are likely to take away the Rights of the whole People, or aim at changing the Form of the Government, subverting the Laws.[45]

Atwood believed that these occasions would "cry aloud." But all the same, at least in the case of England, there "was and is an establish'd Judicature for the great Case in question." This was the "Lords and Commons in full Parliament." Their role was testified to by precedents stretching back to Saxon times.[46] Thus by the 1690s, Atwood was asserting the constitutional supremacy of parliament. He had moved a long way from his defence in the early 1680s of the common law view of the balanced constitution. In summary, the constitution now consisted of " the express Original and continuing Contract between Prince and People ... with the Legal Judicature enpowered to determine concerning it."[47]

The second problem that Atwood felt obliged to overcome when arguing that the English constitution countenanced resistance involved showing that resisting the monarch did not cause a breakdown in the constitution. Were it have done so, he would have been obliged to admit either that the Revolution was unconstitutional but necessary, or that it was lawful according to some other standard of legality than the constitutional. "The Kingdom I own is founded in Monarchy," he argued, but this did not imply "that the dissolution of the Contract between the immediate Prince and People, should destroy the form of Government."[48] The main difficulty with respect to 1688 concerned the status of the Convention Parliament which, after James II's escape to France, had determined that William and Mary should be offered the throne in his stead. On the one side, the defenders of James II argued that the Convention was an illegal body because a regular parliament alone could resolve constitutional questions but that such a parliament could only be convened by the king's writ. Atwood attacked these arguments as excessively formal. On the other side were those who "suppose the Consequence of a **Dissolution** <of the> **Contract** to be a mere **Commonwealth,** or absolute

Anarchy." The error of these men lay in not having attended to Pufendorf. For, "according to the **Judicious Pufendorf**, by virtue of a double Contract, where the Fundamental Constitution is **Monarchical**, as in England, a **Monarchy** remains."[49]

The neglect of Pufendorf's wisdom was the error of Locke's **Two Treatises of Government.** Locke had published **Two Treatises** anonymously and there is no evidence to suggest that Atwood knew him to be the author.[50] But Atwood considered **Two Treatises** to be "the best Treatises of Civil Polity which I have met with in the **English** Tongue." They successfully refuted the absurdities of Filmer and established government "upon the only true Foundation, the Choice of the People." The only glaring omission of the work could be rectified by resorting to Pufendorf. And Pufendorf's treatises, we may assume from the extent to which Atwood falls back on their authority, comprised the best books on civil polity in any tongue.[51]

It is instructive of Atwood's central concern with the English constitution that in discussing Locke he considered that "his Scheme of Government is not erected as the most perfect, but seems designedly adapted to what he takes our Government to be, tho not expressly named." Since Atwood interpreted Locke in this way he could neglect the part of **Two Treatises** which examined the nature of pre-political man, his natural rights and the law of nature that guided him. He could then conclude that it would be wrong to interpret Locke's argument as involving the dissolution of government in 1688 since although one contract had definitely been broken, any reasonable man like Locke would accept that "there plainly was a farther contract ... to prevent **Anarchy** and, Confusion, at any time when the **Throne** might be **vacant**." And it was precisely because of this second contract that previous examples of removing English kings were lawful and acted as "authentick Presidents for our late Proceedings."[52]

In Atwood's view, then, Locke was correct in arguing that the only legitimate foundation of government was the consent of the governed. But his omission of Pufendorf's two contracts led to errors in understanding the English constitution. Yet Atwood himself was equally guilty of having misunderstood, or misinterpreted, Pufendorf. For Pufendorf had distinguished between the contract whereby a civil society was established and a contract of submission which established and guaranteed a regular government. Both these contracts were only comprehensible in the light of logically prior beliefs in natural rights and natural law.[53] Yet Atwood's interpretation of Pufendorf neglected these beliefs altogether. Pufendorf's complex theory was reduced to two stages of constitution-making. Thus, by the first of Pufendorf's contracts, as Atwood understood it, the English supposedly made "a Provision ... for a Monarchy, before any particular Person was settled in the Throne." By the second, the people simply chose a king.[54] Only then, from the dissolution of Atwood's second contract, could it be argued that the monarchical form of the constitution would remain unchanged.

These, then, are the major propositions involved in Atwood's constitutional contract theory. From the idea that the English constitution was begun by a dual contract, he elicited the first, fundamental, constitutional law of **salus populi**. His theory made it perfectly consistent to argue the case of the constitutional legality of the 1688 Revolution. If the constitution were really as he wished to persuade his contemporaries, then an attempt to remove the incumbent monarch could be styled constitutional, provided two conditions were satisfied. These were: first, that no attempt be made to alter the monarchical form of the constitution; and second, that the replacement of the monarch should be justifiable on the grounds of **salus populi** (with the Lords and Commons acting as final judge in case of dispute). Atwood and many of his contemporaries were convinced that both these conditions were satisfied in the case of the struggles against James II. But it was only possible to accept the satisfaction of these two conditions as evidence of the **constitutionality** of the 1688 Revolution by accepting a contractual view of the English constitution as well. Thus many men, sympathetic both to the dangers of arbitrary government and to the difficulties involved in upholding constitutional contract theory were still faced with a dilemma. Atwood may well have persuaded some that "the People of **England** are actually discharged from their Oaths of Allegiance to James II and were lately restor'd to that Latitude of Choice which ...<is> their Original Right."55 But to those who could not follow him, allegiance still lay with the deposed king. For this group, the distinction between a "**de facto** and a **de jure** king" became increasingly significant and Atwood's solution to their problem by simply denying its existence was of little comfort.56

In the immediate context of the late 1680s and 1690s, then, the principal point of Atwood's constitutional contract theory seems to have been to redefine the idea of rebellion in such a way that the sort of resistance eventually exhibited in 1688 could be argued to have been legal. Unlike many contemporary contractarians, Atwood did not concern himself with examining the principles of consent and contract in terms of natural law and natural rights. The reason for this does not derive from any blind spot in Atwood's theoretical vision. By 1690 he had read Locke, Tyrrell and their opponent Filmer, as well as the works of Pufendorf.57 But Atwood simply took the refutation of Filmerism for granted. From his standpoint, Filmer's notions of patriarchalism and divine right were simply ridiculous or, at most, mere stumbling blocks in the way to a more concrete proof from records of law that the events of 1688-9 were constitutional. Thus Atwood dismissed the whole Filmerian debate in just a few words:

> As to the Nation's rightful Power <to act as it had in 1688>, I shall not go about to refute the fond Notion of an absolute **Patriarchal** Power descending from **Adam** to our Kings in some unaccountable way; because, tho if it were true, there could be no more Compact between Princes and their People, than is between Fathers and Children for establishing the Rights of Fatherhood, yet the differences between a **Patriarchal** and **Monarchical**

> Authority, is so well stated and prov'd by my
> Learned Friend Mr **Tyrril**; that few besides the
> unknown Author of the two late **Treatises** of **Government,** could have gained Reputation after him,
> in exposing the false **Principles** and Foundation of
> Sir Robert Filmer and his Admirers ...
> Wherefore I may well think that I may pass over
> the Stumbling-Blocks which such Men <Filmerians>
> lay in the way to my Proof, that the Power whereby
> this Nation is govern'd, is originally under God
> derived from the People, and was never absolutely
> parted with.[58]

There could be no political power before contract; Pufendorf, Tyrrell and Locke had proved that much. But they had done so by means of philosophical notions of a state of nature inhabited by men with natural rights and guided by the dictates of natural law. Atwood was prepared to adopt their conclusions but not to engage in their sort of enquiry himself. The conclusions, indeed, were necessary postulates for him but his scepticism of "metaphysical" notions seems to have made him hesitate in following the manner of their proofs. His concern, anyway, was with constitutional questions whose solutions he felt must be sought in constitutional law alone. If the original contract were historically valid, establishing fundamental laws that defined and protected the rights and duties of Englishmen, and if the fundamental, ancient constitution could be shown to be the present constitution, then the defence of those rights which Atwood wished to uphold would take an historical or pseudo-historical form without necessitating recourse to "thin and metaphysical Notions." A justification of the 1688 Revolution, then, need only take the form of a correct examination of the constitution, especially as it concerned the monarchy. Disputes about divine right and patriarchalism were needless. All that was required was a knowledge of the provisions of the fundamental, ancient and continuing constitution; or, as Atwood chose to style it, "the fundamental or subsequent Contract."[59] But that constitution, Atwood insisted, had to be examined correctly. By this he meant not only the careful interpretation of historical records but also that, in the absence of records proving certain desired provisions to be constitutional, appeal could be made to "the reasonable." The plausibility of this view, however, depended in turn on the ideas that government was rationally designed and that history embodied a rational purpose.

We may assume that Atwood thought himself successful in proving the historical validity of the English constitution's "express Original and continuing Contract." But, apart from the single reference to the unification of Saxon England that appeared in the **Mirror of Justices**, the only evidence that Atwood brought to support his contract turns out to comprise arguments from reason and not from history. Historical evidence of the contract, in other words, took the form of arguments from the existence of government to categorical statements of what must have been their origins. This, of course, was not to argue historically at all. Beginning from historical evidence, Atwood proceeded to enunciate the necessary conditions for the appearance of that evidence. And whilst we might tentatively accept in historical narrative an argument from what was to what **might** have been, the rationalist argument from what was to what **must** have been is of an entirely different order. Yet Atwood found his argument satisfactory and so did many of his contemporaries. Why was this so?

The problem here has been clearly stated by Behrens in her study of the Whig theory of the constitution in the reign of Charles II. There was, she claims, a clear contradiction, despite "assumptions to the contrary," between arguments from reason and from history:

> <The historical argument> ... involved not merely the idea of a law equally applicable to and binding upon all men, and of justice impartially administered, but also the idea that, in a more extended sense, the law was supreme because its essential provisions regarding the constitution were unalterable.
> How remote all this was from the conclusions dictated by "reason" is equally apparent. If **salus**

populi is **suprema lex** there can be no limit to the extent to which the constitution can be altered.[60]

But in Atwood's work, we find that **salus populi** was the "chief fundamental law" and yet there was a definite limit to how far the constitution could be altered. Before concluding, however, that Atwood was totally confused in claiming that his rational constitution was the product of historical evidence alone, it is necessary to re-examine those "assumptions to the contrary" to which Miss Behrens refers. From this re-examination it will appear that whilst Atwood may well have been mistaken in the conclusions he reached, he most certainly was not confused. For whether reason and history lead to different conclusions depends on how their respective logics and interrelationships are conceived.

Atwood's idea of the extent and limits of the individual's reasoning faculties creates little difficulty for our understanding. As I have indicated, his views seem to coincide fairly consistently with the seventeenth and eighteenth century tradition of rationalist contructivism which Professor Hayek has described. But the extent of his rationalism was to some extent disguised by his frequent appeals to traditional authorities in religion and history. These authorities, Atwood believed, were as unquestioningly to be followed as they had been in previous centuries. But this did not mean that Atwood was any the less rationalist in his approach to them. He still claimed the exclusive right to determine the best interpretation of an authority or to choose who was to be the best interpreter. Thus what was acceptable to Atwood's reason was not offered to his public as a logical consequence derivable from simple, explicit and undeniable premises. Instead it was offered as **the true interpretation** of the traditional, customary or habitual.

He often insisted, as he did in his **Reflections upon a Treasonable Opinion** (1696), for example, that his views were "for the most part, the Result of the Collective Wisdom of the Nation." And he clearly felt a great veneration for the antiquity of English political institutions. At one point he lauded the "**English Parliament in comparison with which we are but of yesterday and know nothing.**" Whilst in a later passage he reaffirmed this idea, so thoroughly anti-rationalist though it seems, by asserting that "Mankind ... have greater Benefit and Freedom by submitting to equal constitutions, long established, than they could reasonably propose to themselves by innovations of any kind."[61] But a closer examination of Atwood's historical arguments reveals that these anti-rationalist statements did not really conflict with the rationalism of the rest of his arguments. He was convinced that the past actually was as he described, even though it included an original contract and could not accommodate the Norman Conquest. His rationally constructed past was, for him, the genuinely historical past.

His view of history was founded upon two main premises. The first was that "the People that is now, in common presumption is the same which first settled the Succession" - that people in the past were exactly the same as people in the present.[62] The second was that "where Authorities <in history> are received, and the only question is about the Sense of them, the true Sense is as capable of demonstration, as any proposition in Euclid."[63] From the first premise, it was possible for Atwood to argue that, since he could conceive of no obligation without consent, men at the beginning of history **must** have thought the same. Furthermore, the actual propositions that Atwood would consent to in the late seventeenth century must have been those consented to in the past.[64] Times did change, Atwood was not denying that, but the more reasonable the actors in history, the less change would occur. New problems might arise in politics requiring changes to existing laws but the principal problems had been inviolably solved by the original contractors. It was these solutions that most concerned Atwood and his method of ascertaining what they had been was such that history was bound to reveal the answers he wanted. It was bound to do this because, according to the second premise, historical actions must be understood by the light of reason. Thus, for example, when analysing the relationship between England and

Ireland according to the laws of the historical contract constitution Atwood could argue:

> 'Tis certain, that whether we consider the people of the same Nation, or the relation which one Nation has to another, their state or condition, must depend upon Constitutions and Agreements, express or tacit ... what Constitutions and Agreements are binding, and for what time, will fall under the considerations of Reason, either of itself, or aided and assisted by Revelation.[65]

This declaration occurs at the beginning of a study supposedly concerned with the historical and legal relations of England and Ireland. But the ultimately rational basis of the forthcoming history is plainly visible. For all his assertions that the constitution was the product of the "Collective Wisdom" of the ages, each constitutional provision had to stand or fall by the test of reason. It was not the antiquity of the provisions, it was rather "those Laws of **Reasonable Nature, and of Nations**, which ⟨ultimately⟩ oblige Men to keep to the **Contracts** their Forefathers entred into."[66] The assistance that reason might possibly require from revelation in this did not spring from any inherent limitation in reason's power. Not only was it true that "the Scriptures meddle, not with particular Constitutions," but any positive law "if it have due regard to ... the **Supream Law**, the good of the People, is that which Induces or Occasions the **Divine Right**."[67] God was on the side of reason - indeed, He was rational - and anything in the political world which reason supported could **ipso facto** claim God's support. Divine help explained the endurance of legitimate government, not the reason for its legitimacy.[68] The majority of men were not sufficiently aware of their true interests, as the diversity of history proved, but history also showed that they could not be kept in subjection for all time.

God was truly the ruler of the universe but He ruled according to rational principles. The principles by which He ruled were discoverable through the exercise of right reason alone. But because most men did not use their reasoning faculties to the full and because reason could only claim to make faith redundant at the cost of charges of blasphemy, reason still required acknowledged assistance and confirmation from revelation.[69] In Atwood's works this acknowledged assistance was gained by drawing God into partnership with man and by attributing to Him the mental processes of man. God's will in respect of human affairs was knowable by His actions. But His actions were comprehensible because they accorded with what rational man would do.

Divine intervention was "proved" by the endurance of legitimate "Kingdoms and Common-wealths" but there was no possiblity of arguing from endurance to legitimacy. Atwood's criterion of legitimacy was determined independently of his historical studies and was used as the key to understanding, in particular, English constitutional history. This was the point of the maxim "Quod initio non valet, tractu temporis non convalescit."[70] The legitimacy of a government was determined by its birth. The idea of legitimacy, therefore, was a construction of reason and since the history of a legitimate government consisted of re-affirmations of its birth, that history too was a rational construction. The history of illegitimate governments was also an essentially rational construction because the same criterion of relevance had to be applied to whatever evidence existed. Available historical evidence did impose some limits upon what a particular history could contain. But since the discipline of history was conceived as a didactic enterprise in which meaning was "as capable of demonstration, as any proposition in Euclid," then those limits were so wide as to be practically insignificant.

As far as Atwood was concerned, then, the universe was actually created and ruled by God, but God was as a rational man. History was the story of God's rule, therefore history was rational. On this view of the world and the nature of history, it was perfectly consistent for Atwood to argue that since reason taught that contract was the only proper foundation of legitimate government, then this **must** be historically valid. All legitimate governments existing in the world were actually founded by an historically specifiable contract. Furthermore, since all contracts embodied the will of the contractors, if followed that the **raison d'être** of all legitimate governments was **salus populi**. **Salus populi**, therefore, was necessarily the highest law of the contract constitution. These views and the idea of history that gave them coherence were widely shared in the late seventeenth century.[71] But the practical political message associated with constitutional contractarianism was by no means always the same. I have so far considered the nature and coherence of constitutional contract theory. Atwood's writings have served as one of the clearest statements of the doctrine. Robert Ferguson's career and writings will reveal just how various the practical political recommendations to be derived from constitutional contract theory might be.

CHAPTER 5

ROBERT FERGUSON

The political career of Robert Ferguson "the Plotter" was remarkable. It contained all the intrigue and conspiracy necessary to justify the epithet that has become attached to his name. Yet Ferguson, like Atwood, has been neglected by modern historians. As a pamphleteer, he was prolific. And his writings, judging by the replies and comments they elicited from contemporaries, were widely read. His name constantly cropped up in court cases, official letters, pamphlets and gossip about suspected conspiracies throughout the period. Educated as a nonconformist divine, Ferguson was one of several Scotsmen to move to England in the 1650s and enter public life as a controversialist and political activist. In 1663, he was imprisoned for "treasonable practices." This, however, was the only term of imprisonment that he served in his life. He was involved in practically all the conspiracies against Charles II, James II, and William and Mary that were discovered and he wrote popular defences of each side involved in the constitutional upheaval of 1688. He seems to have had a passion for losing causes. All the plots in which he played a prominent part (including the Rye House Plot, Monmouth's rebellion and Lord Atholl's Plot) were failures. He appears not to have had any significant involvement in the only successful rebellion of the period, the 1688 Revolution, and after the Revolution he stopped supporting the victorious side and devoted his energies to the Jacobite cause.

The not entirely unusual **volte-face** in Ferguson's career during 1690, from support of the successful William and Mary to the defence of the claims of James II, earned Ferguson the contempt of many contemporaries and has confused historical judgments of his life and ideas.[1] In 1704, for example, an anonymous opponent reflected:

> Now since Mr. **Ferguson's** whole Life has been one continued **Maze** of Intricate **Windings, Turnings, Shiftings, Doublings, Sculkings, playing** Bo-peep, and **Dissembling, Prevaricating** and **Betraying** (like a perfidious Jesuite) all Mankind he has treated with, ... he has made it a Herculean Task to find out what he truly is.[2]

In fact, Ferguson seems to have shared (though very early and in an extreme way) the fairly widespread Whig disillusionment with William's policies. The courting of Tories, the foreign favourites, William's stiff manner, continued corruption in government, and the possibly imminent return of James, all of which led the Whigs to be cautious in their dealings with William, led Ferguson towards angry opposition. And when William introduced an Indemnity Bill (1689) into the Commons, Ferguson's opposition turned to a belief that the Revolution was about to be betrayed. The Catholic supporters of James II were about to be given licence to continue their attacks on Protestantism. The way was being cleared for a Catholic resurgence divorced from Jacobitism. And in Ferguson's view, this had always been William's real intention. The English had simply been fooled.[3]

J.R. Jones is one of the most recent historians to make more than a passing reference to Ferguson and not to dismiss him as, in the words of Charles Bastide, simply one of "les vulgaires conspirateurs" of the period. Jones attempts to explain Ferguson's career as a plotter and his dramatic change of sides in 1690 in terms of his supposed moral scruples. Ferguson "worked against every administration because he believed that all ministers were and must, under the existing system, be always oppressive, corrupt, and parasitic."[4] But Ferguson never justified himself on these grounds and since, anyway, he plotted for so many different ends, Jones' attribution of consistent moral principles behind Ferguson's shifting political persuasions would seem beside the point. Gilbert Burnet, Ferguson's contemporary, imputed consistency into Ferguson's career on psychological grounds. Ferguson appeared as a "hot and bold man, whose spirit was naturally turned to plotting" and who was always "setting on some to mischief." Macaulay came to a similar conclusion. Ferguson "could not be quiet. Sedition, from being his business, had become his pleasure. It was impossible for him to live without doing mischief as for an old dram drinker or an old opium eater to live without the daily dose of poison." James Ferguson, Robert's only biographer, attempted to reconcile the conflicting elements of his career by portraying him as the consistent defender of James II. Thus his participation in the plots against Charles II and James II was made to appear as an attempt to thwart them from the inside. The argument, however, rests upon only one piece of evidence and that is Ferguson's own account of his activities during the Rye House Plot, an account written in exile in Holland and in all probability designed to vindicate himself should he be caught.[5] A final suggestion, that I owe to Professor M.M. Goldsmith, is that Ferguson was simply very susceptible to being bought off. But although this may have been the case (it was certainly suspected by John Oldmixon in 1735), I have been unable to turn up any evidence to support the idea.[6] Much more to the point, however, in the present context, is the recognition that Ferguson was "the most active and important" of radical Whig propagandists.[7] He was a man committed to intrigue and action and his success as a pamphleteer depended upon his command of all the resources of contemporary practical political rhetoric.

The many pamphlets that issued from Ferguson's pen between 1679 and 1709 all had an immediately practical character. Their main concern was to gain support for the variety of causes Ferguson championed and to this end all else, including coherence and consistency in ideas, seems to have been subordinated. This makes any interpretation of the meaning of the concepts he employed somewhat difficult. There is a danger of imputing not only precision where none in fact existed, but also of consistency where the tactics of dispute might have necessitated contradictions. But in these circumstances it is remarkable to note that all of Ferguson's political arguments draw upon a constitutional theory similar to William Atwood's. The central propositions of this theory were that the English constitution both embodied and was the historical product of an original contract and that in disputes over the requirements of constitutional law reference must be made to the intentions of the original contractors as well as to statute and common law. The distinctions between reason, natural law and civil law were accordingly blurred and almost anything that Ferguson believed reasonable could be presented as legal.

In 1679/80 Ferguson wrote the first of a long series of political pamphlets designed, in the most general terms, to secure political safeguards for the Protestant religion.[8] More specifically, his pamphlets of the 1680s were intended to support the causes of the Exclusionists and the Duke of Monmouth. After the failure of Monmouth's rebellion, he turned simply to oppose the king and eventually (for a short period) he wrote in support of William of Orange.

Practically all the anti-royalist writers of the 1680s took considerable trouble to defend the legality of their standpoints. Ferguson was no exception. He insisted that he was "of most sincere loyalty to the King and Government."[9] But mere assertions to the contrary could not avoid the accusation that he and "his **Party,** ... would willingly be at the old game of **Forty** and **Forty one** again."[10] Ferguson's activities invited the attack that he was plotting "to have all things in Common, to have the Power in the People," and was holding out "that Common-wealth **Prize**" as the "Reward" for anti-monarchical activities. Indeed, attacks on the Shaftesbury Whigs, of whom Ferguson was the leading pamphleteer, for being regicides and commonwealthmen were frequent.[11]

To be accused of being a commonwealthman was a serious matter in the 1680s. Hardly anyone wished to experience anew the upheavals of civil war or to be held responsible for causing them. Thus to combat these accusations Ferguson adopted the arguments of Sir William Jones, Attorney General at the time of Exclusion Parliaments. Jones' pamphlet was originally published in 1681 and Ferguson republished it with minor alterations (though without acknowledgment) in 1689.[12] In a clever and somewhat devious passage, Ferguson borrowed an argument attempting to make the accusation of commonwealthman rebound on the accusers. He noted:

> It is strange how this **Word** <commonwealth> should so change its signification with us in the space of twenty years. All **Monarchies** in the world, that are not purely Barbarous and Tyrannical, have ever been called **Commonwealths**. Rome itself altered not that Name, when it fell under the Sword of the **Caesars** ... And in our days, it doth not only belong to **Venice, Geneva, Switzerland,** and the **United Provinces** of the **Netherlands,** But to **Germany, Spain, France, Sweden, Poland,** and all the Kingdoms of **Europe**. May it not therefore be apprehended that our present Ministers, who have so much decried this **Word** so well known to our Laws, so often used by our best Writers, and by all our Kings until this day, are Enemies to the thing; And that they who make it a brand of Infamy to be of **Commonwealth Principles,** that is, devoted to the good of the People, do intend no other but the hurt ... of that People?[13]

By thus redefining commonwealth to mean a state governed for the good of its citizens, Ferguson was able to accuse his attackers of a "fondness of ... Arbitrary Power, and ... design to set it up, by subverting our Ancient Legal Monarchy, instituted for the benefit of the Commonwealth." But this was clearly achieved by simply redefining the term in a way that was unacceptable to his opponents. Commonwealthmen had become people "passionately devoted to the Publick good, and to the common Service of their Country." They were men "who believe that Kings were instituted for the good of the People, and the Government ordained for the sake of those that are to be governed, and <who> therefore complain or grieve when it is used to contrary ends." Royalists may well have disagreed with these principles but they would certainly not have recognized them as the essence of the commonwealth cause. To them, the distinguishing character of the commonwealthman was not that his ideas might lead him to complain or grieve about abuses of government. It was rather that they would lead him to a "design of setting up a Democratical Government, in Opposition to our legal Monarchy:" exactly the design which Ferguson wanted to dissociate himself from.[14]

In all his anti-royalist writings of the 1680s, Ferguson claimed that there was "no mark of an Intention to change any part of the Ancient Government, but to provide against the Violation of it."[15] It was his opponents who were acting against the constitution. Thus the issue at the centre of constitutional controversy in the early 1680s - Parliament's right to alter the succession - became for him a legal right never "questioned or gainsaid till a few Mercinary People <during the Exclusion Crisis> endeavoured to obtrude upon us a pretended Divine, and unalterable Right to the Succession." These were the people who, in Ferguson's eyes, were guilty of designing constitutional innovations.[16]

Even the 1688 Revolution, as we have seen, was defended by many as constitutionally lawful along these lines. The ancient constitution had at length been saved, they claimed, and the opposition to Charles II and James II over the previous decade had thus truly been based on positive law. Ferguson was amongst this number and his claim to justify resistance to James II "from Principles which our Constitution and Laws do administer" followed a familiar pattern. His argument focused on James II's "breach of all stipulations and Promises ... his violating the Original Contract."[17] The theory of government and law involved here was implicit in Ferguson's earliest political writings. In the **Second Part of No Protestant Plot** (1682), for example, he argued that:

As the Law is both the Measure and Bond of the

Subjects Duty and Allegiance, so it is not only the best security which they have to trust unto for their peace and safety, and the established fence and hedg for the protection of their lives and properties; but it was intended, and always ought to be the Rule and Standard by which the Prince is to defend and govern his people.[18]

The law, then, was above king and people. Yet the law was designed for the people's "preservation." The people were "obliged by their Interest, as well as by the ties of Conscience, to honour and maintain all due **Allegiance** to their Supreme Governours." Rulers were "not only bound by the **Stipulation** which they have made with their people, but by the respect which they bear to the preservation of the Constitution and the safety of their Crowns." Thus it was effectively only rulers who were under an onerous obligation. For rulers must avoid ruling in such a way that their subjects might fear for their own safety. If this were not avoided then rulers simply forfeited the "due **Allegiance**" of the citizenry. Ferguson was explicit about this. It followed, he warned, that "whensoever Laws cease to be a security unto men, they will be sorely tempted to apprehedn <sic> themselves cast into a state of War, and justified in having recourse to the best means they can for their shelter and defence."[19]

By 1689, however, a very explicit justification of the legality of resistance was required if the Revolution were to be defended as constitutionally lawful. This need spurred Ferguson to write his single most extensive analysis of the nature of government and the English constitution. Since government, he observed, "derives its Ordination and Institution from God," it is also limited by God. Emphasis was still being placed on the ruler's rather than the subjects' duties, but now those duties were formalized into a compact between God and king. Rulers were now portrayed as "under Pact and Confinement" to God. God required them "to exert their Governing Power, for the Safety, Welfare, and Prosperity of those over whom they are Established." The consequence which Ferguson drew was clear and unequivocal.

There was no need of "previous Compacts, and Agreements, between Princes and Peoples" to establish the universal rule that government should be conducted for the good of the people and the honour of God. The compact between God and the magistrate established that. Thus whoever "refuseth to Govern in Subordination unto and for God, and in order to the protection and benefit of the Community, ceaseth to answer the Ends unto which Magistracy was Instituted." And ceasing to answer these ends meant losing the right to the subjects' obedience.[20]

But it still seems that Ferguson believed this compact between God and ruler was of far too general a nature to provide a community with a workable constitution. God simply laid down the general character of government and no-one subsequently had a right to change it.[21] But the constitutional detail necessary for the practical working of the government ordained by God had to be established through a constitutional contract:

> Now God having in the Institution of Magistracy, confined such as shall be chosen Rulers, within no other limits in reference to our civil concerns, save that they are to Govern for the good of those, over whom they come to be Established, it remains free and entire to the People at their first Erection of, and Submission to Government, to prescribe and define what shall be the measures and boundaries of the publick Good, and unto what Rules and Standards the Magistrate shall be restrained ... And every one being equally Master of his own Property and Liberty, antecedently to their Agreement with one another, and to the compact of the Universality, or at least of the Majority, with Him or Those whom they call to Rule over them; it evidently follows, that those who come to be cloathed with Magistracy, can lay claim to no more Authority ... than what the Community conferred upon them, ... upon the prospect of the advantages arising unto them from their living in Societies and under Magistrates.[22]

The familiar contractarian ideas and assumptions

about the origin and purpose of government are all contained in this passage. Governments were founded by the conscious design of prospective citizens who, obeying the will of God and realizing the potential advantages of civil society, agree to set them up. The act of combination consisted of outlining and agreeing to a body of constitutional laws and naming the principal office-holders. The contractors' main concern was to protect their antecedent property and liberty. The form of government erected was inevitably some kind of limited government. The only somewhat extraordinary aspect of Ferguson's theory thus far was the emphasis placed on the role of God in these proceedings. But in this, Ferguson was harking back to much earlier contractarian treatises like that of the **Vindiciae contra tyrannos**.[23]

Ferguson's theory, however, was far from comprehensive. Many enquiries were left unconsidered. No attempt was made, for example, to consider questions of the artificiality of contract society, or of life in a state of nature, or of natural rights and natural law. But Ferguson's concern was essentially the practical one of justifying the activities of William of Orange and the resisters of James II. His attention was thus focused on the English constitution even though he felt compelled, perhaps because of the peculiar case that he wished to defend as constitutional, to enquire into more general questions about the nature of government. Thus he began his argument by remarking that the "Consideration of Government in general, is none of my Province at this time; farther than to observe ..."[24] But he then devoted a quarter of his lengthy pamphlet to summarizing his contractarian general theory. The reason for so long an introduction to the pamphlet's main concern was that his main constitutional arguments depended upon it for their coherence and persuasiveness.

In the course of Ferguson's outline of government in general, it becomes clear that "Force and Conquest give no just nor legal Title over a People, ... until they by some consent either **tacit** or **explicit**, declare their submission ... upon the best Terms which they can obtain."25 The idea of legitimacy involved here coupled the legal with the just. The two were related through a notion of consent - a notion which Ferguson understood in terms of contracts and agreements. The association of law, justice, consent and contract enabled Ferguson to argue that:

> no Government is lawful, but what is founded upon Compact and agreement between those chosen to govern, and them who condescend to be governed; ...<and> the Articles upon which they stipulate the one with the other, become the Fundamentals of the respective Constitutions of Nations, and together with superadded positive Laws, are both the limits of the Rulers Authority, and the Measures of the Subjects Obedience.26

With ideas like these, Ferguson set the scene for a consideration of the English constitution. Like many of his contemporaries, he believed the English constitution of unrivalled excellence. But its unique excellence he understood in a way that only contractarians would have accepted. England had been the "most provident and careful of all Nations in reserving unto itself, upon the first Institution of, and its submission unto Regal Government" rights and liberties exactly appropriate for upholding the good of the people. And throughout history, England, "with a Courage ... peculiar to it, maintained its Priviledges and Liberties."27

It was by reference to this rationally constructed English constitution, preserved and augmented throughout history, that Ferguson examined the legality of the anti-royalist movements of the 1680s. He did this secure in the knowledge that if a conflict arose between law and reason the latter might override the former. After all, to subordinate positive law to the dictates of reason was simply, on his view, to remove inconsistencies from the constitution by referring to the most basic constitutional laws. The problem, then, of the legality of resistance could be easily resolved. No real restriction was placed on the scope of Ferguson's argument by his acceptance of the common belief that

English kings "can claim nothing for what they enjoy, or claim, but fundamental and positive Laws" and that the subjects' rights and privileges had a similar source.[28] Certainly, he still devoted much effort to finding authorities in Law Books and precedents. But disputes were not settled according to the strongest legal case. Whenever Ferguson ran into legal or historical difficulties, he took recourse in reason.[29] And this, according to the constitutional theory which he shared with Atwood, meant simply appealing to a higher or more basic judge which was not in the least less legal nor was it an appeal to legality of a different kind.

Ferguson upheld a view of the English constitution as a balance between king and parliament, although the balance was tipped in the latter's favour. He defended this view with essentially the same mixture of arguments from the ancient constitution and from reason as those we have already seen in Atwood's writings. Thus the Norman conquest was not a conquest at all: William I conquered no-one save Harold and his few associates.[30] The absence of records showing the foundation of an institution deemed good by the writer proved that that institution was "co-eval with the first Constitution of our Government" and thus inviolable. Englishmen's rights were derived from the original contract and the immemorial constitution, not from the grant or concession of kings. And finally, Magna Carta was not forced from King John but was simply a reaffirmation of the "ancient Rights of the People."[31]

Ferguson thus portrayed the balanced constitution, just as Atwood did, issuing from the wisdom of our ancestors.[32] It was they who established that the executive power was "conveyed unto and vested in the King" not as a personal right but as something "delegated ... as a Trust." Nothing was left "to the King's private discretion, much less to his Arbitrary Will." Instead, he had "assigned to him the Laws as the Rules and Measures he is to govern by." The House of Commons was given the principal function "to search into all the Oppressions and Injustices of the King's Ministers."[34] And in order to ensure effective performance, even against the wishes of the king, Ferguson asserted that the "Wisdom of our Ancestors had provided, by diverse Statutes, both for the holding Parliaments annually, and oftener if need be; and that they should not be Prorogued or Dissolved till all the Petitions and Bills before them were answered and redressed."[35] The most interesting general function of the Lords, indeed, "the very end of a House of Peers," was to maintain the balance between king and Commons, "to prevent his Invading the Priviledges of the People, and them usurping upon the Prerogatives of the Crown."[36] These constitutional arrangements, then, were set up by a set of wise ancestors. And in referring back to them, Ferguson gained plausibility for his highly questionable views of the nature of the English constitution. Referring each pretended law to the intentions of our ancestors meant, in the last resort, that attention was directed away from the judgments of legally qualified contemporaries and towards the supposed design of the original contractors.

Ferguson's handling of the principal constitutional issue of the 1680s - the question of the succession to the throne - led to some interesting conclusions. He attempted to justify a parliamentary right to modify the succession by referring back to the original contractors. Parliament's right, he claimed, had existed "from the first Original of the Government" and had continued to exist despite the "coming in of the **Norman** Race."[37] Although historical examples could show that the Crown had at times descended in irregular and unusual ways and that the hereditary principal had not always governed the succession, Ferguson's difficulty was to prove that these historical examples constituted legal precedents. He set about doing so by extending Parliament's right far beyond the question of succession. Thus instead of attempting to make out the strongest legal case for an ultimate parliamentary right to determine the successor, Ferguson proceeded first of all to elicit a parliamentary right to determine any constitutional question. Parliament became both the interpreter of the "Interest of the Publick" and the ultimate interpreter of the constitution. To have a parliament now appeared as "the most Fundamental and essential" of all "the Rights and Priviledges appertaining unto us." By parliaments, society was preserved and the temporal and spiritual welfare of the subjects advanced.38 The constitution consisted of "the **immemorial** course of Administration, with the sense of the whole **Society** signified by their **Representatives** in **Parliament** upon emerging occasions." And this parliamentary voice alone was of relevance in determining questions of constitutional law. In no case were "the **Opinions** of particular men of what Rank or Order soever they be" to be admitted.39 Thus parliament, as distinct from the king, became the dominant partner in Ferguson's constitutional theory. It was both the interpreter and the guardian of that ancient constitution which had been set up by contract in order to fill in the details of the lawful government ordained by God. This view of the English constitution provided Ferguson with the means to argue that the 1688 Revolution had been perfectly legal.

James II, Ferguson argued, had committed a number of "unlawful" acts and these were the things "whereby our lately departed King hath unqualified himself."40 By dispensing with oaths, encouraging papacy, attacking the corporations and law courts, and by refusing a parliament, James had destroyed "the legal and regular Monarchy of the Nation" and turned it into "an Arbitrary and Despotick Power." The result was "that all the Franchises and Rights, which by Original Contracts and Subsequent Laws had been reserved unto the People, were entirely overthrown, or enjoyed precariously."41 In short, James' policy amounted to "a plain destroying of all natural as well as **Civil Liberty**." And the consequence on Ferguson's constitutional theory could be no other than to release Englishmen "from the ties, which by vertue of **fundamental Stipulations**, and **Statute Laws** we formerly lay under."42

The character and some of the implications of Ferguson's political vocabulary are fairly clear from these constitutional arguments. The vocabulary is one of fundamentals which associates original contracts with subsequent laws, fundamental stipulations and statute laws, civil liberty and fundamental constitutions. The questions he was considering were matters of English constitutional law and practice. All this, including the causes on behalf of which Ferguson wrote, serves to underline the similarity of his ideas to those of Atwood. But one point of apparent difference should be clarified before pursuing Ferguson through his change of political allegiance in 1690. For unlike Atwood, he chose to designate James' attacks on Englishmen's rights as an attack on natural as well as civil liberty and he described the interregnum up to the crowning of William and Mary as a "state of nature."[43] These uses of a more philosophical vocabulary should not surprise us, however. It is clear from the context of his argument that he did not understand them in the ways we will find them being used in philosophical contractarianism. He was simply drawing upon common terms and giving them a narrow and specific meaning in arguments of his own.

For example in the state of nature created by James II, Ferguson insisted that it was lawful, albeit "both Lawful and Necessary, to recover that by Force, which had been wrested from us by Usurpation." Now the only law that could give this use of force a legal character was natural not constitutional law. Ferguson, however, was not content to justify the use of force against James solely in moral terms. He believed he was justifying the Revolution "from Principles which our Constitution and Laws do Administer." James' actions it appears had only rendered the English constitution momentarily inoperative. The **government** had been dissolved but the former subjects remained Englishmen. They remained in that union set up by original contract with the mutual rights and obligations that had then been agreed to. This severely limited the range of possibilities open to them in what Ferguson chose to call the state of nature. Thus although Ferguson accepted that in that state the only rule of what should be done was the people's "Will, guided and regulated by the Measures of what is most conducible to the publick good," what it amounted to was little. All that Englishmen had to do was "to declare the Prince of Orange **King**." For, as he explained, "until then, the Government can exert itself but in few of its proper operations; nor can it either Repeal ill Laws, nor Enact such good ones as we want and need." Thus although James's actions had restored "the People to their State and Condition of Primitive Freedom," government and law still operated after a fashion, actions might still be judged lawful or unlawful according to constitutional law, and all that was required to rectify the situation was to declare William king.[44]

But having produced these elaborate arguments against James II and on behalf of William of Orange, Ferguson changed sides almost immdediately. Within eighteen months of William's successful expedition to England, Ferguson was suspected of being engaged in Jacobite plots.[45] Although he continued to escape arrest, when he next appeared in print it was as an ardent opponent of the Revolution. He acknowledged that the reader might be "surprised to hear this kind of Theology and Politics from me" but he explained that he had hitherto been misled by "false Notions" and "Hypotheses" about government which he had come to realize were "neither reconcileable to our Laws, nor to the Peace of Communities."[46]

The ideas that Ferguson now wanted to reject were of considerable practical importance. But what is most significant for our purposes is that he never abandoned the idea that the English constitution was essentially contractualist. His opposition to William III, his defence of James II and his calls for a "legal" revolt against the new regime were all defended on exactly the same basis as their opposites had been in the 1680s.

The Revolution certainly took on a different colour from the perspective of Ferguson's Jacobitism. He was now convinced that it "was neither King **James's** Interest to destroy, or the Prince of **Orange's** to protect the **Protestant Religion.**"[47] England had been deluded by William III and its citizens "translated out of a **Canaan**, where too much Safety, Ease and Plenty, made them complain, and brought into an unpresidented and intolerable Thraldom."[48] The supposed threat to Protestantism had been an elaborate hoax. The Whigs were a

"Compound of the Atheistical of all Opinions and Persuasions whatsoever."[49] The Revolution had in fact been a Catholic rather than a Protestant plot. Catholics "undertook the deposing a Prince of their own Church, because he would not support the Supremacy of the Pope." They "procured Resolutions from Rome ... to authorize the Catholicks in **England** to transfer their Allegiance from King **James** to King **William**." And this was not as self-destructive as might appear, since William was a Catholic in "disguise."[50] Ferguson's view here certainly was extreme. But Protestant Jacobitism seems to have mustered quite considerable support.[51]

He began to subscribe to doctrines that were commonplace in Tory and Jacobite argument and this led Ferguson to reverse his previous judgments on the requirements of English law. He now asserted, as the best of Tories had done before 1688, that:

> in no Circumstances of Danger into which our Religion and civil Liberties could be brought nor under any Hazards we could fall into of losing and having them suppressed, we were either permitted or impowered, by the Fundamentals of our Government, the rules of our Constitution, or by the common or statute Law of the Kingdom, to rebel against the King, or to dethrone or drive him away.[52]

There simply was "no Law or Contract, existent in the King's time" that "provided that we might fly to Arms" to protect legal rights. Rather, there were several statutes that made it "**Treason to take up Arms ... upon any Pretence whatsoever.**"[53] Furthermore, since the "Wisdom of our Ancestors made it an **Axiom** of our Government and State, **That the King could do no Wrong**," it followed that "no Accusations of him could be justified, and much less any Force against him lawful."[54]

In similar style as before, but with obviously different content, then, Ferguson now began promoting the Jacobite cause. He still asserted that "the great End of the Laws <was> the Publick Good" and that the "first and the highest Law of the Society ... is that of **Salus Populi**," but he drew very different constitutional conclusions from those he had drawn in the 1680s. He retained the basic belief that the English constitution was essentially the product of an original contract, supplemented and modified through time. The source of determining legal rights and duties thus remained the intentions of the original contractors and the rational constitution that they were supposed to have established. Instead of James II, it was now the Convention Parliament that had destroyed the constitution, "As to what it was, and what it still ought to be, according both to the Fundamentals of our first Establishment into a **Polity**, and the Common and Statute Laws of the Kingdom."[55]

The royalist constitutional theories of Robert Brady and Edmund Bohun, which formed the basis of some of the most frequently voiced attacks on the Revolution, played no part in Ferguson's Jacobitism. Such theories as these, deriving Englishmen's rights from the concessions of absolute monarchs whose titles to rule depended either on conquest or patriarchalism, were explicitly rejected by Ferguson. In 1695, for example, he made his point in a manner that could well have appeared in any of his pre-Revolution tracts:

> For, Sir, suffer me to tell you, That a Right and Title to the Freedom of our Persons ... doth not accrue and arise unto us either from **Magna Charta**, the **Petition of Right**, or the Staute of **Habeas Corpus**; but it was reserved unto us, and we were kept in Possession of it, by the very Nature and Frame of our Constitution. For our whole Government was founded upon the Supposal and Concession, That it was to be a Government of and over Freemen ... And the **Great Charter**, and the **other Laws**, which I have mentioned, did not create and give us a Right to the **Freedom** of our Persons; but they did only assert, vindicate, and fence it about. They were not Laws of manumission from Bondage, but Declaratory of our antecedent and inherent Title to Liberty.[56]

Royalist constitutional history, then, was deficient as an account of the origin of Englishmen's rights. But Ferguson did make one concession to it and by so doing he implicitly outlined a solution to a major contemporary problem of constitutional interpretation. The extreme royalists were arguing not only that Englishmen's rights originated in monarchs' concessions but also that it was lawful for monarchs to withdraw those concessions. Many of the anti-royalists believed, as we shall see, that Englishmen's rights were something like the natural rights of man made specific and practicable by the original contract which established the English constitution. They then argued that defending these rights by arms could be constitutionally justified. Both sides argued from fixed points of historical origin to the provisions of the seventeenth century constitution, without allowing for any significant changes in the intervening centuries. When, however, Ferguson argued that "unquestionably many Things were at first vested in the Crown" which no longer are, he acknowledged the possibility of a divorce between historical origins and later justifications of laws and institutions. He did not make use of this, however, in his own constitutional analysis. To have done so would have questioned the relevance of the historical original contract for understanding the contemporary constitution. But he did modify his understanding of the original contract. The constitution was still regarded as beginning by a contract but that contract became one of many agreed to between rulers and ruled whereby the constitution had been altered as circumstances required. In this fashion Ferguson defended James II not only for having had no "ill Design against our Religion" but also for having been prepared "to have granted a Stipulatory Law, which should have the Force and Virtue of a **Magna Charta,** or **Constitutional Contract,** and to have made the Protestant Religion ... a Fundamental in the Government of all other Reigns."[57]

With this far from unprecedented equation of constitutional contract and important constitutional law, Ferguson demolished the Whig theory of a constitutional right of resistance. **Salus populi** was still the supreme law but in the ancient English constitution:

> there is no **Original Contract**, nor stipulatory Agreement, by which it is provided, That if Princes do not as they should, they do either forfeit their Soveraign Authority, or that we may lawfully rebel against and dethrone them. Nor do any Presidents or Examples ... shew, that it was lawful, or a Thing that either the Constitution, or subsequent Laws, did authorise and countenance; but they only declared what a provoked People will sometimes do ... And **via facti** is not always **via juris**.[58]

The Revolution of 1688 had been illegal. The only proper course for Englishmen had been preached by the upholders of passive obedience and non-resistance.[59] There certainly had been a contract at the basis of the old constitution but this was interpreted much more loosely than before:

> And as for that **Contract** (if it might be called one) which was involved and tacitly wrapt up in the Constitution, the whole Import of it was, to declare the Ends for which our Princes were to rule ... and to teach and instruct them, that they were to govern us by Laws; but it in no ways provided, that they should be accountable unto, or arraignable by their Subjects, if they did not; leaving them for that only responsible to God.[60]

Contractualism, passive obedience and divine right, then, were harmoniously incorporated in the pre-Revolution constitution. But the case was otherwise with the new constitution of 1689. For "whatever there was of an **Original Contract** between former Kings and the free People of these Kingdoms, yet it is undeniable, there is a very **formal** and **explicite One** between K. William and them."[61] Juggling with Whig, Tory and Jacobite arguments, Ferguson turned this interpretation of the situation against the new regime. The king was in a worse than precarious position having been put on the throne by men who had flouted all law to satisfy their whims.[62] But the men of the Convention who had contracted with William had no right to act on behalf of the people. The government they had established was illegal. William was "only King **de facto**, not **de jure**."[63] His rule was nothing less than "the Prince of Orange's Tyranny" and it was necessary to oppose force with force.[64] Such force would be lawful, Ferguson argued, but this time it was to natural law that he appealed. Constitutional law no longer existed not even implicitly. Recourse must be had to natural laws "which put us upon a common level with those that were antecedently our Rulers." But even in this situation Ferguson was concerned to add that such force was necessary to "defend our selves and our Government by Laws established."[65] Constitutional right had to be incorporated.

Here then, we have the basic propositions and arguments of Ferguson's constitutional contract writings both for and against the 1688 Revolution. Perhaps what emerges most clearly is the extent to which ideas of a constitutional contract had penetrated into practical political debate of the late seventeenth century. Ferguson's writings provide one of the clearest indications of the connection between constitutional law and original contract in the political ideas of the time. His insistence that "no government is lawful, but what is founded upon Compact," and that "the Articles upon which ⟨the contractors⟩ stipulate the one with the other, become the Fundamentals of the respective Constitutions of Nations"[62] provided exactly the connection between civil law and reason that enabled reasonableness to be credited as a standard of lawfulness.

The loose way Ferguson used the idea of contract indicated both his concern with practice rather than theoretical profundity and that he felt considerable capital could be made by employing the term. He sometimes used the idea to explain the historical origin of the English constitution; sometimes to explain the historical origin of all just constitutions; and sometimes, indeed most frequently, as little more than a synonym for constitutional law. In doing this, and especially the last, we should not understand Ferguson as in any way innovatory. We have become so accustomed to think appeals to contract involved an elaborate theory that considerable evidence of quite other usages has been quietly passed over. The elaborations of contract theories in writers like Atwood and Ferguson were novel. Nothing quite like them had been presented before. But the association of the term contract with constitutional law and the use of the word for constitutional law occurred very early in the history of modern political thought. A rapid glance at late sixteenth century French political literature might cure us of too hasty an attribution of novelty (or absurdity) to the use by Ferguson and the rest of the term contract as a synonym for constitutional law.

For in the literature of the French Wars of Religion it is possible to detect some of the earliest associations of contractualist ideas with speculation about fundamental laws. The term "lois fondamentales" only begins to appear in French constitutional writing around the middle of the sixteenth century.[67] Initially, discussion about what were referred to as the "lois fondamentales positives ou particulières" - the specific constitutional laws of France - usually asserted that such laws were the gifts of kings but that custom had given them a force independent of the ruling monarch's will. This appears to have been the view of Jean du Tillet, Estienne Pasquier and Du Haillon.[68] And it was this idea which Hotman challenged in **Francogallia** (1573). Hotman's argument was that French kings had been instituted by the people and that at their institution they had been restrained "by defined laws and compacts."[69] **Francogallia** was widely read and quoted. And even such an arch-royalist as Du Haillon is to be found engaging in archive ransacking and reconstructing, in his **L'Histoire de France** (1576), a romantic account of the French people setting up their supposed first king, Pharamond, by agreement.[70] Hotman's reflections on French fundamental law were associated in many quarters with the contractualist arguments of the **Vindiciae contra tyrannos** (1579). Indeed, it was long suspected that Hotman had written both works.[71] Understandings then, similar to Ferguson's, that basic constitutional law was "un pacte conclus entre la nation et le roi" were far from unusual even in the literature of late sixteenth century France.[72] In Beza's **Du Droit des Magistrats sur leur suiects** (1574) we encounter arguments referring to "the fundamental laws of the French kingdom established at the time of its foundation."[73] And in **Apothègmes et discours notables recueillies de divers autheurs** (1573) we find very general references to basic constitutional laws as simply "les contracts."[74]

We might trace similar usages through French, Scottish, Spanish and English political literature from the sixteenth to the early eighteenth century. But the point is perhaps sufficiently made that Ferguson's reference to constitutional laws as contracts were far from idiosyncratic. That there were differences in understandings of what this meant, as between sixteenth century writers and Ferguson and the others at the end of the seventeenth, is not in doubt. When French writers during the Wars of Religion referred to constitutional law, fundamental law and contract they could not possibly have meant to convey any of the associations with debates about the ancient constitution and the feudal law that were the immediate reference point for much of Ferguson's writings. But in terms of understandings of contract in late seventeenth century English political argument, Ferguson's writings deserve attention for one further reason. His arguments indicate that during the 1680s and 1690s there was no inevitable connection between having Whig sympathies, viewing the constitution or the nature of the state in terms of a contract, and supporting William III and the Revolutionary Settlement. And when Ferguson's appeals to contract in the Jacobite cause are recognized as far from unqiue, Charlwood Lawton and Robert Jenkin were doing much the same thing,[75] the excessive simplicity of our text book histories might finally be abandoned.

PART III

CHAPTER 6

PHILOSOPHICAL CONTRACTARIANISM

In a paper written the year before his death, Locke noted some **Thoughts Concerning Reading and Study for a Gentleman.** The paper contained, amongst much else, an examination of the nature of political studies and a selected list of suggested reading. Locke wrote: "Politics contains two parts very different the one from the other, the one containing the original of societies and the rise and extent of political power, the other, the art of governing men in society."[1] Locke might be thought here to be distinguishing between an historical enquiry into the origin of society and government and a practical, 'manual for governors,' sort of enquiry. But this turns out not to be the case. His reading lists and further comments indicate that the origins he was concerned with were rational, not historical. History and experience were relevant to the second part of politics - the part concerned with the study of policy in particular constitutions. For an understanding of the first part, Locke recommended the first book of Hooker's **Ecclesiastical Polity** and Sidney's **Discourses Concerning Government.** These, he claimed, were "the most talked of" books of this kind in English, but added that he had never read Sidney. He then proceeded: "Let me here add **Two Treatises of Government,** printed 1690, and a treatise of **Civil Polity,** printed this year <1703, written by Peter Paxton>. To these one may add Pufendorf **De Officio Hominis et Civis,** and **De Jure Naturali et Gentium,** which last is the best book of that kind." It is significant that Locke bracketed his own **Two Treatises** with these other texts of which Pufendorf's **De Jure Naturae et Gentium** was the best example. It is also significant that he should confess to never having read Sidney. For Sidney's work was the only one in the list that dealt explicitly and in detail with the specifics of the English constitution and by doing so it shared many of the characteristics of the works recommended by Locke for the student of the second part of politics.[2]

This second part, Locke explained, "concerns the art of government." It was "best to be learned by experience and history, especially that of a man's own country." He went on to expand:

> And therefore I think an English gentleman should be well versed in the history of England, taking his rise as far back as there are any records of it, joining with it the laws that were made in the several ages as he goes along in his history, that he may observe from thence the several turns of state, and how they have been produced. In Mr. Tyrrel's **History of England** he will find all along those several authors which have treated of our affairs and which he may have recourse to concerning any point which either his curiosity or judgement shall lead him to enquire into.
>
> With the history he may also do well to read the ancient Lawyers, (such as are Bracton, Fleta, Henningham, **Mirrour of Justices**, My Lord Cook on the second **Institutes**, and the **Modus Tenendi Parliamentum**, and others of that kind whom he may find quoted in the late controversies between Mr. Petit. Mr. Tyrrel, Mr. Atwood, etc., with Dr. Brady; as also, I suppose, in Sedler's treatise of **The Rights of the Kingdom, and Customs of our Ancestors** ...) wherein he will find the ancient constitution of the government of England.

It is worth dwelling on Locke's statements about political studies because they reveal something of the distinction in Locke's mind between a constitutional and a philosophical contractualism. In accepting the traditional distinction between theoretical and practical writing, he recognized that both contained arguments using the notion of contract. The theoretical and practical treatments are distinguished by their terminology, at least in the first instance. In the practical literature that Locke recommends we constantly run into terms like fundamental law, fundamental rights, fundamental liberties, fundamental or original contract and ancient or fundamental constitution. In the theoretical literature, we constantly meet terms like state of nature, natural law, natural rights, original or social contract and civil or political society. These differences in vocabulary reveal much more significant differences between the two types of contractarian argument. The questions posed in each were different. Philosophical contractarians addressed questions of a much more general kind than those which concerned constitutional contract writers. No doubt the questions and issues actually at stake were often the same. But at least in appearance, the terminology of social contract was invoked in answer to questions of a universal kind whereas constitutional contract was concerned with particular issues and events. Theorists of a social contract tended to ask: why is civil society necessary, what is the essential nature of civil society and what sort of government should men have? They were not concerned with the questions that preoccupied theorists of constitutional contracts: how did the English (or any other particular) constitution originate, what sort of constitution was it, what specific rights and liberties did its laws define and guarantee and what did all this imply for the conduct of present political affairs? Just as the different vocabularies reveal that different questions are being asked, so they highlight that different evidence is being appealed to. For constitutional contractarians the evidence of law books and history was essential (even though such evidence might be interpreted in a very cavalier fashion); social contract theorists did not require this evidence for the coherence or persuasiveness of their arguments. In social contract writings the crucial concept was the natural, in constitutional contract arguments it was the fundamental. By tradition, speculation about the natural concerned reason and the divine law whereas the fundamental was firmly wedded to history and human law.

   We have here, then, an initial characterization of two very different kinds of contractualist talk. Locke's use of the traditional distinction between practical and theoretical political writing has revealed some awareness on his part of these two types of contractual language. But theoretical, in Locke's discussion, does not mean philosophical. Much of the reading that he recommends to the would-be student of the theoretical part of political studies turns out to be fundamentally practical in character. Nonetheless, I have called the contractualism that appears in this writing philosophical contractarianism in order to capture the distinctive connotations (rather than denotations) of the language employed. The terms and concepts were part of a philosophical language and those who employed them tended to have far greater theoretical ambitions and to aim for a much greater generality of thought than those who employed the alternative language. Frequently the terms were merely borrowed from philosophical language and put to use in practical political argument. It will be a part of my enquiry to assess when this is being done. Some distinction must be made between genuine and sham philosophy, since the understanding of contract exhibited in each will be different. This point will become clearer as my enquiry advances. But sufficient has been said to expose the limitations of my initial characterization of the differences between constitutional and philosophical contractarianism. Differences in vocabulary may serve to indicate differences in meaning, but the use of a standard vocabulary is no guarantee of a similarity in meaning.

   In the remainder of this chapter, then, I will be concerned to portray what sort of theory was involved in philosophical contractarianism during the Revolution period. I shall try to exhibit the soil of speculation in which the late seventeenth century modifications of the theory grew and consider how radically the theory differed from constitutional contractarianism. Finally, I shall consider the question whether all examples of the consistent employment of the vocabulary of philosophical contractarianism were genuinely philosophical writings.

During the seventeenth century, those writers who have usually been considered social contract theorists sought to explain the rationality of civil society by locating its source or origin in the nature of the individual. The enterprise was informed by the resolutive-compositive method of the famous Paduan methodologists. Thus the complex relations of civil society were broken down into their simplest parts and were then reconstructed anew from them. The process of analysis was essentially one of rational abstraction. The process of reconstruction essentially involved the pursuit of the logical consequences of the interactions between "natural men." This was the kind of enquiry referred to above as rationalist constructivism.[3] But although the procedures of analysis were abstractive and hypothetical, although the state of nature to which civil society was reduced was in essence a rational construction, this did not mean that history and empirical evidence were irrelevant to the enquiry. Social contract writers of the seventeenth century did not always make rigid distinctions between the provinces of reason and history. At the very least most of them believed that the evidence of history and experience should not contradict a true account of the state of nature and the characteristics of natural man. In some works this interweaving of rational, historical and empirical enquiries reveals that a particular Christian view of the universe is being appealed to. This view presented the universe as the creation of a divine will; it presented human affairs as guided by that divine will; and it understood the divine will as a rational will. In other works, this interweaving reveals simply that the writer is engaged in political controversy and is concerned to cover his flanks from all anticipated attacks. We shall meet some peculiar results of the appeal to both reason and history when examining the literature of what I have called integrated contractarianism.[4] But even the great seventeenth century social contract theorists like Althusius, Grotius, Hobbes, Spinoza, Pufendorf and Locke were not always clear about the role of historical and empirical evidence in their theories.[5]

In the late seventeenth century, Pufendorf's reputation clearly marked him out as the foremost proponent of social contract theory. He provided a model of the standard theory for his contemporaries and worked it out in a very clear fashion. Of English writers, Locke alone had the distinction of writing purely in social contract terms. Both Pufendorf and Locke, then, demand our close attention if we are to understand the nature of social contract thought in late seventeenth century England. I will examine Locke's work in detail in the next chapter. He is by far the most famous of the English contractarians with whom we are concerned and the status of his work has been the subject of great disagreement. An examination of Pufendorf's ideas will provide an idea of the distinctiveness of social contract theory. This, in turn, will cast light on the disagreements over the intellectual status of Locke's **Two Treatises of Government**. After all, as we have just seen, Locke believed that Pufendorf had written the best book of the same kind as **Two Treatises**: a book, that is to say, which would instruct the reader "in the natural Rights of Men, and the Original Foundations of Society, and the Duties resulting from hence."[6]

Pufendorf's importance in the present context derives from his immense stature in the European republic of letters of his time. Practically all his works on philosophy, law, politics, history and religion were reviewed favourably in contemporary learned journals like Pierre Bayle's **Nouvelles de la république des lettres**, Henri Basnage's **Histoire des ouvrages des sçavans** and J.C. de la Crose's **The History of Learning**. His excellence was so widely acclaimed that it moved Andrew Tooke to note in the preface to his English translation of **De Officio Hominis et Civis** (1691) that: Pufendorf had "had as great regard paid him from Personages of the highest degree, as perhaps ever was given to the most learned of men."[7] Most of Pufendorf's works were translated into English, or summarised in English, between 1690 and 1705. They were all well received. In particular his political works were found most illuminating by Atwood and Locke. Indeed, to Atwood, Pufendorf appeared as the "judicious Civilian **Pufendorf**, one of the Ornaments of the present Age" and his **De Jure Naturae et Gentium** was "that Book of his which is counted the Standard of the Law of Nations."[8] Pufendorf's European reputation is well attested by the German jurisconsult Johann Wolfgang Textor who, in his **Synopsis of the Law of Nations** (1680) acknowledged Pufendorf as master in the field.[9] In England, Locke's and Atwood's theories, as well as many others, contain distinctive echoes and explicit references to Pufendorf.

Pufendorf himself regarded his enquiries in the **Elementorum Jursiprudentiae Universalis** (1660), **De Jure Naturae et Gentium** (1672) and **De Officio Hominis et Civis** (1673) as contributions to the same line of enquiry as had engaged the attention of Grotius and Hobbes. Indeed, Pufendorf saw one of his main tasks as reconciling the insights of Hobbes with those of Grotius. Grotius appeared as the culmination of the Aristotelian-Christian tradition, Hobbes appeared as the exponent of a new rationalist-individualist critique of that tradition. Grotius himself had already indicated the lines along which some such reconciliation as Pufendorf had in mind might occur. Following Grotius' writings, natural law theorists of the seventeenth and eighteenth centuries attempted to ground natural law on reason alone since this appeared, in the light of rationalist-individualist critiques, a more promising and self-sufficient foundation than theology. They attempted to explain the moral and political world by reference to supposedly undeniable facts of individual human existence alone. Human reason unaided by authority and revelation was thought capable of demonstrating with a certainty approaching the mathematical the requirements of the moral law. In their essentially political writings, these post-Grotian natural law theorists attempted to reconcile the Hobbesian idea that community and sovereignty can only be explained by reference to individual willing with the Aristotelian-Christian notion that community and sovereignty were natural phenomena deriving from the condition of mankind or the will of God.[10]

Pufendorf's natural law theory exhibited these characteristics of the post-Grotius natural law tradition. In the preface to **De Jure Naturae et Gentium**, for example, Pufendorf declared "this study concerns not Christians alone but all mankind." He would not begin an account of the moral law from Christian doctrines of the Fall or original sin. Instead he sought to found his enquiries on "such a principal as no one, provided he be of sound mind, can deny:" the Aristotelian dictum that man is by nature sociable."[11] In his **Elementorum Jurisprudentiae Universalis**, Pufendorf asserted that his purpose was to establish certain knowledge of the moral law where hitherto it had been felt that "all knowledge of such matters rests upon probable opinion only." Previous theorizing about moral law, that is, had been defective because it had not been "embodied in sure demonstrations."[12]

These characteristics of late seventeenth century natural law theory reflected two more general features of the century's intellectual life: the passion for certainty and the rejection of traditional authorities. As Professor Krieger has noted, in "politics as in natural science and philosophy the characteristic intellectual of the seventeenth century sought a new axis of explanation."[13] And this search has been perceptively summarized by Professor K.R. Minogue in term of the rise of a "quite new mood in intellectual history, one in which men for the first time rejected their intellectual heritage and began the work of understanding (as they thought) anew."[14] Knowledge came to be conceived as if it were a building with rationalist philosophy attempting to construct new foundations. A new division between empiricists and rationalists came to the fore in philosophy: empiricists putting their faith in observation of the world, rationalists seeking to build the house of knowledge on "the solidities of reason," while both rejected traditional authorities. Even though we might acknowledge with W. von Leyden that the differences between early empiricism and rationalism was more a difference of degree than of kind, the essential point remains: in the seventeenth century schools of philosophy the search for certainty took the form of a search for the irreduceable sources or origins of knowledge and the mechanical construction of the world from them.15

Pufendorf attempted to construct the political world after the manner of Hobbes and, especially, Grotius using materials drawn from both. He believed Grotius to have been correct in both emphasising man's natural sociability and in grounding his account of civil society upon it. But Grotius' account was also defective for a number of reasons. In particular, it underrated the great force of self-interest in human activity and it perpetuated traditional confusions by upholding the doctrines of divided sovereignty and natural property rights pre-contract. Hobbes, on the other hand, had overplayed the importance of selfishness and egocentricity. Thus his portrayal of the state of nature and his rigorous account of political obligation suffered from being one-sided. Pufendorf was willing to acknowledge that Hobbes' **De Cive** was "for the most part extremely acute and sound," especially with its insistence that the state was an "artificial man." But Hobbes' writings "savoured" of the profane and Hobbes had confused matters by regarding the terms supreme power and unlimited power as interchangeable.16 Pufendorf's argument here was that the authority of rulers is supreme but not unlimited. He agreed with Hobbes that the governed **community** could not possibly have rights against its governor, but he insisted that **individuals** had more substantive and defensable rights against their rulers than simply the defence of their lives.17

Pufendorf's endeavours to reconcile the insights of Grotius and Hobbes and to do justice to both rationalist analyses of natural man and empirical and historical evidence issued in the construction of a social contract theory which, if not directly the inspiration of all English social contract writing of the late seventeenth century, was at least reflected in its principal formal characteristics. But unlike many subsequent writers, Pufendorf was very clear about the kind of enterprise that he was engaged in. His first major work, the **Elementorum Jursiprudentiae Universalis**, began with the statement that he was writing about the "science of law and equity, which is not comprehended in the laws of any single state, but by virtue of which the duties of all men whatsoever toward one another" are determined. He was enquiring into "matters of morality" not questions of specific constitutional arrangements.[18] And when he did address himself to the latter, unlike the English constitutional contractarians, Pufendorf never had recourse to notions of contract.[19]

The **Elementorum Jurisprudentiae Universalis** contains a significant clue to the resolution of a difficulty that has long troubled students of post-Hobbesian social contract theory: the apparent contradiction in writers like Locke between the portrayal of the state of nature as social and rule governed on the one side and as near anarchic on the other, therefore necessitating the construction of civil authorities. The clue can be found in Pufendorf's analysis of "the principles to which in juridical demonstrations one ultimately ascends." These turn out to be of two kinds: the rational and the experimental. Pufendorf explained the difference between them as follows. The truth of rational principles:

> their certainty and necessity, flows from reason itself, without the perception of individual details, or without instituting a discussion, merely from the bare intuition of the mind. But the certainty of <experimental principles> is perceived from the comparison and perception of individual details uniformly corresponding to one another. These latter we shall call **Observations**, as we shall call the former **Axioms**.[20]

Amongst the rational principles, Pufendorf included "the common axioms ... derived from prime philosophy." Such principles were that man is rational, that he is created by God and that he has a moral law to guide him. Observation, however, led to such experimental principles as that man is fundamentally selfish but with a lesser, though nonetheless natural, inclination to live in association with others of his kind.[21] The distinction between rational and experimental principles of juridical demonstration seems to highlight the common enough distinction between man as he ought to be and man as he is. Recognition of the moral dilemma of Fallen Man seems to be leading to the construction of two separate standards of morality: the ideal and the practical. This, however, Pufendorf avoided by recourse to an argument from design. The natural inclinations observable in man are portrayed as "by the intention of nature, so to be tempered" that pursuing society does not contradict man's concern for his own well-being.[21] The rules, then, governing man's social intercourse serve rather than hinder human selfishness although, once again, observation of particular human conduct reveals that the realisation of this can only generally arise "by cultivation" in societies. Indeed, this realisation is "the principal fruit produced by societies."[23]

Given the belief that a juridical demonstration of the nature and necessity of the state required appeal to axioms and observations, and given similar characterizations of those axioms and observations to Pufendorf's, it is hardly surprising that the state of nature should be portrayed in such a way as to appear ambivalent. Some kind of social arrangements were necessary in the state of nature if the cultivation of individuals capable of living in states were to occur. Accordingly and consistently, social contract theorists of the late seventeenth century restricted this social experience to associations smaller and different in kind from the state. Their concern was merely with living together. Societies like the family, relations of master and servant, or whatever, could give rise to awareness of what was involved in this as well as the potential advantages of civil association. But without that awareness, the explanation of the transition to civil society would have been much more problematic. The problem with Hobbes' portrayal of the state of nature, as far as Pufendorf was concerned, was precisely that it was consistent with Hobbes' faulty presuppositions. In Hobbes' one-sided axioms and observations, the state of nature was consistently viewed as "the war of all against all, which is the very life of beasts."[24] But beasts, as a matter of observation and principle were incapable of framing civil societies. Axioms and observations appropriate to human conduct would lead to a much more complex state of nature - one which might properly be styled natural since it accorded with the intentions of nature's creator and one which might account for the artificial or conventional origin of civil society.[25]

Pufendorf's model of the state of nature was the most complex of all seventeenth century social contract theories. He presented a two-part state of nature: the "purely natural state" and the "modified" or "mixed" state of nature. The relationship between them was one of increasing correspondence to the complexities of the real world. The purely natural state was the state of individual man abstracted from all social and divine relationships. It was an entirely rational construciton, explicitly acknowledged never to have existed. Purely natural man was identified by the characteristics of "weakness and natural helplessness" and "self-love." These characteristics underscored man's natural "sociability" since only by living in company with others could natural weakness be overcome and the self protected. The mixed state of nature was the state of mankind living in societies but in the absence of political arrangements. The mixed state of nature, Pufendorf believed, had once existed and still did exist in the form of the relations between independent political communities.

The pure state of nature was inhabited by naturally free and equal moral persons. Natural equality consisted of the absence of authority relations between individuals and natural liberty was expressed in the right of self-preservation. The mixed state of nature introduced that authority involved in social relations but did not compromise natural liberty. The governing rules of the mixed state of nature were the laws of nature: moral laws which Pufendorf, following Grotius, declared "would have had a perfect force to obligate man, even if God had never set them forth also in His revealed word."[26] In an elaboration of Hobbes' "first, and fundamental law of nature; which is, **to seek peace, and follow it**,[27] Pufendorf identified the fundamental prescription of natural law as that "Every man, so far as in him lies, should cultivate and preserve towards others peaceful sociability, which is suitable to the nature and goal of universal humanity."[28] This fundamental prescription was the source of many less fundamental dictates. These were all derivable from "sound reason alone" - they were rational axioms rather than matters of observation.

Pufendorf classified these axioms under three heads: the rules governing man's conduct towards God, towards himself, and towards other men.[29] The third of these is of most relevance here in attempting to characterize Pufendorf's contract theory. The duties of man towards his fellows were subdivided into two kinds: "absolute duties" of anybody to anybody and "conditional duties," those owed "only towards certain persons, a certain condition or status being assumed."[30] The absolute duties consisted of not injuring others, of recognizing natural equality and treating all men as equal, and of promoting "the advantage of another," as far as conveniently can be done.[31] Conditional duties comprised all the other obligations that a man might enter into with others and in all cases these duties "presuppose an express or tacit agreement."[32] The foundation of all these conditional duties, then, was "the general duty which we owe under natural law ... that a man ... fulfill his promises and agreements."[33] This postulate of a natural law duty to keep promises was crucial for the logic of Pufendorf's account of political obligation and his theory of the social, mixed state of nature.

Pufendorf argued that the obligations imposed on individuals by living in any particular societies, including civil societies, arose from consent and therefore involved conditional duties. Here, then, he would seem to be presenting a version of the contractualist theory of political obligation attacked by Hume in **A Treatise of Human Nature** and **Of the Original contract**.[34] But Hume's attack on contractualist confusion is no more appropriate when levelled against Pufendorf than it was, as we shall see, when levelled against Locke. For both writers grounded the natural law obligation to keep promises on religious conceptions which appear to have escaped Hume's notice entirely. Thus Pufendorf very explicitly asserted that the dictates of natural law acquired their obligatory character only when God was recognized as their author:

> although those precepts of natural law have manifest utility, still, if they are to have the force of law, it is necessary to presuppose that God exists, and by His providence rules all things; also that He has enjoined upon the human race that they observe those dictates of reason, as laws promulgated by Himself by means of our natural light. For otherwise they might, to be sure, be observed perhaps, in view of their utility, like the prescriptions of physicians for the regimen of health, but not as laws.[35]

Since "Natural reason" alone could be counted upon to discover that the obligation to obey natural law ultimately rested on the will of God, the natural state of human relations, the mixed state of nature, could be portrayed as a social state. And this could be done even though observation might disclose that natural society would be very precarious all the same. Pufendorf in fact located the institutions of property, marriage, the family and slavery (supposedly the extreme form of the master-servant relationship) in the mixed state of nature. Each of these institutions was in essence contractual. They originated with, and embodied, the mutual consent of individuals and that consent was taken to be conditional. They were natural institutions in the sense that they did not depend for their existence and right upon civil law and nor, therefore, could civil law abolish them. The function of civil law was simply to protect these natural institutions and to specify the practical rules necessary for their conduct.

The institutions themselves all involved relationships of an authoritative kind - based immediately upon consent but ultimately on natural law and God's will. Thus the natural equality of the purely natural state was compromised in the mixed state of nature. But this compromise did not constitute a negation of natural liberty. Natural men limited their right to all things in the interest, ultimately, of self-preservation when consenting to the institutions of the mixed state of nature. The limitations arose from enlightened self-interest and were confined to the ends for which the institutions were established. The end of the institution of property was the satisfaction of physical need. For this **private** property was necessary "to avoid quarrels and to introduce good order."[36] The end of marriage was the propagation of children and the end of the family was the care and education of those children. The end of slavery (including the master-servant relationship) was the advantage to be gained by all parties from "exchanging material necessities for material conveniencies."[37]

The primary distinction between the institutions of the mixed state of nature lay in their different "ends." Political society too had a distinctive end - "mutual defence" - and it was this which all the prepolitical institutions were incapable of securing and which therefore necessitated transcending the state of nature.[38] One problem, however, was clear. The mixed state of nature had been so portrayed that it appeared "there is scarcely any pleasure and advantage" that could not be satisfied in it.[39] By rejecting a Hobbesian state of nature, Pufendorf seemed to have removed the **"Impelling Cause"** for setting up states in the first place. The problem was confounded by his rejection of the Aristotelian and Christian notion that human nature itself compels the formation of states. Given his belief that the state was something artificial, he had to show that the state arose because men "had regard to some utility" which they would derive from it for themselves.[40] The utility had to be sufficiently great to outweigh the considerable costs to natural liberty which citizenship undoubtedly involved.[41]

In explaining why these costs should be willingly incurred, Pufendorf emphasised those characteristics of natural man that Hobbes had exclusively concentrated upon. But here Pufendorf's point was to draw on **observations** of the actual conduct of men and to underline his argument that only in society could men be so cultivated as to balance their two natural inclinations to selfishness and love of their fellows. Selfishness all too easily dominated especially amongst the "great multitude of those to whom every right is worthless, whenever the hope of gain has enticed them, or confidence in their own strength or shrewdness" leads them to believe that they may "be able to repel or elude those whom they have injured."[42] Such conduct gave rise to the principle which explained the necessity for the state. It showed that "no animal is fiercer or more untameable than man, and more prone to vices capable of disturbing the peace of society." And from this Pufendorf concluded: "Therefore the genuine and principal reason why the patriarchs, abandoning their natural liberty, took to founding states, was that they might fortify themselves against the evils which threaten man from man. For, after God, man can most help man, and has no less power for harm."[43] But none of this meant contradicting his previous argument. Natural law was still law and social life of a rudimentary kind was possible in the absence of civil arrangements. All it meant was that the laws of nature would, as a matter of fact, be sometimes broken and that social life outside civil society would be precarious. Problems arose because "with many, through defect of training and habit, the force of reason grows deaf as it were. The result is that they aim at things present only, indifferent to the future, and are moved only by what strikes upon the senses."[44] Thus the search for security gives rise to the state.[45]

In order to show how these short-sighted, self-seeking individuals might become integrated into the moral and political community of the state, Pufendorf elaborated the most complex series of contracts since Althusius. The exercise, he acknowledged, was not an historical one. The historical origin of most states was "unknown, or at least ... not entirely certain." The origins he was concerned to portray were thus not historical. But neither were they "imagined." Rather, he considered himself concerned to portray the "necessary" origins of the state: necessary for a proper understanding of the nature of contemporary civil society and of political obligation. The contracts that he elaborated, then, were necessary truths knows "by reasoning" about the origins of states from the existing fact of them.[46]

Thus "for a state to coalesce regularly," Pufendorf argued, "two compacts and one decree are necessary." The first compact was a unanimous agreement of each of the future citizens with each other "to enter into a permanent community." This had to be followed by a decree stating the form of government which the permanent community was to have. And finally, "another compact is needed, when the person, or persons, upon whom the government of the nascent state is conferred are established in authority." This second compact consisted of the mutual exchange of promises, the future governors binding themselves to "care for the common security and safety, the rest to yield them their obedience."[47] The state thus created united the individual wills of each citizen by subordinating them to the single will of the sovereign authority. At the same time that sovereign was endowed with the power to punish offences against its will by either forcing the individual will's compliance or by eliminating it. The state, then, was "defined as a composite moral person, whose will, intertwined and united by virtue of the compacts of the many, is regarded as the will of all, so that it can use the powers and resources of all for the common peace and security."[48]

The only way that such a uniting and intertwining of wills could legitimately occur was through the consent of all those concerned. This fundamental proposition of philosophical contractarianism, however, was not understood by Pufendorf to entail any radical political conclusions. There was no suggestion, as supremely exemplified by Fichte a century later,[49] that the private will might withdraw its consent and forcefully resist established government. There was not even any insistence that the consent necessary for legitimate government must in some way be formally and freely given. On the contrary, Pufendorf was quite prepared to accept that "sometimes a people is compelled by the violence of war to consent to the authority of the victor."[50] We have already encountered a version of this argument from consent amongst some of the defenders of the 1688 Revolution. It was certainly a fairly common Civil War argument.[51] But its revival in 1688 may well have had something to do with Pufendorf's reputation in England at that time.

Pufendorf appears also to have been at least one of the sources for another important contractualist doctrine widely held in England during the late seventeenth century. This was the doctrine that the original contractors (those whose consent was necessary for the legitimate foundation of a state) were only the "heads of households," or the "fathers and masters of families."[52] Thus, for example, Pufendorf defined democracy as that form of government in which "supreme authority is in the hands of a council composed of all the heads of households." And this section of the population alone was what was meant by the term "the people."[53] We will meet similar ideas in the writings of Algernon Sidney, James Tyrrell and others, where they are invoked to identify that section of the community which can legitimately determine when the sovereign has broken his contract. In Pufendorf's theory, the ideas are woven into the logic of the transition from the purely natural state of individuals, to the mixed state of nature, to finally the civil state. As we have seen, individuals in the purely natural state are driven to make contracts with one another to set up the institutions of the mixed state of nature. The family is one such institution. It was described by Pufendorf as "the fountain-head and seed-plot, as it were, of all societies."[54] Although it differed in its purpose from civil society, Pufendorf nonetheless admitted that in families outside a state the father "will have over his own family what amounts to supreme authority, and so, whatever prescript he has laid down ... will have the force of a civil law.[55] Men are superior to women in this theory. In marriage, fathers acquire rights springing from generation over their children. Essentially, however, these were rights not directly arising from the fact of birth but rather from a tacit contract whereby the father ensured the care of the children and the children returned reverence to the father.[56] But the children could only be released from their duty by the consent of the father.[57] In the mixed state of nature, then, the fathers of families alone had the freedom to contract with other heads of families to ensure the institution of that security which was the end of the state. The state, in short, was as much a union of families (rather than free and independent individuals) for Pufendorf as it had been in the contractualism of Althusius.[58]

Nor were the implications that Pufendorf drew from his contractualist account of the state any more favourable to general rights of resistance than those drawn by Althusius and Grotius before him. Considerations of interest and convenience led heads of households to enter civil societies. Consent was essential for particular persons to incur obligations to particular societies but the obligation to continue obeying civil authorities was rooted in conscience conforming to God's will. Civil authority was "from God" and He "is understood antecedently to have enjoined upon the now numerous human race to establish states, which are animated, so to speak, by their highest authority."[59] Civil authority was "supreme" and unaccountable "to any human being."[60] It was "absolute."[61] The holder of civil authority "can neither be judged nor punished" in a human court and no matter what specific "obligation he has contracted towards his own subjects, provided only that he has preserved the right of supreme authority unimpaired" subjects have no right to try him for violations nor to "apply force to him."[62] In a "pure kingdom" even parliaments have no rights against the king in these respects for "they have the authority of counsellors only."[63] And thus the doctrines of popular sovereignty and tyrannicide that Pufendorf found in **monarchomachi** and English Civil War literature were condemmned as "an extremely perilous error."[64]

But all this meant neither that all government was necessarily unlimited, nor that all commands of the sovereign must be obeyed. **Salus populi** was still the "general law of rulers" since "authority was conferred upon them, with the intention that the end for which states have been established, should be insured."[65] Experience had shown that under absolute monarchy this end might easily be perverted. Thus "it has seemed wise to some nations to circumscribe the exercise of this authority by certain limits." Coronation oaths, fundamental laws, regular parliaments appear to be what Pufendorf had in mind here.[66] But in all kinds of government, natural law and the divine will provided a limit on what sovereigns could legitimately command. Citizens were "not bound by any commands of the civil sovereignty, which are confessedly and openly repugnant to a command of God."[67] A sovereign who persisted in demanding action that was morally wrong "treats me no longer as a subject but as an enemy, and he himself is understood to have remitted the obligation by which I was bound to his authority." The result was a matter of definition. By being forced to do wrong "I pass from being a subject into being a free enemy"[68] and can then "rightly employ against him also the means customarily used against an enemy."[69] Yet as individuals, as with Hobbes, citizens could only forcefully resist when faced by imminent death. Pufendorf's advice to the oppressed subject was to endure patiently or to flee but never to disturb further the stability and quiet of civil life.

This call for passive obedience could not be extended to the people as a whole. In cases of extreme danger a whole people might legitimately resist its sovereign. But Pufendorf's point here was to warn against too liberal an interpretation of the right of resistance. That some such right existed was the inevitable consequence of his analysis of the nature and end of the state. His concern was to distinguish between two seemingly similar propositions which had been confused in the literature which lay to hand but which he believed were in reality worlds apart. The one proposition was mistaken, the other correct. The mistaken proposition was that "'A People has authority to bring even absolute monarchs to order, if, indeed, these have not ruled according to its liking.'" The correct proposition, the logical consequence of his analysis of the state, was rather that "'A people properly has the right, in a case of extreme necessity, namely, when the prince has become an enemy, to defend its safety against him."[70] For in this case, they are no longer citizens or subjects but have been restored to their rights in the state of nature by the very actions of their ex-sovereign to which they are now opposed.

Such conclusions about the right of resistance were intended to counsel caution in making practical political judgments. They did not deny a right of resistance but nor were they tied to any assertions on Pufendorf's part about any particular state of affairs in past or contemporary Europe. In this respect, they fitted in with the temper of all Pufendorf's enquiries into what he called "universal jurisprudence" or the "science of law and equity, which is not comprehended in the laws of any single state."[71] And in this respect, too, his enquiries are most sharply differentiated from those of the constitutional contractarians. Pufendorf's social contract theory, his philosophical contractarianism, was not constructed primarily with a view to recommending intervention in the practical affairs of his day. Nor was he concerned to justify any particular activities. He was interested instead in portraying and accounting for the phenomenon of the modern state as a complex of interrelated powers, rights, and duties. His enquiry was aimed at a proper understanding of the state rather than to recommend or justify changes within any particular state. His dispute was primarily with other theorists like Grotius and Hobbes. It was not with contemporary politicians. His evidence was not that of particular laws or the history of particular countries, it was the evidence of rational and empirical principles. How far could this be said of those English writers of the late seventeenth century who employed the vocabulary of social contract?

In many cases it most clearly could not. Perhaps the best example of this body of social contract literature is T.H.'s **Political Aphorisms: Or, The True Maxims Of Government Displayed ... By way of a Challenge to Dr. William Sherlock** (1690). Here the author was concerned to transcribe (though without acknowledgement) passages from works by contractarian writers that might prove useful in arguments about the Revolution. His chosen sources ranged from Pufendorf, Hooker and Locke, to Gilbert Burnet. And the point, as his title indicates, was a very practical one. Similar examples of practical social contract arguments appear in the two anonymous pamphlets **An Argument for Self-Defence** (1689) and **A Political Conference between Aulicus, a Courtier: Demas, a Countryman: and Civicus a Citizen** (1689). The first endeavoured to prove that the threat of violence against James II was perfectly legitimate. The second attempted to prove to men of "Ordinary Capacity" that government originated by contract, or rather by a Pufendorfian double contract, and that by this means resistance in 1688 could be justified. The author of **A Discourse concerning the Nature, Power, and proper Effects of the Present Conventions in both Kingdoms** (1689) introduced notions of state of nature, natural law, and double contract into an argument designed to prove that the Convention Parliaments in England and Scotland were constitutionally legitimate bodies.[72] These pamphlets evidence a typical expedient of polemicists to resort to handy higher principles; but doing this does, of course, have the effect of transforming Pufendorf's theoretical arguments into something quite different. For those arguments are lifted out of their philosophical context and are placed in another. They are informed with particular meanings. A narrow and specific relation to particular events or institutional arrangements is imposed upon them. And they are employed as weapons in the cut-and-thrust of a practical debate that has meaning only for a particular place at a particular time.

A practical concern, then, predominates in much literature employing the language of philosophical contractarianism in the late seventeenth century. But what of the more famous theoretical and contractarian writings of the time: those of Sidney, Tyrrell, Locke and Paxton? At first glance, Locke's work at least seems very similar to Pufendorf's. Locke did, after all, rely exclusively upon the vocabulary of philosophical contractarianism and he did suggest that his own work was like Pufendorf's. But although the more obvious stylistic differences might be accounted for in that Pufendorf was writing in a tradition heavily influenced by Roman law whilst Locke was not, the closer one examines Locke's **Treatises** the more the similarity with Pufendorf becomes problematic. Tyrrell's and Sidney's works, too, contain extensive sections of a highly theoretical kind. Yet once again when their complete works are considered, the theoretical sections acquire a very different character from Pufendorf's. I shall consider these writings in detail in the following chapters but it should be noted at the outset that the most obvious characteristic that these English writings share, a characteristic which separates them quite obviously from Pufendorf, is an urgent concern to refute a specific practical argument: that of Filmer. The urgency of these writings is only comprehensible when it is recalled that Filmer had become the theorist of a powerful political faction, a faction which threatened the political forces supported by Sidney, Tyrrell and Locke. Thus theirs was an attack on Filmerism. It was an attack on Filmer's theory as it appeared in the late seventeenth century and in the practical implications that were currently being drawn from it.

Of these more famous writings, only Peter Paxton's **Civil Polity** (1703), which was written relatively late in the period, escapes from the concern with Filmer. The tone of his argument is more reflective and he is not concerned to recommend or justify changes in the English polity. But even though much that he wrote might well have commanded the assent of Sidney, Tyrrell, Locke[73] or Pufendorf, his work was devoted to answering different questions from any of these. Paxton was concerned to portray "from what Source such a Diversity of Customs, Manners, Usages, Laws, and Methods of Living, that are daily to be observed amongst the Sons of Adam, do proceed."[74] And in this he never had recourse to notions of contract.

English writing employing the vocabulary of philosophical contractarianism, then, appears varied in nature but generally much more concerned with the specifics of current political practice than Pufendorf's

PHILOSOPHICAL CONTRACT

Elementorum Jursiprudentiae Universalis, De Jure Naturae et Gentium and **De Officio Hominis et Civis.** Locke's **Two Treatises of Government** is the most famous late seventeenth century English work in this social contract genre. If we look more closely at Locke's theory and the controversies that surround its intellectual status, we may begin to appreciate more distinctly the implications of philosophical contractarianism for Englishmen during the late seventeenth century.

CHAPTER 7

JOHN LOCKE

Studies of Locke's political works have multiplied enormously in recent years. But a very confusing picture of Locke has emerged. The once undisputed exponent of the "principles of 1688" and the "champion of constitutional democracy" has become a much more complex, contradictory and devious character. Occasionally the more traditional Locke - the champion of individualism and the elaborator of modern Liberalism - still musters support. But that Locke now contends with a series of new Lockes - a champion of majority rule, an ideologist of the emergent bourgeoisie and a tacit exponent of Hobbism.[1] Again, although the Locke who was once an original and profound political thinker still has his defenders, he is now challenged by Lockes who expressed nothing but "parochial political orthodoxy," or who simply reestated the "familiar principles ... forged by the heirs of John Calvin."[2] Indeed, one of these new Lockes so disappointed his creator that the **Two Treatises**, appeared as "too quaint and insubstantial to deserve the admiration it has received."[3] Practically all of these interpretations of Locke acknowledge that the argument of **Two Treatises** is presented in a loose and unrigorous way; and, at least in part, it is this acknowledgement that has sometimes led to Locke's relegation from the rank of political philosopher to that of party pamphleteer or tract-writer. It is the issues involved in this question that will occupy much of our attention in this chapter. They are central to my overall concern with whether the understanding of contract presented in **Two Treatises** is essentially the same as that presented in Pufendorf's **De Jure Naturae et Gentium**.

JOHN LOCKE

I propose to examine this broad question by considering a number of narrower, more specific ones. First, what occasioned Locke's writing the **Two Treatises**? What effect did he hope his writing and publishing the work would produce? Second, what was the character of Locke's notions of the state of nature and the social contract? Were they understood historically or, as by Pufendorf, as hypothetical and necessary concepts for a proper understanding of the state? Third, is the argument of **Two Treatises** more appropriately viewed as political philosophy or as political rhetoric? And finally, how did Locke's contemporaries view the argument of **Two Treatises**? What impact did the work have on political debate, especially in England, during the first two decades after its publication? I will look at each of these questions in turn.

Locke students are now agreed that the **Two Treatises** was largely written some years before the 1688 Revolution. Peter Laslett's detailed research during the 1950s revealed that the two essays of the **Treatises** were conceived as a single work, that they were simply revised for publication after Locke's return from exile in 1689, and that they had initially been written between 1679 and 1681.[4] The considerable textual, biographical and historical evidence which Laslett presents for the earlier dating appears sufficient to uphold his basic thesis. But it is worth remembering that the case has not been established beyond doubt. Part of Laslett's historical evidence about the relevance of Locke's arguments to the Exclusion Crisis rather than the Revolution, for example, is questionable.[5] Yet, from his enquiries, Laslett convincingly argues that Locke wrote the **Treatises** as a propaganda piece for a projected rising by the Earl of Shaftesbury.

The contention that **Two Treatises** was a pièce d'occasion, a propaganda piece, does not preclude, as E. S. De Beer has recently suggested, that it was also a "speculative treatise written in answer to a speculative treatise."[6] It clearly was the case that one of Locke's purposes in writing the work was that which is expressed in their title. The **First Treatise** was designed to "detect and overthrow" the **"False Principles and Foundation of Sir Robert Filmer** and his Followers;" the second was intended to display the "True Original, Extent and End of Civil-Government." The connection between the first and second parts was quite simply, as the first review of Locke's work pointed out, that the first revealed the shortcomings of the principal royalist theory of political legitimacy, whilst the second provided an alternative and supposedly much more adequate theory.[7] Locke himself explained the purpose of the **Second Treatise** along these lines in its first paragraph. It was an enquiry to "find out another rise of Government, another Original of Political Power, and another way of designing and knowing the Persons that have it, than what Sir **Robert F.** hath taught us." [8]

The anti-Filmer design clearly runs through the whole of **Two Treatises** and it is difficult to see why commentators like R. I. Aaron should want to insist that Hobbes as well as Filmer was Locke's target in the **Second Treatise.**[9] Locke and Filmer in several respects were much more akin to one another than either was to Hobbes. Both accepted that Man was a creature made by, for and in the image of God, that God had ordained government in the world, that the Bible contained a valid, and in no sense simply metaphorical, account of the first ages of the world, that the Bible was absolutely authoritative in all moral questions. And both agreed, too, in the broadest of terms, on the methods of argument appropriate to resolving disputes.

It was precisely this considerable agreement between Locke and Filmer on certain fundamental issues that made the republication of the latter's works such a serious challenge to the Shaftesbury Whigs with whom Locke was associated. The arguments of Hobbes' **De Cive** and **Leviathan** for the necessity of absolute sovereignty simply did not carry the same weight as Filmer's during the late seventeenth century. The judgment of Filmer himself on Hobbes might be taken as representing that of even the most ardent royalists. "I consent with him about the rights of exercising government," he declared, "but I cannot agree to his means of acquiring it ... I

... praise his building, and yet mislike his foundation."[10] Indeed, the seemingly atheistic theory of Hobbes was practically universally spurned in the very religion-conscious political literature of the Restoration and Revolution. As we have seen, almost the only references to Hobbes in political debate, particularly after the mid-1680s, were as contemptuous labels for categorising opponents. It was Filmer and not Hobbes who was the principal authority for late seventeenth century royalists.[11]

Hobbes' political writings, then did not attract any significant following during the late seventeenth century, whereas Filmer's did. Filmer's major works were first published at the height of the Exclusion Crisis as an act of policy by the royalist, anti-Exclusionists. The works were warmly recommended to the public by the official paper, "the Publick Gazette."[12] It was, furthermore, Filmer and not Hobbes who appeared as the principal opponent of all those pro-Exclusionist writers who were concerned to raise their argument above mudslinging and gossip.[13] And finally, it was Filmer and not Hobbes who remained the principal authority of all those defenders of the English monarch's absolute power during the two decades following the Exclusion Crisis - men like Edmund Bohun, Jeremy Collier and Charles Leslie. In these circumstances, it is not surprising that Filmer should have appeared as the most significant exponent of absolutist theory in the late seventeenth century and that a writer of a different persuasion, like Locke, should have found it necessary to devote considerable effort to attacking Filmer so that his own theory would stand more chance of acceptance.

Two Treatises, then appears to have been written by Locke with a clearly practical political end in view. to undermine the theory of the principal royalist authority and establish an alternative theory to which Whig politicians could appeal. This end **Two Treatises** shared with a number of other political works composed at approximately the same time - most notably, Sidney's **Discourses Concerning Government** and Tyrrell's **Patriarcha Non Monarcha**. But Locke's work differed from these others in the narrowness of its critique of Filmer and the generality of its alternative theory. Sidney and Tyrrell, as we shall see, were concerned to refute not only Filmer's theory of political legitimacy but also his notions about the English constitution. And the general social contract theory that they outlined was integrally connected to their views on English constitutional history and law.

Filmer's political works were indeed much more wide-ranging than Locke's **Two Treatises**. Apart from the famous enquiry into the nature of political power, Filmer's writings contain commentaries and critiques of Aristotle, Hobbes, Milton and Grotius, as well as detailed examinations of the power and interrelations of the various constitutional authorities in England. His general theory of the necessity for an arbitrary, unlimited, sovereign, monarchical power, however, pervades the whole of his work. Indeed, the work in which he most carefully outlines this general theory was conceived, as its sub-title indicates, with English affairs in mind.[14] And his argument proceeds in a single development from a refutation of "Natural Freedom" (the basic principle of his opponents), to a justification of the naturalness of absolute monarchy, and on to an examination of the English constitution supposedly proving it to be such a natural constitution.

Locke's published work did not follow Filmer into the specifics of English constitutional law. This remarkable fact has never been fully appreciated. But we can never be sure that Locke never attempted any such enquiry, especially in the absence of the missing part of the **Treatise**.[15] The lost part of **Two Treatises** supposedly pursued Filmer "through all the Windings and Obscurities which are to be met with in the several Branches of his wonderful System."[16] Yet if there were any such missing papers it is difficult to imagine what they could have contained if not, in part at least, a refutation of Filmer's theory of the English constitution. One of the most prominent branches of Filmer's enquiries - occupying about one third even of the **Patriarcha** itself - was concerned with the English constitution.[17]

But no matter what the missing papers may have contained, the **Treatises** as published were unique. Locke published, as he wrote, with a practical political end in view. The work, he hoped, was "sufficient to establish the throne of our Great Restorer, Our present King **William**."[18] But Locke, unlike all the other defenders of the Revolution, made no attempt to prove that the establishment of William and Mary on the English throne had been warranted expressly or tacitly by English constitutional law. His reference to William as the "Great Restorer" was certainly a reference to constitutionalist justifications of the Revolution, William had supposedly restored the ancient constitution but Locke's argument did not continue in this vein.

It seems, then, that in terms of the circumstances of their creation and publication, **Two Treatises** and Pufendorf's works were very different. But what of the character of the concepts of state of nature and social contract that each explored? As we have seen, Pufendorf understood these concepts to relate to neither the historical nor the conjectured origin of the state. They were rather the logically **necessary** concepts for a proper understanding of the nature of contemporary society. Locke's understanding of state of nature and social contract, however, has been the subject of numerous, conflicting interpretations. A glance at these controversies will provide a clearer view of the character of Locke's social contract theory.

Commentators hardly differ over the function of the state of nature in Locke's argument. It is accepted as establishing the natural, pre-civil rights and duties of man and as indicating why civil government is necessary for social life. But controversies have arisen about its status. Some have argued that it is a purely expository device, others that it is partly expository and partly historical, and others still that it is principally historical.[19] Again, it has been viewed as an exposition of the pre-social, pre-political, or pre-civil condition of man.[20] It has also been argued that Locke has not one, but two conflicting notions of the state of nature

– the one a state of peace, the other a state of war.[22] And finally, Locke's state of nature has been considered as either an abstract construction of reason, or as based on "experience, and on the observation of the actual behaviour of men," or as essentially a theological axiom.[22]

Some of these characterisations are plainly wrong according to explicit statements by Locke, but others have strong textual evidence to support them. Locke's views on the status of the state of nature are far from unambiguous and it is thus unlikely that any account will prove finally conclusive. The most that can be hoped for is an account which does least injustice to the evidence of Locke's text.

We may begin by considering what the state of nature most clearly was not. In the first place, it was not a pre-social condition. Life in the state of nature was depicted as one in which family life existed on a grand scale, with families consisting of relationships between "Man and Wife, which gave beginning to that between Parents and Children; to which, in time, that between Master and Servant came to be added."[23] It was also a form of social life in which "Promises," "Compacts" and "Bargains" could be effectively made since "Truth and Keeping of Faith belongs to Men, as Men, and not as Members of <civil> Society."[24] This, then, was as social a state of nature as Pufendorf's "mixed state of nature." Secondly, the state of nature was not a Golden Age in the development of mankind – a virtuous, harmonious state into which corruption penetrated, eventually necessitating the harsh controls of civil society. There are elements of this view in Locke,[25] but he refers to the "Golden Age" as rather the early stages of government than any pre-governmental period.[26]

Locke most frequently defines the state of nature in terms of it not being "Politick Society." It is the state "all Men are naturally in ... and remain so, till by their own Consents they make themselves Members of some Politick Society."[27] But, still, the state of nature is not a pre-political society in the sense that political power does not exist within it, at least in embryo. For **Political Power** is that Power, which every Man, having in the state of Nature, has given up into the hands of the Society, and therein to the Governours."[28] Political power is derived from the aggregation of the executive power of the law of nature which each exercised independently in the state of nature. Thus the state of nature is examined as the state of mankind in the absence of organised government. And the point of the enquiry is to show first, that man stands in dire need of government; second, that only a certain (though very general) form of government organisation can properly be seen as government at all - in particular, that arbitrary, absolute rule is, properly speaking, not a form of government.

Here then are three things which the state of nature most definitely was not. But from what sources did Locke derive his conception of the state of nature and, in particular, what role did historical evidence play? Locke, of course, was aware that state of nature arguments and original contracts had been objected to on the grounds that they were not evidenced in history. Yet he believed the objection could be easily countered. His answer was twofold: first, there was ample evidence in history and current practice of the state of nature and original contracts; and second, even if history appeared to lend support to the patriarchalist case, this could not undermine his own argument. It is this last point, that his contractarianism was immune from historical criticism, that linked Locke's theory with Pufendorf's **De Jure Naturae et Gentium** and separated it, as we shall see, from the apparently similar works by Sidney and Tyrrell.

Locke insisted that "the World never was, nor ever will be without Numbers of Men in that State <of nature>." And he pointed to the rulers of independent states and invoked Hooker's authority for evidence of this.[29] He often spoke of the state of nature and it supersession by contract as an historical event, and in this context he countered the objection that history did not support him. In the first place, he argued, "it is not at all to be wonder'd, that **History** gives us but a very little account of Men, **that lived together in the State of Nature.**" But this was not because it had not happened in the past. The reason was rather because the period of the state of nature was exceedingly short and had existed in Europe before there were any records. Yet what little evidence did remain of the origin of governments, Locke claimed, did support his argument. The accidental records "we have, of the beginning of any Polities in the World," he declared, "excepting that of the **Jews,** where God himself immediately interpos'd, ... are all either plain instances of such a beginning as I have mentioned, or at least have manifest footsteps of it." And he pointed to Rome, Venice and the emigrants who left Sparta with Palantus as historical examples of original contracts; and to "many parts of America" (which was "still a Pattern of the first Ages in **Asia** and **Europe**") as evidence of the continuing existence of states of nature.[30]

Despite all this evidence from history and contemporary experience, Locke denied that such evidence could either support or refute **in any conclusive respect** the principal argument of **Two Treatises.** His argument was about right rather than fact. Thus, Locke noted, even if history supported the patriarchalist case, "one might, without any great danger, yield them the cause." He could concede that in the past governments began in paternal rule and yet the argument of **Two Treatises** would be substantially unaffected. The argument there was about right and, according to Locke, "at best an Argument from what has been, to what should of right be, has no great force." The only occasion when such an argument might have force was where "the want of such ⟨historical⟩ instances be regarded an argument to prove that Government were not, nor could not be so begun."[31] Since this was not the case, and since, anyway, history did provide instances of original contracts, then one main objection to contractarian arguments could be rejected.

Throughout his own contractarian argument, Locke's appeal was primarily to reason. History was evoked simply as evidence that the conclusions of reason were not at variance with the practices of mankind. Reference to history was important because of the current state of debates about contract. As we have seen, practically all Locke's contemporaries who appealed to contract believed it to have been an historical occurrence, and one of the most troublesome criticisms was the absence of historical evidence. Thus in arguing that history and reason were not at variance, and at the same time immunising his idea of contract from historical criticism, Locke's contract theory could accommodate any historical evidence whatsoever. Indeed, having considered the historical objection to his theory, Locke proceeded to note the historical evidence of the rise of government. His point was to prove that reason and history were not discordant by showing "that as far as we have any light from History, we have reason to conclude, that all peaceful beginnings of **Government** have been **laid in the Consent of the People.**"[32]

Locke began this examination by acknowledging, with the patriarchalists, that the earliest recorded governments were usually monarchies. He was even prepared to admit that in certain circumstances the monarch might well have been the father of his people.[50] But this evidence, Locke insisted, "destroys not that, which I affirm, (**viz.**) that **the beginning of Politick Society** depends upon the consent of the Individuals, to joyn into and make up one Society; who, when they are thus incorporated, might set up what form of Government they thought fit."[33] The evidence merely suggested that there must have been good reasons why the first framers of government should have decided upon, and been content with, monarchy rather than any other form of goernment. These reasons, Locke felt, were so simple and obvious that in "the first Ages of the World" it was "almost natural" for family government to change into political government. It would be brought about by a "scarce avoidable consent" and the change would be "insensible."[34] Thus the historical evidence advanced by anti-contractarians could be accepted without destroying Locke's basic contentions about the state of nature and the original contract.

It would seem, then, that those interpretations of Locke which insist that his state of nature and social contract are based on historical or empirical evidence are wide of the mark. Recently, however, an alternative view of these concepts has been suggested: that the state of nature is essentially a theological axiom. Now whilst both Polin and Dunn have convincingly argued that a religious conception lay at the bottom of Locke's reflections on the nature of man and the law of nature, this hardly warrants the further contention that it was religious conviction rather than rational enquiry that led Locke to his views on the state of nature. For Locke himself believed that his basic religious ideas were themselves capable of rational demonstration. God was a rational being whose existence could be rationally proved and His ways for man portrayed a rational design. Thus only by expanding the notion of a theological argument to include any discussion about the nature of man as a rational being could we conclude, with John Dunn, that the "state of nature is a topic for theological reflection, not for anthropological research."[36] In Locke's understanding, it was both. But on Dunn's argument, the distinction between anthropology and theology is collapsed in Locke by the former being subsumed under the latter.

Locke's state of nature seems to have been essentially an expository device of a rationalist kind. It established the natural rights of man, indicated the necessity for civil society, and provided the key for distinguishing between the legitimate and illegitimate exercise of political power. Both the state of nature and the original contract were viewed by Locke as evidenced in history, but their status in the argument of the **Treatises** was not dependent upon that. They served as crucial concepts in a rational explanation of the nature of political society, rather than in an historical account of the rise of government. As rational constructions, they were not susceptible to refutation by anything but similar arguments from reason, as far as Locke himself was concerned. His description of life in the state of nature supposedly accorded with the evidence of reason, history, experience and theology. And though evidence from the last three of these could conceivably cast doubt on the validity of his arguments, none could disprove them.37

So far we have seen that Locke's **Two Treatises** were conceived and published as contributions to the practical political conflicts of late seventeenth century England. In this respect the **Treatises** were very different from Pufendorf's **De Jure Naturae et Gentium** and **De Officio Hominis et Civis**. But the understanding of state of nature and social contract expressed in the argument of the **Second Treatise** appears very similar to Pufendorf's. Considerations such as these have given rise to widely different interpretations of the general nature of Locke's social contract theory. On the one side, it is asserted that Locke's theory represents a philosophical enquiry into the nature of the state, whilst on the other it is insisted that the **Second Treatise** is essentially sham philosophy, a work of political rhetoric. The debate is important for our purposes because the character of Locke's appeal to contract depends upon it. What then are the sources of these disagreements and how might Locke's argument best be represented?

I shall argue that in part these disagreements arise from the preconceptions of Locke scholars, and in part from the writings of Locke himself. In outlining the first of these, I shall concentrate upon the two opposed accounts which seem the most coherent and substantial in this respect: those of Peter Laslett and Raymond Polin. In examining the second, I shall concentrate on Locke's notions of natural law and consent because these notions have been at the centre of most disagreements over the general nature of the **Treatises**.

In the introduction to his critical edition of **Two Treatises**, Laslett asserts that to call this work "'political philosophy', to think of <Locke> as a 'political philosopher', is inappropriate." The observations he makes in defending this view are persuasive. **Two Treatises**, he shows, was intended as a call for revolutionary action rather than as a justification for a revolution that had already occurred. It was intended to justify the activities of the Shaftesbury Whigs. It was a **pièce d'occasion** and that alone. According to Laslett, Locke, on his own testimony at the time he was writing the **Treatises**, believed that true knowledge of things political was impossible. Politics was the sphere of opinion and probability which by its nature eluded the philosophical understanding. And thus, Laslett asserts, with this view of politics it was hardly unlikely that Locke would have attempted to write political philosophy.[39] Locke's indisputably philosophical work, the **Essay Concerning Human Understanding**, expresses ideas, especially in respect of natural law, which are irreconcileable with the views contained in **Two Treatises**. It is only posterity that has looked upon the **Essay** and the **Treatises** as "complementary" - Locke himself was anxious that they should be seen apart (he was, of course, most reluctant to admit his authorship of the political work). The **Two Treatises** were not written according to the "plain, historic method" of the **Essay**. Had they been, Laslett asserts, they would have insisted on the limitations of our social and political understanding. Locke would have demonstrated his conclusions by arguments proceeding from definitions of simple ideas to the construction of complex ideas in a way capable of "entering into a mathematically demonstrable morality." Instead of this, most of the notions that are crucial to the argument of the **Second Treatise** - notions of natural law, consent, freedom, law, reason, will government, justice - are "nowhere discussed as subjects in themselves." The ideas of political power and property, Laslett admits, are defined in the **Second Treatise**, but they are defined "not in philosophic terms, on nothing like the principles laid down in the **Essay**."[40] From all these observations Laslett concludes that **Two Treatises** should be viewed as the work of a man who wrote on economics, on toleration, on religion, on education, who was **also** an epistemologist. Each enterprise was different and therefore it is "pointless to look upon Locke's work as an integrated body of speculation and generalization, with a general philosophy at its centre and as its architectural framework."[41]

JOHN LOCKE

It was precisely this final point of Laslett's that Polin set out to reject in his **La politique morale de John Locke**. All Locke's speculations on matters moral and political, Polin argues, were informed by a rational theology. Locke's philosophy, he asserts, is "inseparable from his religion" because "throughout his philosophical works Locke appealed to God, and without this recourse to God, all the coherence of his philosophy would dissolve."[42] Thus in Polin's understanding, Locke's enquiries into morals, politics, religion and epistemology are just so many parts of a single philosophic enterprise. Polin accepts Laslett's arguments that the **Treatises** were composed around 1680 as part of the attempt to exclude the Catholic Duke of York, the future James II, from his right to succeed to the throne. But he refuses to follow Laslett in taking the further step of arguing that because the **Treatises** was thus a **pièce d'occasion**, a work of circumstance, it could not be philosophy. In Polin's view, the circumstance of the Exclusion Crisis simply gave Locke the impetus to consider the "universal problems of politics." The constant interest which philosophers have shown in the **Treatises** is indicative, he argues, of the extent to which the work escaped from the circumstances of its creation. Yet, as well as being an enquiry into the eternal truths of morals and politics, the work had a practical message too. It was concerned **both** to counsel and to justify a set of present political activities **and** to explain the essential nature of moral and political experience.[43]

It is apparent from these sketches of Laslett's and Polin's interpretations of the general character of **Two Treatises**, that they express different conceptions of the nature of philosophical enquiry. To Laslett, philosophical enquiry is necessarily non-practical - it is enquiry conducted in a particular way for the sake of truth, and this inevitably precludes a concern to justify or counsel intervention in practical affairs. To Polin, philosophy can **both** justify or condemn political practice **and** illuminate universal and eternal truths. Political philosophy and political doctrine are one and the same, or can be - all that matters is that the argument be pitched at a sufficiently general level. In Polin's work philosophy and **Weltanschauung** are equivalents (or at least compatible), in Laslett's work they are mutually exclusive categories. It is this sort of disagreement that constitutes one of the main sources of confusion in the current literature on the character of Locke's work on government. Recognition of this basic point helps explain why so many contemporary Locke scholars can agree that **Two Treatises**, considered in isolation from the rest of Locke's writings, appears confused, repetitive, unrigorous and so on, and yet they can differ so widely in their interpretations of the general nature of the work.

The second source of confusion for Locke scholars arises from Locke's own writings and reflections about the general character of the argument of **Two Treatises**. Locke was a very self-conscious writer. His journals and letters contain interesting reflections on the nature of political studies, the nature of philosophical argument in moral and political affairs, and on the sort of work that he believed **Two Treatises** to be. A consideration of these reflections and an examination of the argument of the **Treatises** in the light of them will help to clarify the nature of Locke's social contract theory.

We have already seen that Locke distinguished between theoretical and practical enquiries into politics and classified his own **Two Treatises** as a theoretical study, the best example of which was Pufendorf's **De Jure Naturae et Gentium**.[44] It seems that this distinction between the theoretical and the practical has a counterpart in Locke's general distinction between the two kinds of knowledge that the human mind is capable of acquiring. He outlined this general distinction in a note in his **Journal** of 1681. It is this note which Laslett interprets as an argument against the possibility of certain knowledge in political affairs and uses as evidence that the **Two Treatises** could not have been intended as political philosophy. Locke's note contains the following observations:

There are two sorts of knowledg in the world,

generall and particular, founded upon two different principles, i.e. true Ideas and matter of fact or History. All generall knowledg is founded only upon true Ideas and soe far as we have these we are capable of demonstration or certain knowledg. ⟨Just as in mathematics⟩ he that as ⟨sic⟩ a true Idea of God, of himself as his creature, or the relation he stands in to God and his fellow creatures, and of Justice, goodnesse, law, happinesse, etc., is capable of knowing morall things or Laws, ⟨of having⟩ a demonstrative certainty in them. But though I say a man that hath such Ideas is capable of certain knowledg in them, yet I do not say that presently he hath thereby that certain knowledg ... He may believe others that tell him ... but know it not till he himself hath ... made to himself the demonstration i.e. upon examination seen it to be soe.[45]

If we interrupt Locke's reflections at this point we may emphasise a number of considerations that are important for his conception of philosophy, morals and politics. In the first place, for Locke the philosophical concern with knowledge and truth was a concern with "true Ideas" - and this concern involved a clear understanding of the limited capacity of the human understanding for apprehending true ideas, and hence the necessity and grounds for opinion and belief. The **Essay Concerning Human Understanding**, of course, had this as its central concern. Secondly, the essential nature of true knowledge was that it was both general and demonstrable. Thirdly, moral laws were presented as capable of mathematical demonstration, and hence were proper subjects for philosophical enquiry. And, finally, some aspects of human experience were inherently incapable of the demonstrative certainty necessary for true knowledge. In the remainder of Locke's reflections, he notes that "physique ⟨medicine⟩, politie, and prudence" are three such areas in which demonstration is impossible and hence they concern merely opinion and probability. His conclusion is instructive:

Knowledg, then, depends upon right and true ideas;

Opinion upon history and matter of fact. And hence it comes to pass that our knowledg of generall things are eternae veritates and depend not upon the existence or accidents of things ... But whether this course in publique or private affairs will succeed well, whether rhubarb will purge or Quinquina cure an ague, is only known by experience; and there is but probability grounded upon experience or analogical reasoning, but no certain knowled <sic> or demonstration.[46]

It is clear that what Locke means by "politie" here is **policy**, not all things political. Thus Laslett's inference that Locke excluded politics from the proper field of philosophical enquiry cannot be sustained. Indeed, Laslett was forced to argue that Locke changed his mind on this point. For only in this way could he account for Locke's view, expressed in 1697, that "True Politics I look on as a part of moral philosophy."[47] And, anyway, in the **Essay Concerning Human Understanding**, Locke did present two examples of how certain knowledge was ascertainable in political studies. He considered two propositions - "'Where there is no property, there is no injustice'" and "'No government allows absolute liberty'." Provided we have true ideas of the concepts of property, justice, government and liberty, Locke asserted, and provided we use the terms consistently, then the truth of these propositions can be demonstrated.[48]

So far we have seen that Locke believed his **Two Treatises** was a contribution to that branch of political studies that "was very different from" the concern with policy; that Pufendorf's **De Jure Naturae et Gentium** was the best treatise of the same kind as his work; that within this branch of political studies certain knowledge was possible; and that the purpose of philosophical enquiry into morals and politics was to demonstrate, according to the mathematical method, the eternal truths that this area of enquiry admitted. But if we now look at the way the arguments of the **Treatises** are constructed, it becomes extremely difficult to see how Locke could have considered the work philosophy of a

Pufendorfian kind. The **First Treatise** is nothing more than its title indicates - an attempt to detect and overthrow "**The False Principles and Foundation** of Sir **Robert Filmer** and his Followers." It is a classic example of a piece of rhetorical writing with arguments of all kinds and from all sources being introduced to persuade the reader that the principal text of Locke's royalist opponents was worthless, even ridiculous. The **Second Treatise**, however, is more problematical. Its title asserts that it is concerned to portray "The True Original, Extent and End of Civil-Government," a genuinely philosophical concern according to Locke's view of political studies. The chapter headings seem to indicate that the argument will parallel the middle part of Pufendorf's **De Jure Naturae et Gentium**. And the **Treatise** begins, as it must if Locke were going to pursue a philosophical enquiry according to his own method, with a **definition** of political power and a declaration that his task was "To understand Political Power right, and derive it from its Original."[49]

But Locke does not sustain the initial promise. His argument does **not** proceed from definitions and the establishment of fixed and definite ideas to the demonstration of more complex but equally certain truths concerning politics. Several ideas crucial to Locke's argument - like, for example, natural law, consent, liberty and obligation - are not defined at all. Others, of similar importance, are not employed consistently according to the definitions initially established. Property is a well-known case in point. Also, the notions of "Society," "Politick Society" and "Civil Society" are often used interchangeably even though a crucial point of Locke's argument is to indicate how natural society differed from civil society. And still other notions, like the nature of man and God's purposes for him, are introduced in a casual way almost as an after-thought, yet they are essential for the coherence of the argument.[50] All this is fairly familiar. But considerations such as these do indeed invite us, as Laslett has suggested, to look upon **Two Treatises** as something other than political philosophy. How is it, then, that Locke could insist that his work was of the same kind as Pufendorf's? If we look at Locke's references to natural law and consent in the **Treatises** and compare them with Pufendorf's supposedly similar references, we may begin to gain a clearer perspective on this problem.

In the schema of the **Second Treatise**, natural law guarantees to natural men their natural rights and teaches them their duties in respect of one another. It provides an eternal standard for judging the rectitude of positive human laws. And it provides the ultimate grounds for resistance. But neither the **First Treatise** nor the **Second** is concerned with the questions which concerned Pufendorf about natural law. In his **De Officio Hominis et Civis** - Pufendorf's shortened version of the mammoth **De Jure Naturae et Gentium** - he noted that his concern with natural law was to portray its "character" and "necessity" by examining "the nature and disposition of man."[51] And this involved enquiring into the nature of human action, exhibiting the characteristics of moral experience, and distinguishing between the spheres of rational morality, civil legality and moral theology - all of which had become confused, he thought, in the moral discourse of his day.[52] Locke's **Treatises**, however, were concerned with no such enquiry as this. Indeed, Locke claimed that "it would be besides my present purpose to enter here ⟨in the argument of the **Second Treatise**, that is⟩ into the particulars of the Law of Nature, or its **measures of punishment**." All that Locke was interested in was that his reader should acknowledge that "it is certain that there is such a Law, and that too, as intelligible and plain to a rational Creature, and a Studier of that Law, as the positive Laws of Commonwealths, nay possibly plainer."[53]

The essential point here, which neither Laslett nor Polin consider, is that Pufendorf's work contained a consistent argument deriving the rights and duties which defined natural law from an initial characterization of the nature of man and of moral experience, wheras Locke's did not. The point that divides Laslett and Polin is whether Locke's statements about natural law were inconsistent both within the **Two Treatises** and between the **Treatises** and Locke's other writings. Laslett, as we have seen, argues that Locke's references to natural law in the **Essay** and the **Treatises** are inconsistent and this provides him with one of the main reasons for denying that **Two Treatises** represents Locke the philosopher's understanding of politics. Polin argues that Locke's religious ideas provide the common ground to which his statements about natural law must be referred: statements, that is, in the early **Essays on the Law of Nature** (1664), in the **Essay Concerning Human Understanding** (1690), in the **Two Treatises** (1690) and in **The Reasonableness of Christianity** (1695). If this is done - and here Polin has John Dunn on his side - Locke's references to natural law portray a remarkable coherence and consistency stretching over the last forty years of his life.[54] But in so far as these disputes amongst Locke scholars are intended to clarify the general character of Locke's social contract theory, they miss the essential point. That point emerges readily from a comparison of Locke's and Pufendorf's works.

Pufendorf's discussion of civil society arose out of a concern to explain the kinds of rights and duties that men in contemporary society possessed. The purpose of his enquiry is encapsulated in his concluding chapter entitled "On the Duties of Citizens." Locke's discussion of civil society in the **Treatises** arises from no such concern as this. His purpose appears rather to be to characterize political society in such a way that the common association of resistance with sinfulness (notions tied together in the Church of England's doctrine of passive obedience) could be severed, and thus an acceptable justification be rendered for resisting incumbent magistrates. That this was Locke's point seems to emerge from the argument running from his summary chapter "Of Paternal, Political, and Despotical Power, considered together," to his conclusion "Of the Dissolution of Government." In arriving at his conclusion, Locke utilised propositions and arguments from his own philosophical works and, indeed, from Pufendorf's as well. But these propositions and arguments were neither employed nor established to demonstrate the eternal truths of moral and political experience. They simply served as maxims or premisses from which to argue a case that was published in order to persuade his audience that the 1688 Revolution was justified and that William and Mary were legitimate monarchs.

If, then, an essentially practical political, an essentially rhetorical purpose gave rise to the argument of the **Second Treatise,** it is no longer surprising that that argument does not follow Locke's own philosophical method. It is not surprising, in respect of natural law, that Locke declared it besides his present purpose to examine the "particulars" of that law. It certainly can be persuasively argued (as Polin does) that Locke's references to natural law in the **Treatises** are all consistent with his extended discussions of that law in other works. But even if this is accepted, it does not provide sufficient reason for categorizing the **Treatises** as political philosophy. Yet neither does the argument that the statements in the **Treatises** are irreconcileable with those elsewhere (Laslett's argument) provide sufficient reason to deny the **Treatises** that status.

Similar problems arise from Locke's references to consent in the **Second Treatise.** Most contemporary Locke scholars have followed Hume in believing that the **Two Treatises** contains Locke's explanation of the nature and grounds of political obligation. Locke, it is thought, reduces the obligation to obey government to the obligation to keep promises: and this is supposedly the central feature of his discussion of consent.[55] This belief tends to perpetuate the view that the **Treatises** are really a work of political philosophy. It is perhaps not too unfair to represent a prevailing view as follows: all works of political philosophy are concerned with political obligation; Locke's discussion of consent in the **Second Treatise** is an account of political obligation; therefore Locke's **Second Treatise** is a work of political philosophy.

Now, not only is this a false syllogism, but also Locke's discussion of express and tacit consent is misunderstood if it is regarded as his account of political obligation.[56] Locke did not commit the errors of which

Hume accused him (of reducing one sort of obligation to another, whilst explaining neither), nor was he guilty of the confusions and inadequacies of which many of his more modern critics accuse him. His discussion of express and tacit consent is not a confused attempt to reconcile the express consent involved in contracting with the grounds of political obligation in post-contractual situations.57

It is certainly true that Locke's references to consent in the **Second Treatise** have something to do with political obligation. But that they do not express the **grounds** of political obligation is manifest from the rest of Locke's writings. Locke seems to have distinguished between three related questions; first, why men are **obliged** to create government; second, how **particular** governments were established; and, third, what constituted the legitimate limits of political power. The **Second Treatise** was concerned more with the last two of these questions than with the first. Consent explains how it is that men **incur** obligations to any particular governments. It explains the limits of political power and how legitimate governments can arise. But it does not explain why men are obliged to obey the governments they have thus consented to. Locke's explanation of this referred to natural law, to the necessities of organised social life and to the instincts of man; but ultimately the explanation rested on God's command. The obligation to obey **legitimate** government (i.e. government that elicited the consent of its citizens) was ultimately an obligation to God. Thus in his Journal for 1679, for example, Locke noted:

> If ⟨man⟩ finds that God has made him and all other men in a state wherein they cannot subsist without Society and has given them the judgment to discern what is capable of preserving and maintaining that society can he but conclude that he is obliged and that god requires him to follow rules which conduce to the preserving of Society.58

Men are created by God, they are His servants, and they are set in the world about His business. They belong to

God, and hence they cannot have a right to destroy themselves. Indeed, the right of self-preservation is itself a duty to God. All men's responsibilities and duties are ultimately owed to God. Hence, as Locke noted in his early **Essays on the Law of Nature**, "all obligation leads back to God."[59]

But if Locke's discussion of express and tacit consent was not an account of the grounds of political obligation, what was it? One plausible way of interpreting this discussion is to see it as a theory of citizenship which has significance in the argument of **Two Treatises** because it identifies that section of society that might properly be styled **members** of political society whose judgment will determine when government is "dissolved." In other words, it can be seen as an attempt to theorize the **activity** of being a citizen in late seventeenth century England, rather than as an attempt to theorize the **condition** of being under an obligation. And that this is not too unlikely an account of Locke's discussion is suggested by the apparently similar concern of Sidney and Paxton with the distinction between "citizens" and "mere inhabitants."[60] In the late seventeenth century only a small proportion of the population was accorded the fullest rights and duties of citizenship, and the import of Locke's discussion of express and tacit consent was precisely that it explained how this situation could legitimately arise. That this was at least one purpose of the discussion can be seen from the conclusion Locke draws:

> submitting to the Laws of any Country, living quietly, and enjoying Priviledges and Protection under them ⟨i.e. tacit consent⟩, **makes not a Man a Member of that Society** ... Nothing can make any Man so, but his actually entering into it by positive Engagement, and express Promise and Compact ⟨i.e. express consent⟩. This is that, which I think, concerning .... that **Consent which makes any one a Member of any Commonwealth.**[61]

Membership of civil society was reserved for those who had expressly consented to it, although at any given time the government of that society could exact obedience from all those residing within, or passing through its territory. All those who were thus subject to the government, but who were not fully members of the society, had tacitly consented to obey. Men became subject to a government by their own consent (either express or tacit), but they only became members of a society through express consent. But this notion of express consent Locke nowhere explains. He simply asserts that "no-one doubts" that express consent entitles an individual to full membership of a commonwealth.[62] His meaning can only be guessed or interpreted as referring to social presuppositions and the like - to ideas such as, that it was gentlemen who expressly consented at their coming-of-age by accepting (or rejecting) their political responsibilities; or that taking oaths of allegiance, as practically all public officials did in seventeenth century England, constituted the express consent Locke had in mind here.[63] But no matter what use we make of Locke's social presuppositions to elucidate his meaning, it is clear that his discussion of express and tacit consent is not an account of what it means to be under an obligation to someone. Yet this is precisely the point of Pufendorf's superficially similar discussion of consent in his **De Officio**.

It appears, then, that Locke's discussion of consent in the **Second Treatise**, like his discussion of natural law, did not arise from considering the same questions as Pufendorf. Apparently similar statements that occur in Pufendorf and Locke are only superficially so. Locke's **Second Treatise**, like the **First**, is fundamentally a piece of rhetorical writing. Despite its generality, it does not exhibit the characteristics of philosophical enquiry that Locke himself outlined. Despite Locke's assertion that it was a work of the same kind as Pufendorf's, a comparison of their writings reveals considerable differences. Despite the almost complete absence of any direct references to English politics, the argument was concerned to persuade Englishmen to take a particular stance in relation to the major political conflict of the day. It was published to defend the 1688 Revolution, some of its arguments are only properly intelligible within the social context of late seventeenth century English politics, and, as we shall see, the first reactions to the work interpreted it as directly related to English constitutional conflict.

But if the **Treatises** is essentially a piece of political rhetoric, the problem still remains of accounting for Locke's view that it was a work of the same kind as Pufendorf's **De Officio** and **De Jure Naturae et Gentium**. Two considerations seem relevant here. The first concerns Locke's notion of the theoretical study of politics; the second concerns a common misunderstanding of the nature of rhetoric. We may conclude this part of our enquiry by briefly examining these.

The reading that Locke suggested to the would-be student of the theoretical part of politics indicates that he himself made no distinction between philosophy and rhetoric. Pufendorf's **De Jure Naturae et Gentium** was represented as the best book of the same kind as not only the **Two Treatises**, but also Hooker's **Ecclesiastical Polity**, Sidney's **Discourses** and Paxton's **Civil Polity**. Now none of these works, apart from Pufendorf's, even begin to construct arguments along the lines that Locke believed necessary for the establishment of certain knowledge. All of them were general, in the sense that they contained theories about government, society and law, but two of them at least were particular and practical as well. These were designed, that is to say, to persuade their audiences to adopt a particular stance in relation to major, practical political issues of their day: to reject Puritan opposition to the Elizabethan Church Government in Hooker's case, to reject Filmerian Royalism and establish (or re-establish) parliamentary supremacy in Sidney's case.

These other works, then, in Locke's first kind of political study were themselves rhetorical in the sense that I am using the term here. They were concerned with opinion and persuasion, rather than with truth and demonstration. But by calling them rhetorical, I do not mean that there was anything necessarily insincere or misleading about their arguments. Many writers in the modern world have emphasised these negative connotations of the idea of rhetoric. Kant, for example, in his **Critique of Judgement** (1790), notes a common meaning of rhetoric as "the art of persuasion, i.e. the art of deluding by means of a fair semblance."[64] Locke shared this common belief that rhetoric was somewhat disreputable - he tended to associate it with the excesses of Scholastic disputation and did not regard it as a suitable subject to be taught.[65] We may surmise, then, that Locke would not have welcomed an interpretation of his work as a piece of rhetoric. He believed that the principles and propositions employed in the **Treatises** - especially those concerning natural law - could all be established as certain knowledge through mathematical demonstration. But this belief alone, as I have argued, is not sufficient to warrant interpreting the **Treatises** as political philosophy, even according to Locke's own view of what philosophical argument should look like.

By rhetoric here, then, I mean simply a piece of writing that has as its principal organising idea, in Aristotelian terms, the concern to persuade its readers to think and act in a particular way rather than to logically demonstrate certain propositions.[66] There are, of course, many different ways of pursuing this aim and there are, accordingly, many different kinds of rhetorical works. So simply to call **Two Treatises** rhetoric does not add a great deal to our understanding of the work. But it does clarify some of the problems concerning the nature of Locke's social contract theory. If we regard his argument as rhetoric rather than as political philosophy, then many of the disappointments that Locke scholars have encountered, and that I have noted, can be removed: they are born of the wrong expectations.

Two Treatises, then, presented an argument in social contract terms designed to have a specific impact on late seventeenth century English political practice. But how effective was it as a piece of rhetoric? I will conclude this survey of Locke's theory by attempting to answer this question.

Clearly the **Treatises** were eventually very successful. The **Second Treatise**, in particular, came to be regarded as containing the "Principles of 1688" and it supposedly supplied the Whig party of the mid-eighteenth century with its "philosophical or speculative system of principles."[67] Yet the immediate reaction to the work seems rather surprising. It occasioned no replies until 1703, and it was not until 1705 that any extended attempt was made to refute Locke's arguments.[68] The work did not straightway become the principal authority of the Whigs. In fact, it did not introduce any startlingly new ideas into political debate. Its main outline was to be found in Tyrrell's **Patriarcha Non Monarcha** (1680), Sidney's **Discourses Concerning Government** (published in 1698 but written before 1683) and Pufendorf's **De Jure Naturae et Gentium** (1672) and **De Officio Hominis et Civis** (1673). The first two of these contained much more besides, but this will be examined in the last part of my enquiry. In most Whig writings it was as much, if not more, to these authorities (and the authorities like Hooker and Grotius that they had used) as to Locke that reference was made. Indeed, it appears that Locke was so far from occupying the front place amongst Whig authorities that Benjamin Hoadly could write a work in the same idiom as Locke's (in 1710), and be commended in the Commons for it, with only one brief reference to **Two Treatises**. And that reference simply recommended the reader to look at the **First Treatise** for a criticism of "Some Branches" of the "Patriarchal Scheme." That part of Hoadly's argument that parallelled the **Second Treatise** was presented simply as a "Defence of Mr. Hooker's Judgement."[69]

In the learned periodicals and book reviews of the day, **Two Treatises** had a similarly far from excited reception. On the Continent, the **Bibliothèque universelle et historique,** produced by Locke's friend Jean le Clerc, received both the English first edition and the first French translation (of only the **Second Treatise**) very enthusiastically.[70] But Henri Basnage's **Histoire des ouvrages des sçavans** was not taken by it at all. The review of the French edition simply concluded coldly:

"C'est dommage que l'Auteur n'a pas toujours bien dégagé ses pensées, ni bien développé ses sentimens."[71] The most notable of the English journals, including Peter Motteux's **The Gentleman's Journal**, J.C. de la Crose's **The History of Learning**, John Dunton's **Athenian Gazette**, Richard Wooley's **The Compleat Library**, the **Mercurius Reformatus** and **Mercurius Britannicus** and the mammoth **History of the Works of the Learned** were all apparently unimpressed by the **Treatises**; none either reviewed any of its editions or mentioned it in any of their other reviews. Yet each of these journals carried notices of political works, and some reviewed in detail books by Pufendorf, Tyrrell, Sidney and Paxton as well as Locke's own **Essay Concerning Human Understanding** and his educational works.

This remarkable lack of immediate response seems to indicate that hindsight has inflated our sense of Locke's importance as a political writer during the late seventeenth and early eighteenth centuries. One recent historian, John Dunn, has noted this. But his account is both exaggerated and somewhat away from the point.[72] From the more ephemeral party literature and from contemporary letters and reports of conversations, a slightly more familiar picture of Locke's influence emerges. But it is a Locke who is as significant for his **First Treatise** as his **Second**, and one who shares a growing reputation with Sidney, whilst both he and Sidney were overshadowed by the "judicious Pufendorf."

That Locke's work did not pass unnoticed by the press is evidenced from a number of sources. In August 1690, **Two Treatises** was apparently the subject of admiration and speculation amongst some circles of learned society in both Oxford and London;[73] a popular Whig pamphlet entitled **Political Aphorisms** (1690) summarised and quoted extensively (without acknowledgement) from the work;[74] William Atwood, as we have seen, adopted some of Locke's arguments in his **Fundamental Constitution** (1690) and referred to the work as "the best Treatises of Civil Polity I have met with in the **English** tongue;"[75] and by 1693 Pierre Bayle could report to his Italian correspondent Minutoli that the theory of government outlined in the **Second Treatise** was "l'Evangile du jour à présent parmi les Protestants."[76]

During the early years of the 1690s, James Tyrrell placed Locke's **Treatises** in the public eye by numerous references and quotations from them in his popular compendium of political argument, the **Bibliotheca Politica** (1692-4). But it is interesting to note that the references all occur in the first three dialogues (i.e., those concerned with the refutation of patriarchalism and the establishment of a right of resistance) and that by far the majority of them were from the **First Treatise**. In 1694, Locke appeared to Matthew Tindal, the Deist, as a "wonderfully Ingenious and Judicious Author" who could readily be followed in arguments about consent and citizenship.

In the late 1690s, Locke's **Treatises** continued to feature as an authority in some political argument. A second edition of the work was published in 1694, and a third in 1698. During 1698 the argument of the **Second Treatise** became the subject of a minor sectarian quarrel. This quarrel began when Locke's friend, William Molyneux, adopted the arguments of the **Treatises** to make a case for Irish independence. In particular, Molyneux used Locke's authority to deny that the English could have any right of conquest over the Irish, and to assert that the Irish had a natural right to a government of their own choice.[78] The argument soon occasioned replies from Simon Clement, John Cary and Charles Leslie. Clement and Cary acknowledged that they were supporters of Locke, but they refused to allow that his arguments applied to the Irish situation. Simon Clement, for example, insisted that Molyneux's:

> plausible Arguments for the Liberty and Right of all Mankind; that Conquests cann't bind Posterity, Etc. are wholly misapply'd in this Case, and he abuses Mr. **Lock**, or whoever was the Author of that Excellent Treatise of Government, in referring to that Book on this occasion; for that Worthy Gentleman doth therein argue the Case of the People whose just Rights are violated, their Laws

subverted, and the Liberty and Property inherent to them by the Fundamental Laws of Nature, (which he accurately describes) is invaded and usurp'd upon, and that when this is as evident and apparent as the Sun that shines in a clear day, they may then take the best occasion they can find to right themselves. This is a Doctrine that all good Men may assent to, but this is in no wise the Case of Ireland.[79]

Charles Leslie entered the dispute against Molyneux. He was no Lockean, but his argument against Molyneux played on the authority of Molyneux's master. Locke had founded political authority on consent, Leslie noted, and two successive Irish Parliaments (1692 and 1695) had submitted their allegiance to William and Mary. Since the Irish parliaments had thus consented to English rule, Molyneux's authority in fact testified against him and he should concede the argument.[80]

The reputation of **Two Treatises** was thus certainly growing throughout the 1690s. Practically all references to the work were favourable, and more often than not the author was referred to as "Learned and Ingenious," or the like.[81] But this evidence only serves to modify the initial impression that the **Treatises** occasioned no great immediate response. In all the arguments where appeal was made to Locke, he appeared simply as one amongst a number of authorities and never as **the** authority. His work never attracted the attention of journal reviewers whereas the similar works of Pufendorf, Tyrrell and Sidney did. And it was not until as late as 1703 that any Tory or Jacobite considered it worth his pains to engage in a critical examination of the **Treatises.**

One explanation of Locke's **relative** insignificance in the 1690s is that the **Treatises** were written in the same tradition (to all appearances, at least) as the works of two men of outstanding contemporary reputation - Pufendorf and Sidney. The one was a man of continental reputation. The other was a great "martyr" for English liberty, whose reputation initially depended more upon the circumstances of his death than on anything he wrote. Furthermore, the reputation of the **Treatises** was probably slower in gaining ground because its author was not widely known until Locke's death in 1704 (even though the truth had been suspected from the very beginning). The book's official anonymity may well have adversely affected the attention paid to it, and hence its authority. For Locke's reputation as a philosopher and educational writer was great and the **Treatises** may have been more widely read had it definitley been known that he was the author.

Perhaps a more substantial explanation, however, lies in the argument of the **Treatises** itself. It was not, as Dunn suggests, that the **Treatises** contained nothing but "principles of the most indubitable and parochial political orthodoxy" (or were read as if they did) that they did not create a considerable stir when first published.[82] It was rather that they were not exactly fitted to perform the task Locke intended in publishing - the justification of 1688. The acuter minds of the time saw that too "philosophical" a justification could not but overreach itself. What it gained in scope and grandeur it lost in precision and application to **all** the relevant details of the actual situation. Their political wisdom was clearly more sophisticated than Locke's, for Locke had been led astray, as it were, by rationalist tendencies, derived, in part, from Pufendorf. That this was the problem with Locke's argument for the defenders of the 1688 Revolution can be seen most clearly in William Atwood's qualified praise of **Two Treatises**. The **Treatises**, Atwood suggested, were unacceptable as a justification of 1688, even though they contained the best examination of "Civil Polity" in English. If they were accepted, then the ancient constitution would be endangered, because the people would be at liberty to alter that constitution as they thought fit. Even though Locke's argument was clearly written with English affairs in mind, the Revolution required a more legalistic justification. It required an argument that did not rest upon appeal to natural law, natural right, and the dissolution of government, but which appealed instead (or as well) to the constitutional rights of Englishmen and which restricted the limits of constitutional change to the restoration of the ancient constitution.[83]

The Lockean argument that resistance to constitutional authorities might be morally justifiable or even a moral duty if those authorities encroached upon men's natural rights was altogether unacceptable to the Convention Parliament. Serjeant Maynard at one point interrupted the complicated legal disputes about the place of "abdication" and "vacancy" in English law and suggested that perhaps the attempt to reconcile resisting James II with the strict requirements of constitutional law was misguided:

> If we look but into the law of nature (that is above all human laws), we have enough to justify us in what we are now a doing, to provide for ourselves and the publick weal in such an exigency as this.[84]

But his voice was simply ignored, the debate continued, and his argument formed no part of the Commons case argued by Somers, Holt, Sacheverell and Pollexfen.

The argument of the **Second Treatise** was thus felt not to be "sufficient," as Locke had hoped, to justify the Revolution. The **First Treatise**, however, was far less contentious, even though it was incomplete. It was from this that Tyrrell quoted most extensively when compiling his **Bibliotheca Politica**. According to Atwood, it was the brilliant exposure of "the false **Principles** and Foundation of Sir Robert Filmer and his Admirers" that accounted for the **Treatises** "gaining reputation."[85] It was to the **First Treatise** that Hoadly directed his readers in 1710. And the first detailed answer to the **Treatises, An Essay Upon Government** (published anonymously in 1705 and reprinted in 1706), was almost entirely concerned with the **First Treatise**.

Although the **Second Treatise** was quite widely read and admired, as we have seen, still the evidence suggests that the reputation of the whole work depended as much, if not more, on the **First Treatise**. Patriarchalism and divine right were by no means extinguished by the Revolution. In the early years of the eighteenth century they in fact gained one of their most able and effective champions, Charles Leslie.[86] Thus the issues discussed in Locke's **First Treatise** remained points of contention until well into the eighteenth century.

The **Second Treatise** did eventually eclipse the reputation of the **First**. The **Treatises** became the principal authority of the mid-eighteenth century Whigs and the argument of the **Second Treatise** was regarded as the core of the work. The beginnings of this fascinating change can be seen from 1698 to 1705. In 1698 Walter Moyle, one of the more radical Whigs, described the **Second Treatise** as containing "the first Rudiments" of politics; he even knew of someone, he said, "who calls it the A.B.C. of Politicks." But the point of so characterizing it was not to recommend it as an unquestionable authority, but rather as a good introduction to the study of Sidney.[87] Sidney's reputation stood very high in Whig circles, and, indeed, he was the only contemporary authority referred to in the most prominent Whig political newspaper (John Tutchin's bi-weekly **Observator**) between 1702 and 1705. Sidney there appeared as the writer who best understood "the constitution of the ENGLISH Government."[88] Even when the **Observator** defended the right of resistance, it invoked the authority of Grotius, not of Locke.[89] But is from Charles Leslie's rival paper, **The Rehearsal of Observator**, and from Leslie's political pamphlets, that Locke's growing reputation can best be seen.

In 1698, whilst opposing Molyneux's **Case of Ireland**, Leslie simply noted that Molyneux had taken over from "Mr. **Lock**, etc." arguments which could more plausibly be used against him.[90] By 1703, however, when Leslie turned once again to consider Locke's arguments, it was the "Great **L-k** in his **Two Discourses of Government**" who was attacked, and whose notion of consent was declared "**Nonsense**."[91] And when he returned to the attack in the following year, it was against "Mr L-K ... in his so much Fam'd **Two Treatises** of Government."[92] In his weekly **Rehearsal**, begun the same year (1704), Leslie rebutted again and again the "Great Lock." Locke and Sidney were singled out as the two "men of **Wit**" in the Whig party.[93] But it was as the "Great **Lock, and Sidney**" that they appeared,[94] and it was the "great **Oracle** Mr. **Lock**" whose **Treatises** was subjected to a detailed scrutiny and criticism which occupied the bulk of eight weeks' issues.[95] Yet even still, although it was Locke's notion of consent that Leslie most frequently criticised, the detailed examination of the **Treatises** was concerned mainly with arguments from the **First Treatise**.[96]

As a work of political rhetoric, then, **Two Treatises** was not an immediate success. Its argument was too general to satisfy the contemporary demand for a legalistic justification of the Revolution. It was most successful in its critique of Filmer, and in this the **First Treatise** was at least as significant as the **Second**. But the weakness of the **Second Treatise** in the particular circumstances of the late seventeenth century turned out later to be the strength of the work as a whole. It was precisely the generality of the doctrine outlined in it that enabled the work to become the principal text of the Whigs in the very different circumstances of mid-eighteenth century politics and beyond.

We have seen that Locke's contract theory was different from Pufendorf's. Locke's work shared the same practical interest as the writings of constitutional contract theorists, but its type of argument was very different from theirs also. Locke's argument borrowed its central notions from contemporary political philosophy rather than from constitutional law and history. It is in this sense, that the connotations of Locke's notions were philosophical rather than constitutional, that Locke's social contract theory is an example of philosophical contractarianism. His argument most certainly was not philosophical in any other sense. **Two Treatises**, then, were unique amongst English contractarian writings of the late seventeenth century. They alone relied exclusively upon the vocabulary of social contract. Much more commonly, we encounter that vocabulary in writings portraying a third kind of contractarian argument during our period. This is the contractarianism which I have called integrated contract.

PART IV

CHAPTER 8

THE COHERENCE OF INTEGRATED CONTRACTARIANISM

At first glance, what I have called "Integrated Contractarianism" appears nothing less than a confusion. In several political works, we find arguments from natural rights, natural law and social contract explicitly invoked to answer questions recognized as concerning constitutional law. Despite the very clear differences between constitutional contractarianism and philosophical contractarianism, many writers used arguments that intermingled the two. Often this intermingling can be fairly easily explained. Political argument has a tendency to be as coercive and as all-embracing as possible in order to persuade and convince its audience. What may not have appeared thoroughly convincing when advocated in constitutional contract terms may have become so if further supported by philosophical contract arguments, and vice versa.

But this kind of consideration seems insufficient to account for a number of rather perplexing arguments and statements that appear in the contractarian literature of the late seventeenth and early eighteenth centuries. We find Algernon Sidney, for example, insisting that Englishmen's civil rights "are innate, inherent, and enjoyed time out of mind."[1] We find Lord John Somers arguing that the right to petition parliament is a "Natural Right of Mankind."[2] We find several writers, including Jeremy Collier, presenting arguments from "the Laws of Nature; which are part of the Constitution of this Realm."[3] And a Whig political bi-weekly can be found asserting:

> For I dare engage to prove that the **Law** and **Constitution** of **England** is according to the **Law** of **Nature**, and prescrib'd by it: Nor are the **Rights** of **Englishmen** in point of **Natural Rights**, different from the **Right** of all Mankind. The farthest Corners of the Earth, and the nearest Parts to Us have all the same Priviledges: They differ only in **Form**, not in **Essence**. We call Ours the **Magna Charta** of **England**; not to distinguish Our Selves from Others in Point of **Native Rights**; but because it is a Summary of what the People of England do claim as their **Hereditary Right** and **Property**, and which is indeed the **Right** and **Property** of the whole People of the Universe: And consequently as all Mankind have **ab Origine** the same Rights with Englishmen: So ought they to have the same sort of Kings with Us: They ought to have the same Currency of **Law** as now we have in **England**, they ought to have a Prince on their several Thrones as is our Queen **Anne**.[4]

I shall argue that statements like these are not always just loose or confused uses of a technical vocabulary. In many writings, arguments from social contract and constitutional contract, from natural law and from fundamental law, appear integrated within a coherent framework. But an objection might be levelled against the enquiry at this point. It could be argued that any apparent integration is either a mere rhetorical device or else the product of confused minds. If it is a device of rhetoric, then we can easily account for it: in political argument there is nothing strange in appealing from particular cases, laws, events or arguments to general principles. If the apparent integration is the product of confused minds, then the arguments themselves can be written off as confused. It is certainly true that these two responses are appropriate in some cases. But we meet integrated arguments very frequently and it is difficult to see them always as mere confusions or rhetoric. At all events, we cannot write off this literature without omitting from our consideration a large number of late seventeenth and early eighteenth century appeals to contract. The persuasiveness of the rhetoric must be explained.

As we look closer into this rhetoric, it becomes increasingly clear that philosophical contractarianism and constitutional contractarianism are being associated together in a very specific way. Notions of state of nature, natural law, natural rights and social contract are merged into the same flow of argument with ideas of ancient constitution, fundamental law, fundamental rights and fundamental contract. But this is not all. For the explicit assumption behind this merger seems to have been that the fundamental laws and rights could be **derived** from their natural counterparts. Yet we have seen a very clear distinction between social contract and constitutional contract: a distinction evident in the sort of questions asked and the kind of evidence appealed to. We must attempt to explain, then, how integration was possible and what made it plausible to both writer and audience. In the end we might still want to assert that integrated contract arguments rested on a confusion. But having explained and accounted for the attractiveness of these arguments, we shall have explained a very prominent strand of late seventeenth century contractarian thought. It will be useful to begin our explanation by considering why integrated contract arguments were presented.

The primary impetus towards integration came from the character of royalist argument during the period. For royalist literature often appeared to marry philosophical, rationalist and constitutional arguments. The republication of Filmer's political works in a single volume is significant here. Filmer's works ranged over many levels of political argument (from the constitutional to the theological and the seemingly philosophical), yet there was a quite explicit connecting thread running through them all. James Tyrrell drew attention to this thread in the Preface to his **Patriarcha Non Monarcha** (1681):

> no man can imagine to what end the **Patriarcha** and

> other Tracts should come out at such a **Time** as they did, unless the Publishers thought that these Pieces, which printed apart could onely serve to ensnare the Understandings of some unthinking Country-Gentleman or Windblown-Theologue, could do no less, being twisted into one Volume, than bind the Consciences, and enslave the Reasons of all his unwary Readers.5

Tyrrell proceeded to devote his own single volume to a rebuttal of **all** Filmer's works.

A specific example of typical royalist argument can be seen in a pamphlet by Robert Brady written against Somers' **A Brief History of the Succession** (1681). Brady, the prominent constitutional historian, entered the dispute over the English law of succession. The question, then, concerned constitutional law. But to defend hereditary succession, Brady felt it necessary to prove that hereditary right was lawful according to the moral law as well as the law of the English constitution. His task, he declared, was to show:

> **First,** That not only all Government, but particularly Monarchy does owe its immediate Foundation and Constitution to God Almighty.
> **Secondly,** That by the Law of God, Nature and Nations the Crown ought to descend according to Priority of Birth, and Proximity of Blood.
> **Thirdly,** That if an Act of Parliament were obtained to exclude his **R. H.** <it> would be unjust, unlawful, and **ipso facto** void, as contrary both to the Law of God and Nature; and the known Fundamental Laws of the Land.6

The integrated contract response to this kind or argument is exemplified by Brady's opponent, Lord John Somers. In his **Jura Populi Anglicani** (1701), Somers set out to defend the Kentish Petitioners.7 His pamphlet blended social contract arguments and an enquiry into English constitutional law. His point was to show that petitioning was rightful both morally and according to specifically English law. But Somers, unlike Brady, attempted to extract constitutional law from the moral law. He interpreted English constitutional history in the terms and categories of his social contract theory. And a principal conclusion that he drew from this exercise was that the right to petition the Commons was an an inviolable "Natural Right of Mankind." Thus he argued:

> If this Right be natural, the People of **England**, who have lost as little by entring into Society as any others, must have as just and ample a Claim to it as any Nation in the World. That they have a Right to represent their Sufferings, and pray for a Relaxation of them, is evident from the Opinions of our Sages of the Law, from what our Kings have permitted and declared, and what has been declared and enacted in Parliament.[8]

Legal history confirmed what his social contract theory had posited. The moral law and positive law were amalgamated together in the same flow of argument.

This amalgamation was effected in two ways: both of them to some extent referred back to medieval strands of argument. The first way involved loosening the conditions of current legal theory. The ambiguities and difficulties concerned with the notions of natural law, equity and "the Reason of the law" were of particular importance here. The central conclusion that integrated contract legal theory upheld was, as one writer asserted, that "the Municipal Laws" were "grounded upon and derived from" the laws of nature and nations.[9] The second way moral theory and constitutional law were amalgamated involved loosening the social contract from its rationalist moorings and interpreting it as an historical event. The plausibility of this historical enterprise arose from the current state of historical scholarship. It was, then, in the two areas of legal theory and history that bridges were constructed between constitutional and philosophical contractarianism. In the remainder of this chapter I will examine each of these bridges in more detail and suggest why they might have appeared plausible and coherent to many Englishmen in the late seventeenth century. First, then, the legal ideas of integrated contractarianism.

We may best appreciate the pecularities of integrated contract legal ideas by contrasting them with the principal legal doctrines of philosophical and constitutional contractarianism. Philosophical contractualism examined the relationship between natural law and positive law. The most characteristic view of this relationship is expressed in Locke's **Essays on the Law of Nature**. Natural law was the ground upon which obligation to obey civil law rested. Without natural law, no compacts would be kept for long, and peace could only be secured by force, not right.[10] Natural law stood as a constant guide to legislators and subjects: it provided an eternal standard to which positive laws and human action should strive to conform.[11] Natural law was the criterion for assessing the justice of positive law. In what we have discussed as constitutional contractarianism, by contrast, positive law consisted only of those pronouncements of a properly constituted legislature that furthered the supposed intentions of the original contractors, the **salus populi**.[12] Salus populi was the criterion for determining the validity of positive law. In integrated contractarianism, these two very different criteria of natural law and **salus populi** were merged. Natural law, or the law of reason, explicitly entered the English constitution and became the most important criterion for determining what was and what was not valid as positive law. The effect of this juncture can be seen, for example, in Defoe's **The Original Power of the Collective Body of the People of England** (1702). Defoe asserts that one of the "maxims" of his argument is: "That Reason is the Test and Touch-stone of Laws, and that all Law or Power that is Contradictory to Reason, is **ipso facto** void in it self, and ought not to be obeyed."[13] The anonymous author of **A Brief Account of the Nullity of King James's Title** (n. d.) was even more explicit. He declared that "It is a Maxim of our Law, That the Laws of God and Nature should take place before all other Laws."[14] And Timothy Wilson reversed the social contract relationship between positive and natural (or divine) law when he asserted that it was the possession of a "Legal and Humane Right" that gave a prince "Gods Authority."[15] It was, apparently, no longer divine law that determined which positive law right was valid, but rather it was positive law that determined divine right.

We are confronted here with the rhetoric of political debate. As I have already suggested, it is not always obvious whether a simple confusion of concepts is occurring, or whether there is a genuine integration of constitutional and natural law arguments. But since we meet assertions like those just noted so often, it seems unwise to write them off immediately as mere confusions. Indeed, if instead of writing them off we take them seriously, we find that we can account for their plausibility and coherence to men in the late seventeenth and early eighteenth centuries.

The integration of fundamental law and natural law in the legal arguments of integrated contractarianism seems to have derived coherence from three main sources: first, one common interpretation of natural law theory; second, a common misunderstanding of the nature of equity; and third, an interpretation of lawyers' arguments from "the reason of the common law". The anonymous author of a pamphlet **Of the Fundamental Laws or Politick Constitution of this Kingdom** (n. d.) illustrates the first two of these sources. He wrote: "The Fundamental Laws of **England** are nothing but the Common Laws of Equity and Nature reduced into a particular way of Policy, which Policy is the ground of our Title to them, and Interest in them."[16] Civil laws were simply "confirmations, or explications of the Law of Nature, or conclusions drawn from it".[17] Ideally, all governments in the world would have the same constitutions. Civil right and natural right were really just two sides of the same coin, or should be. From this theory of natural law, it was a short step to the view that natural law determined which civil laws were properly laws at all. And the step was that much shorter when the common misunderstanding of equity was taken into account. Equity, an eminent lawyer asserted, was the "opposite to regular law."[18] It was a necessary and recognized branch of English law. It was necessary because, as the common lawyer Sir Robert Atkyns argued, "No Makers of Law can forsee all things that may happen, and therefore it is convenient that the fault be reform'd by Equity."[19] There appeared, then, room in English law for the exercise of discretion to ensure justice. But how far did this go? It certainly did not involve the recognition that natural law should determine what positive laws should be accepted as valid - the view involved in integrated contract arguments. Judgments in cases of equity were not given by considering divine law, natural law, **salus populi** or some abstract conception of the just. Rather, as Lord Nottingham explained, in "suits in equity before the Chancellor, the Lord Chancellor must order his conscience after the rules and grounds of the laws of this realm."[20] Yet since judgment in equity was given by reference to conscience, reason and the just, those judgments might **appear** to support integrated contract arguments. For, to the mind untutored in legal technicalities, it did seem that lawyers themselves recognised conscience, reason and the just as arbiters of what law meant and which laws were valid.

In this fashion, the appeals of great common lawyers like Coke and Hobart to "the reason of the common law" might appear to support integrated contract arguments. The lawyers understood by "the reason of the common law" something quite specific. The reason they referred to was supposedly embodied within the history of common law. Only through a knowledge of that history could the reason, the principles, of common law be understood. Yet here, once again, was evidence of lawyers appealing to reason in disputes about the meaning and validity of laws.

In their various ways, then, current notions of natural law, equity and "the reason of the common law" lent credibility to integrated contract arguments. The crucial idea that these notions supported was that natural law was an integral part of the English constitution. The historical ideas involved in integrated contractarianism made this crucial idea even more plausible. Integrated contract arguments borrowed the concepts of state of nature, social contract and governmental contract from the language of philosophical contractarianism and turned them into historical events. This was done both by turning certain historical events (like the Norman Conquest, Magna Carta and coronation oaths) into original contracts (as we have seen constitutional contract theorists doing) and by linking English constitutional history with Biblical history. There was a period in the world's history when political society had not yet been invented. That period lasted from the Creation until soon after the Flood.[21] Indeed, there were still some areas in the world, as contemporary travellers seemed to be reporting, that had not yet adopted civil life.[22] During this time and in these places, people actually lived in the state of nature. In Europe the period of the state of nature lasted until the sons of Japhet spread across the continent settling down into small communities as they went and establishing governments.[23] These first civil societies were set up by contract between the heads of the separate households that were to be incorporated. Each family or household had sacrificed some of its natural rights in order to overcome the disadvantages of the state of nature and to ensure that natural law was made effective. This was the origin of the Gothic constitution, the purest and most just form of government, that had once existed all over Europe, but which, by the late seventeenth century, according to many writers, only remained in England and a few other countries.[24] English constitutional history comprised essentially (as it did in constitutional contract theory and the common law interpretation of the ancient constitution) the so far victorious struggle of the defenders of the pure and free Gothic balance against encroachments by would-be tyrants. With this view of the historical development of the English constitution, notions of state of nature, social contract, natural right and natural law became essential for understanding constitutional law: a law that most accurately followed natural law, it could be claimed, because it was framed by our ancestors whose sole consideration was to overcome the defects of the state of nature and ensure that natural law was made effective.

In part, the attractiveness of integrated contractarianism arose from a general characteristic of much polemical argument, in part, from the peculiarities of political debate during the late seventeenth century. The first of these I have already mentioned: there is a tendency for political argument to be coercive and all-embracing in terms of its audience. Philosophical contractarianism presented theories of political **right**; constitutional contractarianism presented interpretations of the **facts** of constitutional history and law. Both were familiar to audiences in the late seventeenth century, and it is hardly surprising that several writers should have endeavoured to promote their views with arguments from both right and fact. Integrated contract arguments, however, seem to have confused arguments from right with arguments from fact. But the confusion was a far from simplistic one. It was widely recognized that civil right and natural right were notions of different kinds,[25] and writers like Tyrrell and Sidney did consider appeal to moral law to be different from appeal to civil law or history. In discussions about right, Sidney observed, "that which ought not to be is no more to be received, than if it could not be."[26] And when discussing whether there was a **right** of resistance, Tyrrell asserted "that the Question being only Moral, or Political, and not about any point of Faith, or Law, it may be safely maintained by either party, without any guilt, either of Heresie, or Treason."[27] Yet all the same, these writers endeavoured to prove that Englishmen's rights were simple derivations from the natural rights of man, and that English law embodied the law of nature.

A more complete explanation of the attractiveness of this rather peculiar attempt to marry moral right with legal fact requires a consideration of some specific characteristics of late seventeenth century political argument. The attempted marriage was made by writers endeavouring to prove that it was perfectly lawful to exclude James from the succession, and, eventually, to rebel against him. Their principal opposition came from

Filmerian sources. On the question of succession, divine righters argued that "proximity of blood does give a title unchangeable by any human laws."[28] On the right of resistance, the divine right argument was essentially that monarchy was ordained by God; that Adam was the first monarch; that paternity gave rise to political rule; that the bond between father and children was the same as that between ruler and ruled; and that citizens could no more change their rulers than children could their parents. In the debates of the 1680s, most divine righters were concerned to go even further than this, however. They attempted to show what the necessary attributes of monarchical authority were in order to argue that the English king, being properly sovereign, was thus possessed of those attributes by English as well as divine law. Faced with these arguments, Exclusionists were forced back from English law to a consideration of first principles.

The Exclusionist arguments took the same form as the divine righters' arguments and they were directed by the same fundamental conception: all phenomena were either natural or artificial. The form of argument was to begin by eliciting origins. Divine righters insisted that political society was natural, originated by God with his creation of Adam. Contractarians responded that it was artificial, created by human design. But the notion of origins was ambiguous: it might refer to rational origins or historical ones. Divine right arguments appeared to merge the two. The Bible contained a true historical account of the first ages of the world. It portrayed political power originating in Adam's family. Reason, too, taught that royal authority must be deduced from fatherhood.[29] Indeed, the first monarchs in the world were not only **like** fathers of their people, they were also the **actual** fathers of them. A complete contractarian response involved showing that political authority could only be understood if government was viewed **as if** it were the product of the conscious design of its citizens, and that as a matter of **historical fact** government was set up that way. Having established these points, contractarian arguments about particular constitutional provisions of the late seventeenth century

English constitution proceeded after the same manner as divine right arguments. What **was** and what **must have been** in the distant past were made a basis for insisting upon what was the **present** constitutional position.

In these terms, then, the difference between the three theories that were associated with appeals to contract in the late seventeenth century can be clearly seen as three different responses to Filmerian divine right theory. Thus Lockian philosophical contractarianism was a response to Filmer's theory of the nature of political power outlined in the first part of **Patriarcha**. Constitutional contractarianism was a response to the sort of argument about the English constitution presented, for example, in the last part of **Patriarcha** and in **The Freeholders Grand Inquest**. And only the theory of integrated contractarianism was a response to the whole body of Filmer's writings. But we may gain a clearer appreciation of the pecularities of integrated contractarianism if we look in some detail at the writings of Algernon Sidney and James Tyrrell. Sidney's theory of law and Tyrrell's view of English constitutional history will be of particular importance here.

# CHAPTER 9

ALGERNON SIDNEY

Algernon Sidney's name has been linked to the tradition of European radical thought ever since his "martyrdom" for the "Old Cause" in 1683. Various historians have described him as a democrat, a republican, a commonwealthsman, the philosopher of 1688, a tacit proponent of constitutional monarchy, and even as the upholder of the two "ideal" constitutions that achieved their respective realisations in America in 1776, and in England in the mid-nineteenth century.[1] But, somewhat curiously, of all the historians who have mentioned his writings, none have presented a critical examination of his ideas, the purpose for which he wrote, or the coherence of his theories of society, government and law. Yet Sidney's reputation was considerable in the late seventeenth century.[2] He was the author whom Locke ranked with Hooker, Pufendorf, Paxton and himself as recommended reading for the student of "the Original of Societies, and the rise and extent of political power."[3] The surprising lack of critical work is even further underlined by the fact that it was largely on the evidence of his ideas that Sidney was convicted and executed for high treason. The opinion of Lord Chief Justice Jeffreys is sufficiently dramatic to warrant a close enquiry into the ideas of that book which, he said in his summing up, "contains all the malice, and revenge and treason, that mankind can be guilty of: it fixes the sole power in the parliament and the people."[4]

Sidney wrote his manuscript, the **Discourses Concerning Government,** principally to refute Filmer's doctrines and to reassert the idea of man's natural liberty to set up the civil society of his choice and control it throughout all its constitutional development. Many of Filmer's basic assumptions about the relationship of man to God, the importance of scripture as history, and of the necessity of enquiring into origins to settle questions of right, were shared by Sidney. But Sidney totally disagreed with the principles that Filmer had deduced from these premises. **Patriarcha**, he declared, was "grounded upon wicked principles, equally pernicious to magistrates and people." For, as far as his reading of the work was concerned, it declared the opinion that:

> all men are born under a necessity derived from the laws of God and nature, to submit to an absolute Kingly government, which could be restrained by no law, or oath; and that he that has the power, whether he came to it by creation, election, inheritance, usurpation, or any other way, had the right; and none must oppose his will, but the persons and estates of his subjects must be indispensably subject unto it.[5]

The opposing views which Sidney claimed to have defended in his writings were set out in a series of propositions in his scaffold **Paper**. He claimed that God had left men of liberty to set up the form of government of their choice; that magistrates existed for the good of nations, not nations for the good of magistrates; that civil laws defined and limited the right and power of magistrates; that civil laws "were to be observed, and the oaths taken by them, having the force of a contract between magistrate and people, could not be violated without danger of dissolving the whole fabric"; and that usurpation "could give no right."[6]

All these propositions are familiar as the stock-in-trade of late seventeenth century contractarians. In defending them against Filmerian attack, Sidney engaged in detailed and tedious point by point criticism. This common seventeenth century style of criticism tends to obscure the passion, determination and depth of feeling that clearly lay behind the views that Sidney was prepared to die for. The **Discourses** are too rambling and repetitive to present a single developing line of argument. They seem overburdened with an excessive scholarship. Yet a passionate belief is often close to the surface and Sidney was prepared to follow through the consequences of his ideas in a much more rigid way than most other contractarians.

Sidney's critique of Filmer began with an assertion of the far-reaching practical importance of his task. "Such as have reason, understanding, or common sense, will, and ought to make use of it in those things that concern themselves and their posterity," he asserted. "This rule obliges us so far to search into matters of state, as to examine the original principles of government in general, and of our own in particular."[7] The authorities which he claimed were necessary for this examination, and by which he was prepared to be refuted, were those of reason, law, history and scripture.[8] It is in terms of the interdependence of the evidence from these diverse sources that the main characteristics of Sidney's writings as a form of integrated contractarianism can be seen.

The examination of the first principles of government brought Sidney into conflict with Filmer's notion of natural subjection. Against the view that man was born under the dominion of a religiously sanctified absolute monarch, Sidney asserted "that man is naturally free."[9] But this natural freedom was far from unlimited. Sidney disputed only that man's natural obligations involved a political obligation. He accepted much else of Filmer's argument. Thus man, he believed, was born under a complete obligation to God, his creator. But this simply confirmed his own point about natural freedom. For God had created free men.[10] Certainly, too, man was born under an obligation to parents, but this was not a political obligation.[11] Yet this did mean, as we have seen somewhat similarly in Pufendorf, that ultimately only "every father of a family is free, and exempt from the domination of any other."[12]

Basing himself on this qualified principle of man's natural liberty, Sidney proceeded to enquire into the origin of government in a rationalist constructivist manner. Men were equal in respect of natural rights, how then did the patent inequality in existing civil societies arise? The argument from design provided Sidney with the answer. Inequality must have arisen in one or other of the only two types of consciously directed human actions that Sidney could imagine: either "by consent, or by force." The latter, however, could never justify inequality. It could never give a right to governors. Power acquired by force or conquest could never turn into rightful power of itself. Sidney's argument here drew on the maxim that that "which was unjust in its beginning, can of itself never change its nature." We have already met a variety of this maxim in Atwood's "Quod initio non valet tractu temporis non convalescit." Sidney associated it with another maxim, one closer, this time, to Locke. In disputes about right, he added, "that which ought not to be is no more to be received, than if it could not be."[13]

Of the two possible origins of inequality, then, only conscious consent could provide a viable and legitimate explanation of inequality. The manner and extent of consenting was explained by reference to a state of nature and civil contract. It is clear that Sidney understood this as something that had actually occurred in the history of mankind. It was not simply, as in Pufendorf, a hypothetical construction necessary for explaining the relationships inevitably presupposed in social existence. "The first fathers of mankind," Sidney argued, "left their children independent on each other, and in an equal liberty of providing for themselves." Civil society then arose as follows:

> every man continued in this liberty, till the number so increased, that they became troublesome and dangerous to each other; and finding no other remedy to the disorders growing, or like to grow among them, joined many families into one civil body, that they might the better provide for the conveniency, safety, and the defence of themselves and their children. This was a collation of every man's private right into a publick stock. And no one having any other right than what was common to all, except it were that of fathers over their children, they were all equally free when their

fathers were dead; and nothing could induce them to join, and lessen their natural liberty by joining in societies, but the hopes of a public advantage.[14]

The origin of society, then, lay in the rational act of previously free and independent family heads. Natural liberty involved disadvantages, and the intention to overcome these was the only motive for the formation of the association called civil society. "Societies cannot be instituted, unless the heads of families, that are to compose them, resign so much of their right, as seems convenient, into a public stock, to which everyone becomes subject."[15] The public realm was created by a contract imposing restrictions on private right. But the extent of the restriction on natural liberty was left entirely to the subjective judgment of the participants. For, in the last resort, they alone would suffer if a mistake were made.[16]

Thus the first governments were those set up by the consent of the governed. From this Sidney drew certain conclusions about the nature of government which follow, in fact, only when related to his fundamental assumption of the rational design of human institutions:

> If the power be originally with the multitude, and one or more men, to whom the exercise of it, or a part of it was committed, had no more than their brethren, till it was conferred on him or them, it cannot be believed, that rational creatures would advance one, or a few of their equals above themselves, unless in consideration of their own good; and then I find no inconvenience in leaving to them a right of judging, whether this be duly performed or not. We say in general, "he that institutes may also abrogate;" more especially when the institution is not only by but for himself. If the multitude therefore do institute, the multitude may abrogate; and they themselves, or those who succeed in the same right, can only be fit judges of the performance of the ends of the institution.[17]

Government was entrusted to the care of magistrates on condition that its design be fulfilled. Only part of natural liberty was given up on entering civil society, and that only conditionally. The reasons for establishing society in the first place were the continuing ends for which government existed. These ends, according to Sidney, consisted in the public safety being provided for, liberty and property secured, "justice administered, virtue encouraged, vice suppressed, and the true interest of the nation advanced."[18]

The trust involved in government was not without sanctions. Laws originated from attempts to direct and restrain magistrates in the performance of their duties. In variously framing constitutions, all nations retained "their natural right, to be governed by none, and in no other way than they should appoint." A natural right to rebel thus appeared as the inevitable consequence of a proper view of the origin of government. When Pufendorf, Locke and Tyrrell argued for a natural right to resist they qualified and hedged that right round so as not to seem to render government unstable. Sidney's argument, however, contained no such qualifications. In the opening pages of his **Discourses**, he simply declared that the dangers of asserting a right to resist magistrates were exaggerated. What was essential was that government be exercised with justice. "There can be no peace, where there is no justice," he insisted, "nor any justice, if the government instituted for the good of the nation be turned to its ruin."[19] In this statement Sidney summed up an enduring theme of his life in politics. By far the gravest threat to the public well-being came, as he saw it, from existing magistrates. No effort should be spared in opposing their abuses of power. But the citizen body, for its part, almost as an analytic truth would never act contrary to its own interest. It needed no controls. Sidney does not seem to have had any particular communities in mind here. He was simply juggling propositions about the causes of civil disorder.

Here, then, we have the outline of Sidney's theory of the origin of government in general. All his ideas were quite familiar in the late seventeenth century but his unqualified insistence on a popular right of rebellion is remarkable. The idea of contract was crucial to Sidney's notions of society, law and government. Society could only legitimately be set up, and historically the first societies actually were set up, by a contract between the heads of previously independent families. Government was designed to perform the ends adumbrated in the original contract. Laws were designed to ensure that government fulfilled its only legitimate role and punished actions contrary to the terms of the contract. Thus Sidney believed it no exaggeration to say that human societies were, indeed, "maintained by mutual contracts."[20]

Sidney understood the mutual contracts involved in establishing government, society and law not only as historical realities but also as continuing constitutional realities. "I will prove," he claimed, and intended to devote a chapter to that proof:

> in the first place, that several nations have plainly and explicitly made contracts with their magistrates.
> 2. That they are implicit, and to be understood, where they are not plainly expressed.
> 3. That they are not dreams, but real things, and perpetually obliging.
> 4. That judges are in many places appointed to decide the contests arising from the breach of these contracts; and where they are not, or the party offending is of such force or pride, that he will not submit, nations have been obliged to take the extremest courses.[21]

Unfortunately, the rest of the chapter was lost. But sufficient evidence exists, scattered throughout his vast **Discourses,** for us to present a fairly reliable account of what would have been the lines of his proof. His main concern was to establish the existence of constitutional rather than social contracts. The latter were only necessary for him as a weapon against the Filmerian assertion that government had always existed.

But the ultimate justification for both kinds of contract was the reasonableness of believing in their existence and the unreasonableness of their Filmerian alternatives.

Sidney accepted with Filmer that the "Creation is exactly described in the Scripture." But he denied that there was anything to do with the origin of government in the biblical account of the first ages of the world. Our knowledge of what happened between the creation and the flood was so scanty that Filmer "may say what he pleases, and I may leave him to seek his proofs where he can find them." He would never convince Sidney "that any power did remain in the heads of families after the flood, that does in the least degree resemble the regal in principle or practice."[22] Filmer's theory was thoroughly unreasonable since even if "the first fathers of mankind" possessed political rights (which Sidney like Locke, Tyrrell, Hunt and others denied), they "must necessarily perish, since the generations of men are so confused, that no man knows his own original" let alone that of the supposed (and mythical) heir to Adam's power.[23]

Next, Sidney presented his own principles of natural liberty, natural equality, and the contractual origins of government and society as if they accorded with little more than common sense. "Common sense teaches," he confidently asserted, "and all good men acknowledge, that governments are not set up for the advantage, profit, pleasure, or glory of one or a few men, but for the good of society."[24] And this appeal to a supposed common sense was the ultimate "proof" of his general theory that men voluntarily contracted together to set up civil societies.[25]

Yet although nothing more might be required to prove this theory than its patent reasonableness, Sidney laboriously produced further supposed proofs from history, law and scripture. But since all his evidence from these sources was interpreted in the light of what appeared reasonable to Sidney, there could hardly arise any conflict. Indeed, Sidney seems to have believed in a kind of 'scholastic harmony': the universe was so ordered and guided by a rational God that everything in it contributed towards the divine (rational) plan. Any evidence to the contrary was either wrong or had been misunderstood.[26] Thus, for example, in the face of Filmer's demand for historical evidence of original contracts, Sidney simply replied, "if there never were any general meetings of whole nations, or of such as they did delegate and intrust with the power of the whole, how did any man that was elected come to have a power over the whole?" He then proceeded to give several specific examples including the Romans, Goths, Franks, Vandals and Saxons. Indeed, he claimed that the histories of all nations "are so full of examples of this kind, that no man can question them, unless he be brutally ignorant, or maliciously contentious." Sidney's argument here was as much indicative of the very loose way he understood contract as how cavalierly he was prepared to interpret historical evidence.

As for evidence from constitutional law, Sidney claimed that this too supported a contractualist understanding of government. But his argument here was as circular as it was with historical evidence. There was a great variety of constitutions in the world, he asserted, and "no other reason can be given for this almost infinite variety of constitutions, than that they who made them would have it so; which could not be, if God and nature had appointed one general rule for all nations."[28]

The evidence from religion and scripture was dealt with in similar fashion. The reasonableness and necessity of civil society for the life of man, Sidney argued, must be presumed to prove that the contract of civil society was the will of God. God had made man and had ordained that he live in society with others. But he had left man free to choose his own form of government.[29]

The proofs that Sidney might have produced in the missing chapter of his **Discourses**, proofs, that is, of the reality of contracts, are thus ultimately circular.

What accorded with common sense and reason provided the constant reference point for all his enquiries into political affairs. For all his assertions about "the political science, which of all others is the most abstruse and variable according to accidents and circumstances," Sidney's contract theory can only be understood in terms of his rationalism.[30] This can be most clearly seen in his reflections about law and justice.

Sidney declared that his purpose for enquiring into the relative merits of the various forms of government was to "seek only that which is legal and just."[31] We have already seen that the attempt to marry law with morality was a central theme in integrated contractarianism.[32] It involved far more than the common sense idea that there ought to be some correspondence between legal rules and moral precepts. In fact, it seemed to involve a theory of law that bore closer resemblance to mediaeval than to modern ideas.[33] But it is a legal theory of crucial importance for understanding Whig theories of legal rebellion. Sidney's writings contain one of the clearest statements of this sort of Whig theory. The characteristics of the theory emerged during Sidney's search for the lawful and just constitution.

His enquiry, ostensibly, proceeded along both historical and rationalist lines. The outcome of the enquiry was that the lawful and just constitution was that which began in contract and persisted through the continuous consent of the citizens to laws which enshrined their purpose for originally setting up government in the first place. In this constitution "the laws of every people" were indicative of the "reasons for which, or the conditions upon which ⟨their⟩ consent was obtained" to be governed.[34] Justice was possible only if the constitutional arrangements guaranteed the continuous right of the citizenry to alter their laws as they saw fit.[35] Such a constitution, Sidney argued, was no utopian dream. It had been often evidenced in human history.[36]

The best form of government that the world had yet witnessed was that of Republican Rome. It had not been perfect. It had, after all, collapsed. But Sidney's avowed concern was "not after that which is perfect, well knowing that no such thing is found among men." Rather, he was looking for "that human constitution, which is attended with the least, or the most pardonable inconveniences."[37] The consideration of history led him, as it had led many before him, to that classical republicanism for which he is most famous.[38] Ancient Sparta, Republican Rome and contemporary Venice had portrayed most effectively the characteristics of liberty, justice and durability that qualified them as the best models to be followed.[39] Yet Sidney's republicanism was neither populist nor anti-monarchical. Indeed, he declared himself opposed to "pure democracy."[40]

The crucial common attribute of all the constitutions Sidney admired was that they supposedly recognized a perpetual right in the citizen body to change their legal arrangements. This was the very "essence" of the "just constitution."[41] The excellence of this type of constitution consisted in its securing the ideals of justice, liberty and property. By definition the just constitution was a constitution based on consent. The sort of consent that Sidney had in mind here seems to have been of a very explicit kind.

> It is not ... the bare suffrance of a government when a disgust is declared, nor a silent submission when the power of opposing is wanting, that can imply a consent or election, and create a right; but an explicit act of approbation, when men have ability and courage to resist or deny.[42]

The liberty guaranteed by this constitution did involve restrictions. Sidney distinguished liberty from licence very clearly. The liberty he was defending, he claimed, "is not a licentiousness of doing what is pleasing to every one against the Command of God." Rather, it was "an exemption from all human laws, to which men ... have not given their assent."[43] Liberty consisted solely "in an independency upon the will of another" and thus, Sidney concluded, he "is a free man who lives as best pleases himself, under laws made by his own consent."[44]

The contractual origin of civil society, however, did involve sacrificing some natural liberty. This was legitimate provided both that the sacrifice was made willingly and equally by all and also that a sphere of individual liberty remained. Sidney also acknowledged that society might have considerable legitimate interests in the private affairs of individuals. Although the boundary between the public and the private should be very clear, society might legitimately concern itself, for example with an individual's property if the public good so required.[45]

But the sacrifice of natural liberty and the acceptance of possibly considerable interference by society in an individual's affairs were only conditional. The required continuous consent in the just constitution meant, as far as Sidney was concerned, the retention of a natural right to reject the laws of that constitution both by individuals and by the general body of the citizenry. Without these rights, the just constitution would be a mere chimera:

> all laws must fall, human societies that subsist by them be dissolved, and all innocent persons exposed to the violence of the most wicked, if men might not justly defend themselves against injustice by their own natural right, when the ways prescribed by public authority cannot be taken.[46]

Yet this right of resistance was neither a right held in reserve for rectifying intolerable conditions nor was it grounded on natural law alone. It was the outcome of Sidney's complex theories of the origin, design and nature of government. But it also reflected one of the most characteristic beliefs of his classical republicanism: the idea that the virtuous citizen was one constantly involved in doing or monitoring politics. Thus only through the constant operation, or threat of operation, of the right of resistance could the just constitution be retained and corruption avoided:

> Laws and constitutions ought to be weighed; and whilst all due reverence is paid to such as are good, every nation may not only retain in itself a power of changing or abolishing all such as are not so, but ought to exercise that power according to the best of their understanding, and in place of what was either at first mistaken or afterwards corrupted, to constitute that which is most conducing to the establishment of justice and liberty.[47]

And resistance was lawful not only according to natural and divine law but also according to human, positive law. Sidney's argument (which might almost be taken as the fundamental principle of radical liberalism) was the following:

> If the laws of God and men are ... of no effect, when the magistracy is left at liberty to break them, and if the lusts of those, who are too strong for the tribunals of justice, cannot be otherwise restrained, than by seditions, tumults, and wars, those seditions, tumults, and wars, are justified by the laws of God and man.[48]

Sidney acknowledged that it might not seem the case that constitutional laws permit a right of rebellion. Indeed, he noted that "human laws do not, in all cases, make men judges and avengers of the injuries offered to them."[49] But on his theory this presented no major obstacle to maintaining the legality of rebellion. His understanding of law provides the key here.

Law, for Sidney, consisted of rules exhibiting certain distinct and related characteristics. Its origin lay in the attempts by the founders of governments to secure the advantages of social intercourse. Law was thus distinctive in terms of being designed to secure not merely order but good order in society. This design was itself the highest of all human laws. It was the first law in the light of which all other laws must be interpreted. The "general law to provide for the safety of the people" was the highest law, the "municipal laws do only shew how <this> should be performed."⁵⁰ The variety of each country's laws indicated not only the freedom of each nation to frame laws, but also the judgment of each people of what rules best guaranteed their well-being.

Law, then, was the result of the design of rational beings pursuing their own interest. It could be judged either according to the letter or according to the design behind it, because both should point in the same direction.[51] The true intentional meaning of every law was to advance the public good. Law was nothing less than "written reason."[52]

Since law was written reason, the interpretation of it did not involve an enquiry into law books, statutes and cases. It involved simply the application of rational axioms to the letter of the law. It was not the study of past case law that produced legal axioms; instead, the axioms of the law were self-evident in exactly the same way as mathematical axioms were:

> Axioms <in law> are not rightly grounded upon judged cases; but cases are to be judged according to axioms: the certain is not proved by the uncertain, but the uncertain by the certain; and every thing is to be esteemed uncertain, till it be proved to be certain. Axioms in law are, as in mathematics, evident to common sense; and nothing is to be taken for an axiom, that is not so ... The axioms of our law do not receive their authority from Coke or Hales, but Coke and Hales deserve praise for giving judgment according to such as are undeniably true.[53]

Many different rules, decrees and sanctions existed in the world. A rational examination of them not only determined the wisdom or justice of their authors, but also determined which of them were truly laws. It was not the antiquity of a rule nor the reputation of its framers that provided it with the authority of law; it was simply its "intrinsic equity and justice." Thus law and justice were made virtually synonymous, or rather, the name of law was reserved exclusively for just rules. "That Which is not Just," Sidney declared, drawing on an axiom of earlier natural lawyers, "is not Law; and that which is Not Law ought Not to be Obeyed." But just as justice was indispensable for the notion of law, so law was indispensable for the understanding of justice. "If any man ask," he asserted, "what I mean by justice, I answer, that the law of the land, as fas as it is 'sanctio recta, jubens honesta, prohibens contraria', declares what it is."[54] And this question-begging answer, this circularity of reasoning once again, was all that Sidney felt required to give.

He did, however, anticipate a number of questions and objections that might be levelled against his legal theory. His answers were characteristically forthright and, indeed, astonishing. He dismissed the suggestion that it might be difficult to determine which rules in practice should be considered just or unjust by asserting "that as this consists not in formalities and niceties, but in evident and substantial truths, there is no need of any other tribunal than that of common sense, and the light of nature, to determine the matter."[55] To the question "who should judge?," he replied "the people," in the sense of the whole citizen body. His argument was the straight application of a maxim that might be encountered in any number of antimonarchical pamphlets stretching back at least to Mornay, Beza, Buchanan and Parsons in the previous century. "As kings, and all other magistrates ... are constituted for the good of the people, the people only can be fit to judge whether the end be accomplished." Astonishingly, however, Sidney had no reservation to make about the correctness of their estimation. The issues would be straightforward and, anyway, as "long as men retain anything of that reason which is truly their nature they never fail of judging rightly of virtue and vice."[56] This very simple theory of human nature rests uneasily in Sidney's otherwise often thoughtful work. It perhaps serves to emphasise his passionately held belief that magistrates, not the people, represented by far the greatest threat to the public well-being.

Sidney was aware that exception might be taken to his legal theory on the grounds that it effectively dissolved all obligation to obey civil law. He denied that this was so by distinguishing between the obligation owed to magistrates by individual citizens on the one hand and by the people as a whole on the other. This distinction, too, was commonly made in contractualist literature and might be traced back to Beza's **Du Droit des Magistrats sur leur suiects** (1574), the **Vindiciae Contra Tyrannos** (1579), and beyond. But Sidney's appeal to it chose to emphasise the superiority of the people over their sovereign. Unlike, for example Beza, Sidney did not emphasise the unconditional duty of the individual. On Sidney's view, even the individual might be released from his obligation if a magistrate acted contrary to the intention behind oaths and law:

> Allegiance signifies no more (as the words "ad legem" declare) than such an obedience as the law requires. But as the law can require nothing from the whole people, who are masters of it, allegiance can only relate to particulars, and not the whole nation. No oath can bind any other than those who take it, and that only in the true sense and meaning of it: but single men only take this oath, and therefore single men only are obliged to keep it. The body of a people neither does, nor can perform any such act. Agreements and contracts have been made: ... but no wise man can think, that the nation did thereby make themselves the creature of their own creature.[57]

Thus the whole citizen body, whose continuous consent to the law was a prerequisite for the just (and therefore legal) constitution, could not be subordinate to its own creation. The idea of a rebellion by the people was a contradiction in terms. Their consent was a prerequisite of law; the withdrawal of that consent simply involved the illegality of the rules which had previously governed them. "Those who seek after truth," Sidney concluded, "will easily find, that there can be no such thing in the world as the rebellion of a nation against its own magistrates."[58] Civil war was certainly an evil, but it was necessary when the alternative was tyranny. For, although civil war was a "disease," tyranny was "the death of a state."[59] Sidney recognized that civil war would involve extra-constitutional or extra-judicial action. But since law and justice were virtually synonymous, civil war could not involve illegality on the people's side.[60] If the cause were just, then the neglect of the old law could not be stigmatised as illegal.

It is hardly surprising that such doctrines as these should have encountered the censure of late seventeenth century royalists. The right of resistance was made the corner-stone of all legal arrangements. The citizen body was exhorted to constant vigilance over its rights, the laws and the activities of its rulers. The right to resist gave this vigilance effectiveness and meaning. The activity of resisting ensured the continuance of just laws. And all this was left to the conscience not of legal or political experts but of the ordinary citizens. From these ideas Sidney derived a most astounding conclusion: resistance was the foundation of all law. "Whoever disapproves tumults, seditions, or war," he argued, "by which ⟨an evil magistrate⟩ may be removed from it, if gentler means are ineffectual, subverts the foundation of all law."[61] Sidney's notion of the foundation of law, we might be tempted to say, is more like the negation of law. The paradox, once again, seems only comprehensible in terms of a one-sided concern that kings were the only source of political evil to be guarded against.

Since Sidney proceeded to integrate these doctrines of legitimate resistance and deposition of kings into a specific interpretation of the English constitution, it becomes even easier to understand the violence of the royalist reaction against him. His theory of the English constitution shared many of the characteristics of constitutional contractarianism. The present constitution was essentially the same as the ancient English constitution. English constitutional development had been unbroken since Saxon times. There had been neither a Saxon nor a Norman Conquest.[62] The laws of the constitution were initially customary laws and custom was immemorial, though not necessarily unchanging.[63] Not all the laws of the ancient constitution were still in force in the late seventeenth century, but the constitution was in essence the same. Parliament was "as antient as our nation."[64] In brief the ancient constitution was an elective, limited monarchy preserved by resisting and deposing wicked monarchs.[65]

The historical and legal issues of the ancient constitution debate were clearly very important for Sidney. But they did not constitute the basic elements in his theory of the English constitution. Sidney's writings exhibit the tensions between arguments from history and arguments from reason that we have seen as characteristic of constitutional contract theories. But Sidney was even more explicit than the constitutional contractarians in his ultimate reliance upon reason in constitutional analysis and debate. For example, when replying to Filmer's assertion that parliaments did not exist in England until after the Norman Conquest, Sidney argued that such a suggestion was wide of the mark if intended, as it undoubtedly was, to reduce parliament's authority vis-a-vis the king. Sidney accepted that parliament in its seventeenth century form had not existed before the Norman Conquest. He correctly interpreted the royalist challenge to parliament as a challenge to present rights dressed up in historical clothes. Just, indeed, as the constitutional contractarian defence of parliament's antiquity was an assertion of present rights. But Sidney chose to emphasise that "the authority of a magistracy proceeds not from the number of years that it has continued, but the rectitude of those that instituted it." Royalist arguments from history and prescription were falsely founded: "wise and good men do not so much inquire what has been, as what is good, and ought to be." Reason alone was the appropriate test of right. Nonetheless, to cover his flanks and to show that historical evidence was anyway against the royalists, Sidney continued:

> But if that liberty, in which God created man, can receive any strength from continuance, and the

> rights of Englishmen can be rendered more unquestionable by prescription, I say, that the nations, whose rights we inherit, have ever enjoyed the liberties we claim, and always exercised them in governing themselves popularly, or by such representatives as have been instituted by themselves, from the time they were first known in the world.[66]

Thus Sidney believed that history was on his side even though he doubted that historical evidence was of any great relevance in establishing and defending rights of any kind.

These, then, are the basic principles of Sidney's integrated contractarianism and there are only two, apparently significant, differences between Sidney's theory of the English constitution and the general outline of integrated contractarianism that I presented in the previous chapter. The first is terminological. Whereas integrated contractarianism paralleled a theory of social contract with one of fundamental contract, fundamental law and fundamental rights, the distinction between notions of the fundamental and the natural play little explicit part in Sidney's theories. I call this difference merely terminological because, as we have seen, both constitutional and social contract theories contained conceptions of law which at the same time maintained a distinction and a necessary connection between positive and natural law. As far as the coherence of these contract theories is concerned (and therefore their usefulness and apparent relevance for justifying particular actions), it was the supposed connection between positive and natural law that was important. Sidney's theory defined law in terms of this connection. Unjust rules were simply not to be considered as laws. Thus the key for determining whether a particular set of constitutional arrangements was just, and for determining whether a particular law was authoritative, was the same in Sidney's theory as in the general theory of integrated contractarianism. If a constitution could be seen to embody the consent of the governed, then it was just. If a law did not run counter to the supposed requirements of **salus populi**, then, provided also that it had been promulgated in the proper constitutional way, it was authoritative. Irrespective of whether these requirements of consent, **salus populi**, and constitutional procedure were accorded the nominal status of fundamental laws or fundamental rights, the argument was the same.

The second difference concerns the role of historical evidence. Both constitutional and integrated contract arguments appealed to history. But Sidney, as we have just seen, was prepared to argue from reason alone should history conflict with his notion of right. In some respects Sidney's view of history was closer to eighteenth century understandings than to those of his contemporaries. His extensive historical studies led him to a realisation of how varied human circumstances had been. He even developed a notion of historical evolution and progress. Yet in one crucial respect his view of English constitutional history was the same as that of other contemporary contractarians. Many contemporaries took great pains to equate the Saxon constitution with the late seventeenth century constitution and they rewrote history so that it accorded with their understanding of what was rational. Although Sidney did not quite do this (indeed, he acknowledged that many changes had occurred since Saxon times), he did insist that the constitution had remained the same in essence. His history was ultimately as rationalistic as theirs but it allowed for a notion of development which cannot be found within the frameworks of either Whig ancient constitution theory or constitutional contractarianism.

Thus, in company with the constitutional contractarians, Sidney argued for the Germanic or Gothic origin of the pre-Norman English constitution.[67] The earliest English constitution was a limited monarchy, he claimed, and he cited the accounts of Caesar and Tacitus in evidence.[68] After the departure of the Romans, the Saxon constitution could only have been established by a contract. His arguments here were familiar rationalist ones. Since the Saxons "were free in their own country, they must be so when they came hither," so the argument ran.69 Furthermore:

> when the Romans abandoned this island, the inhabitants were left to a full liberty of providing for themselves: and whether we deduce our original from them, or the Saxons, or from both, our ancestors were perfectly free ... whatever they did was by a power inherent in themselves to defend that liberty in which they were born. All their Kings were created upon the same condition, and for the same ends.70

The dependence of this supposed piece of constitutional history upon Sidney's general theory of the way government originates is quite clear. Where historical evidence was lacking, Sidney was as prepared as any of his contemporaries to fill the gap with what he supposed must have been the case. In a situation of natural liberty the only reasonable thing to do was for men to create kings upon certain conditions so as to defend their liberty. But this Sidney presented as historical fact, even though the name of any nation with a legitimate constitution might have been substituted for "Saxon" or "our ancestors" in the above passage.

The constitutional history of England was understood by Sidney as the continued preservation of an association of naturally free citizens. The Normans "inherited the same right" as the Saxons "when they came to be one nation" with them. And having thus assimilated the Norman Conquest into the unbroken development of the constitution, he concluded: "we cannot but continue <perfectly free> unless we have enslaved ourselves. <And> Nothing is more contrary to reason, than to imagine this."71 Once more, then, reason was being turned into the key for understanding historical change. The rights and liberties of Englishmen were not merely historical rights, rather they were "innate, inherent, and enjoyed time out of mind, before we had Kings."72 Englishmen's constitutional rights were nothing less than the natural rights of man guaranteed not so much by natural law as by Magna Carta. Magna Carta, it appears, was made "to assert the native and original liberties of our nation by the confession of the King then being, that neither he nor his successors should any way encroach upon them."[73] England, far from enslaving itself, had been the best defender of its liberty in the world. Neither the Romans nor any other peoples had better defended their liberties.[74] The Saxon laws, Sidney asserted, "continue to be of force among us."[75] The particular laws which he had in mind here were those which concerned the main outline of his idealized view of the Saxon constitution. These ancient laws ensured that the king was below the law. The king must "take the laws and customs as he finds them, and can neither detract from, nor add any thing to them."[76] But the particular laws concerning succession had changed since Saxon times. The monarchy was no longer purely elective. It was now "hereditary under condition."[77] Yet this, Sidney argued, had been brought about by the will of the people - the only legitimate means whereby laws could be changed.[78]

Thus the right of altering law in the English constitution lay in the people, or, more specifically, in parliament as their representative.[79] Even the laws relating to monarchy (or rather especially those laws) could be changed or abrogated only by parliament.[80] The laws in being at any given time received their authority from the consent of the nation. Those laws were of two kinds: immemorial customs and statutes. Custom, however, received its authority not from prescription but from the nation's consent expressed through parliament.[81] Both kinds of law, he argued, "may be, and often are, changed by us" - a rather strange view of supposedly immemorial custom.[82] Law was by no means sacrosanct. It could and should be changed if the people so decided. The only consideration that should guide the citizens was the requirements of **salus populi**. Indeed it was this, the embodiment of **salus populi suprema lex esto** as the highest constitutional law, coupled with the continuous right of the citizens to judge and correct their magistrates that constituted for Sidney the unchanging "essence" of the English constitution since Saxon times:

> Our laws were not sent from heaven, but made by our ancestors according to the light they had, and

their present occasions. We inherit the same right from them, and, as we may without vanity say, that we know a little more than they did, if we find ourselves prejudiced by any law that they made, we may repeal it. The safety of the people was their supreme law, and is so to us: neither can we be thought less fit to judge what conduces to that end, than they were.[83]

In this statement we see how exactly the English constitution seemed to Sidney to portray the essential characteristics of the legitimate contract constitution. His interpretation was not the product of his historical studies even though the arguments we have just considered were woven into the section of the **Discourses** devoted to the history of the English constitution. To be sure, Sidney's analyses of contemporary constitutional problems were often presented as the thoughtful reflections of a student of recent history. But even here his ultimate appeal was to the supposed intentions of our rational ancestors. This emerges very clearly from his analysis of the decline of the nobility.

Sidney, like many others, believed the constitutional balance had become upset in Restoration England. The monarch had risen to an overbearing position in the state. But Sidney did not ascribe the reason for this to either the evil intentions of the king or the laxity of parliament. Rather, he blamed the decline of the traditional English nobility for the contemporary constitutional malaise. His argument was reminiscent of Harrington. The designers of the original English constitution had cleverly counter-balanced the power of the king with "the virtue and power of a great and brave nobility." This ancient nobility consisted of those "with the greatest interest in ⟨the⟩ nations, and who by birth and estate enjoyed greater advantage than Kings could confer upon them for rewards of betraying their country."[84] But in the intervening years this balance had been upset and the virtuous nobility had been reduced to the level of commoners and replaced by purely mercenary and self-seeking men. The result was that the monarch had risen in power because the corruption of the supposed countervailing pressure prevented it from operating as designed. The modern nobility had "neither the interest nor the estates required for so great a work." They could not restore the constitution to its original design.[85] Yet the situation was not irreparable. Englishmen still had the evidence of their ancestors' intentions before them. And thus:

> If we will be just to our ancestors, it will become us in our time rather to pursue what we know they intended, and by new constitutions to repair the breaches made upon the old, than to accuse them of the defects that will for ever attend the actions of men. Taking our affairs at the worst, we shall soon find, that if we have the same spirit they had, we may easily restore our ntion to its antient liberty, dignity, and happiness; and if we do not, the fault is owing to ourselves, and not to any want of virtue and wisdom in them.[86]

These, then, are the principal characteristics of Sidney's theories of both the origin and nature of government in general and the English constitution in particular. His general theory seems to share many of the features of philosophical contractarianism. At least, its vocabulary and the broad outline of how civil society was composed appear the same. But several important differences emerge on closer examination. Sidney's theory was much looser, much less rigorous, than, say, Pufendorf's social contract theory. Sidney was not concerned with the question why civil society was necessary for human life. Many of the central concepts of his theories were presented with little or no critical analysis or clarification. The notion of consent, for example, was hardly examined at all. Similarly, the problem of whether civil society was natural or artificial did not trouble him. His arguments simply presupposed its artificiality and the little that he had to say explicitly on the subject was presented uncritically. Thus he began by arguing that civil society was natural for man but he went on to insist that the establishment of government and the construction of particular constitutions were the result of "an arbitrary act, wholly depending upon the will of man."[87] Civil government was apparently both an artifact and also natural. It was the product both of man's arbitrary will and his reason. The only plausible way of reconciling these beliefs was by defining both nature and man's will in terms of their rationality. This, indeed, is what Sidney did.[88] But then man's rational will could only be considered arbitrary by a thoroughly confused use of the terms rational, natural and arbitrary. Sidney, however, was unconcerned. It was clearly not his intention to work out the philosophical underpinnings of his general theory.

Sidney's general theory, then, was either a very bad example of philosophical contractarianism or it was a theory of a different kind. The latter seems more plausible in that the essential questions that philosophical contractarianism set out to consider hardly troubled Sidney at all. In fact, Sidney's general theory appears to serve the purpose of sustaining his account of the English constitution and providing further justification for the practical political proposals that he was concerned to recommend. His general theory presented a rational account of civil society and this, in turn, organized his researches into constitutional history and enabled him to argue that what appeared reasonable to him was in fact in accordance with constitutional law. Despite appearances, Sidney's rationalist theories of society, government, law and right are never far from the surface in all his enquiries contained in the **Discourses**. The sorts of enterprises in which he believed himself engaged, the methods of his enquiries, the evidence which he considered relevant to justify a particular proposition and the nature of the materials with which he considered himself to be working, were all understood and interpreted according to "the Light of Reason."

This view of Sidney's writings as essentially rationalist is not widely recognized. G.P. Gooch, for example, expressed a generally held opinion when he argued that the "chief merit" of Sidney's theories was their concern with the "historical sanction ⟨rather⟩

than of the law of nature." And W.H. Greenleaf has more recently argued that "unlike Locke, Sidney did not produce a document the essence of which was rationalistic. His book was much more in the normal empirical style, depending for its arguments on the evidence of experience and of history, ancient and modern, sacred and profane."[89] We may conclude our examination of Sidney's ideas by reviewing these interpretations and the light that Sidney's own understanding of history casts upon them.

It has not been my intention to deny that historical evidence played a very important part as justification for the propositions which Sidney wished to uphold, as well as for the preferences that he wished to recommend. My point has been rather, first, that these principles and preferences were regarded by Sidney as ultimately to be justified on rational grounds; second, that history was seen by Sidney in traditional post-Renaissance fashion as a moral frame in which reasonable actions were rewarded and unreasonable ones punished; and third, that even if history were to contradict his rationalistic suppositions, he recognized that this would not destroy their validity.

We have seen that Sidney considered his dispute with Filmer to be one concerned primarily with right and that in this dispute any evidence of what "ought not to be is no more to be received, than if it could not be."[90] This proposition Sidney repeats several times in the **Discourses.** One such occasion clearly indicates how far he was prepared to go to overrule historical evidence if it conflicted with what he believed rational men would consider right:

> Though it should be granted that all nations had at first been governed by Kings, it were nothing to the question <of what now ought to be>; for no man, or number of men, was ever obliged to continue in the errors of his predecessors. The authority of custom, as well as of law ... consists only in its rectitude.[91]

The whole of Sidney's theory of law, his belief that government could be understood as the design of rational men, his fundamental belief in man's natural freedom, equality and rationality were all based on rationalist suppositions, independent of any historical or empirical evidence. Even in his theory of the English constitution, historical evidence was regarded as of only questionable relevance. Much more important was the idea that "in matters of the greatest importance, wise and good men do not so much inquire what has been, as what is good, and ought to be."[92]

Sidney's search for those constitutional arrangements which would best secure the ideals of liberty, justice, property and virtue does seem much more dependent upon his reading of history than any other considerations. He certainly did argue against each of the Aristotelian pure forms of government on the basis of "what history, and daily experience teach us."[93] And he did also argue that historical evidence would justify his preference for a mixed form of government.[94] His belief that perfection was not to be found in human affairs does seem to have been bred from his awareness of historical change. But his understanding of history and the nature of historical change was not entirely divorced from his rationalism. Sidney's understanding of historical change exhibited beliefs in both the progress and refinement of the human intellect and in the more common seventeenth century view that history was a moral story. The first of these beliefs led Sidney to argue that past actions should only be interpreted in their historical contexts. The second belief appears to have persuaded him that there were universal rules in politics just as in other sciences - that changes in the form of government led inevitably to either virtue and persistence or vice and destruction.

The second of these beliefs was dominant in Sidney's historical thought. It restricted how far arguments from historical relativity might be taken and maintained a firm connection of relevance between actions in the past and in the present. In short, there was a tension in Sidney's understanding of history between ideas which emphasised particularity and change and ideas which emphasised universality and constancy. His very wide reading of history led him to the view that political affairs were subject to "mutations" and that "no right judgment can be given of human things, without a particular regard to the time in which they passed."[95] Political change was inevitable because "the wisdom of man is imperfect, and unable to foresee the effects that may proceed from an infinite variety of accidents." But it should be recognized that government was still being regarded here as the result of the conscious design of rational men. Every effort ought to be made "to constitute a government that should last for ever."[96] But since men were imperfect this could never be achieved. Due to the imperfections of human life, the best that could be expected was "such as in relation to the forces, manners, nature, religion or interests of a people, and their neighbours, are suitable and adequate to what is seen, or apprehended to be seen."[97] The study of history, then, taught that government and law should aim at the ideal but be tailored to prevailing customs and manners. It taught, too, that "the laws that may be good for one people are not for all, and that which agrees with the manners of one age is utterly abhorrent from those of another."[98] But in either case an understanding of what constituted the ideal and what constituted the good was presupposed. Yet these, of course, were the conclusions of Sidney's rationalist theories, not his empirical studies.

But aside from these beliefs in historical change and relativity, Sidney's writings occasionally refer to a doctrine of progress. Had this doctrine been developed to the point where Sidney might have asserted that whatever had happened to previous generations was irrelevant to questions of what the present, superior generation ought to do, his historical enquiries would have lost much of their practical importance. History might have become a mere catalogue of falsity and error and the past only useful in the present to show how superior the present was. Arguments from the ancient constitution or the intentions of the Saxon contractors would then have lost all force. But Sidney did not pursue his notion of progress this far. He introduced the idea in order to justify the assertion that Englishmen in the present were not bound to adhere to the laws of their predecessors.[99] And here all that was at stake was a question of improving past laws by adhering to the supposed intentions of the original contractors. He never rejected his rationalist derivation of what those intentions were supposed to be. Deviations from those intentions would ever be attended by hardship. Acting in accordance with them, perfecting their realization, would lead to happiness. Thus:

> nations which have been governed arbitrarily, have always suffered the same plagues, and been infected with the same vices, which is as natural, as for animals ever to generate according to their kinds, and fruits to be of the same nature with the roots and seeds from which they come. The same order that made men valient and industrious in the service of their country during the first ages, would have the same effect, if it were now in being.[100]

The tensions, then, between rationalist and empiricist threads in Sidney's historical thought remained barely concealed in his overall view that history was moral philosophy teaching by example.[101] But my point here has been to emphasise, against the prevailing views expressed by Gooch and Greenleaf, the underlying rationalism in Sidney's thought.[102] His general contract theory served as a basis on which to build a view of the English constitution. A practical political concern ran through all his work. This, I have argued, is most clearly visible in his theory of law. His historical ideas are a little more problematic. They reveal something of the conflict between a past which is useful to the present and a past which is not. Tyrrell's historical thought contained no such conflict. It was much more conventionally seventeenth century in this respect. In Tyrrell's writings, we shall see evidenced how very clearly common seventeenth century notions of history could lend both plausibility and coherence to integrated contract arguments.

CHAPTER 10

JAMES TYRRELL

James Tyrrell, unlike Sidney, was never very actively engaged in politics. It seems that local administration was the extent of his ambition in public life. As the eldest son of Sir Timothy Tyrrell, the heir to an estate in Buckinghamshire, and the grandson of James Ussher, archbishop of Armagh, he seemed to prefer a more secluded and a more academic life. His education was far from unusual for a man of his social position: Gray's Inn, Oxford and then the Inner Temple. But the legal profession proved unattractive. He retired to his estate and became a deputy lieutenant and J.P. In 1687 he was deprived of these offices by James II for refusing to support the Declaration of Indulgence and he devoted the rest of his life to writing.[1]

The Exclusion Crisis occasioned his first major political work. The **Patriarcha Non Monarcha**, apparently written whilst conversing and corresponding with John Locke and William Petyt, was published in 1681 and was concerned to attack Filmer's recently published arguments for absolute monarchy.[2] Tyrrell's book caused some controversy and practically the whole of Edmund Bohun's lengthy introduction to the next edition of **Patriarcha** was written as a reply. Thomas Hunt, the radical Exclusionist, recommended Tyrrell's work as "a very candid and judicious Book" and Locke referred to the "Ingenious and Learned Author of **Patriarcha Non Monarcha.**"[3] It was not until the 1688 Revolution that Tyrrell was once more stirred to bring his views before the reading public. This time he did so in great style, showing, if not the depth, then at least the considerable breadth of his reading. The **Bibliotheca Politica** appeared in the form of thirteen dialogues between the years 1692 and 1694. Two collected editions of the dialogues appeared by 1701 and in 1702 Tyrrell added a separate fourteenth dialogue. Two further collections of all fourteen dialogues appeared in 1718 and 1727. The dialogues take place between Freeman, "a Gentleman," and Meanwell "a Civil Lawyer."[4] Freeman represents a Whig, Meanwell a Tory, and their discussions cover practically all aspects of the current debates about the nature of government, the ancient English constitution and the lawfulness of the Revolution.

The **Bibliotheca Politica** was very favourably reviewed in Peter Motteux's **The Gentleman's Journal**. In the December 1693 issue, for example, the work was recommended as "in effect a whole Library of Politics, and the Sentiments of the greatest Politicians of all Parties are so fairly laid down ... that our Nobility and Gentry will hardly have occasion to read any other <book> to be fully inform'd of the Constitution of our Government."[5] Even in the middle of the nineteenth century, a legal text book continued to recommend Tyrrell's work to students as a "perfect mine of constitutional learning, which the student will be very fortunate if he can succeed in obtaining."[6]

Whilst writing the **Bibliotheca Politica**, Tyrrell published a translation, abridgment and reorganisation of Cumberland's **De Legibus Naturae (1672)**. **A Brief Disquisition of the Law of Nature** appeared in 1692 and ran to one further edition in 1701. Cumberland's work was widely read and was frequently reprinted and translated into English, German and French throughout the eighteenth century. Cumberland's principal opponent was Hobbes and the popularity of his treatise as well as Tyrrell's abridgment should serve to warn against too hasty a dismissal of Hobbes' influence and reputation during the late seventeenth and early eighteenth centuries. Cumberland opposed Hobbes' analysis of human nature and the law of nature that Cumberland outlined had some influence on later Utilitarians.[7] Tyrrell followed Cumberland quite strictly in the first part of his abridgment but added lengthy supporting arguments drawn from Locke's psychology. In the second part he extracted all the arguments Cumberland had used against Hobbes and put them into what he considered a more consistent form. Again, he added some points of his own, principally drawn from history and contemporary travel reports. The **Brief Disquisition** was reviewed favourably in both Wooley's **Compleat Library** and Motteux's **Gentleman's Journal**.[8] And Manningham recommended it to the House of Commons in a sermon preached in 1692.[9]

In 1696 Tyrrell published the first volume of **The General History of England, as well Ecclesiastical as Civil, From the Earliest Accounts of Time, To the Reign of His Present Majesty King William**. Two further volumes appeared in 1700 and 1704 but the history only extended to the end of Richard II's reign. Tyrrell's interest seemed to have waned considerably and the projected abridgment of the first three volumes never materialised. The history, however, was written from the point of view of a Whig constitutional theorist. And from that point of view, as we have seen, a history which covered in detail the period from the exit of the Romans to the reigns immediately following the Norman Conquest had completed the bulk of its task. As D.C. Douglas remarked, Tyrrell's history "never subordinated propaganda to inquiry." The work pleased supporters of the Revolution like Atwood and John Toland, and displeased opponents like Thomas Hearne.[10] Yet all the same, Hearne was moved to remark that Tyrrell was "a learned man, although he runs counter now and again to usually-received opinions."[11]

Tyrrell's work was not that of a first-rate mind. He has none of the stature of Locke or Cumberland and he recognized both Locke and Petyt as his intellectual superiors.[12] But his writings, nonetheless, deserve much more attention than historians have so far given them. No other writer of the late seventeenth century provides anything like as comprehensive an account of the current character of English political controversy. He devoted considerable time to reading the then standard works on politics and history. He was a friend of two of the most influential writers on these subjects: John Locke and William Petyt. His **Bibliotheca Politica** was designed to give the general reader the best arguments out of the best authors on the major problems of political theory and constitutional history. All his work was of this eclectic nature. But it is never very difficult to see where Tyrrell's own sympathies lay. Petyt and Locke influenced him greatly and certainly the best way of characterizing his thought is, as Pocock has suggested, in terms of the "mingling" of them both.[13] Such a mingling, as we have seen, was of the essence of integrated contractarianism.

Tyrrell, like Locke, began his literary career as a royalist.[14] But also like Locke, by the time of the Exclusion Crisis he had come to support the anti-royalist cause. The **Patriarcha Non Monarcha** was directed against Filmerian royalism. Yet Tyrrell, even more than Locke, was so much in agreement with his adversary on fundamentals (especially in the view of man as a creature made by and for God, in the patriarchal origins of society, and in the acceptance of biblical history as valid history) that he constructed a variant of social contract theory characterized by rather tortuous distinctions. Filmer's **Patriarcha** was written "against an Opinion maintained by some Divines, and several learned men, That Mankind is naturally endowed and born with Freedom from Subjection, and at liberty to chuse what form of Government it please; and that the Power which any one man, hath over others, was at first bestowed according to the discretion of the Multitude."[15] Tyrrell was determined to rescue and reestablish these ideas. He adopted current notions of a state of nature as the means to defend those natural rights that Filmer's followers were denying. But Tyrrell believed that the state of nature should stand the tests of historical and empirical analysis. This far from uncommon view was in part necessitated by his interpretation of Filmer.

Filmer's arguments from biblical history were formidable. If government originated with Adam, there could be no doubt that not only government but also absolute monarchy was ordained by God. Tyrrell did not doubt the validity of Genesis, but he felt obliged to dispute Filmer's interpretation of it. His argument depended upon reasserting a traditional set of distinctions between paternal and political power, domestic or economic government, and political or civil government.16 If this distinction could be upheld, Genesis could be accepted whilst Filmer's arguments were refuted. It could be argued that there had been a period in the world's history before civil society existed. This state of nature would destroy the historical foundation of political patriarchalism. If man's condition in the state of nature were then portrayed in natural law and natural right terms, the proposition that "Mankind is naturally endowed and born with Freedom from Subjection, and at liberty to chuse what form of Government it please" could be defended. The state of nature, then, performed a dual role in Tyrrell's writings. It portrayed the historically and empirically verifiable condition of man outside civil society. And it also portrayed man outside civil society so as to establish his essentially natural, as distinct from social, attributes (particularly his natural rights) and thus provide the groundwork for explaining the necessity for civil government. This second role, unlike the first, was not dependent upon historical evidence.

In the first dialogue of the **Bibliotheca Politica**, Tyrrell affirmed that his idea of the state of nature would accord with prevailing Christian belief. Thus, his well-meaning Tory addressed the Whig:

> Pray Sir, begin **first** with the Natural state of Mankind, but remember to do it like a Christian, and one that believes that we are all deriv'd from one **first** Parent, and that we did not at first spring up out of the Earth like Mushrooms, or as the Men whom **Ovid** feigns to have been produc'd of the Dragons Teeth **Cadmus** is feigned to have sown, who as soon as they sprung out of the Earth, immediately fell a Fighting and Killing each other.17

By accepting this as "honest and kind advice," Freeman, the Whig, guaranteed that his state of nature would not be Hobbesian. But exactly what Tyrrell meant by the state of nature is confusing.

At times he refers to the state of nature as the state of innocence before the Fall, at times it appears as the depraved state of post-Lapsarian man.[18] At times, again, it refers to the state of human society in the absence of a particular monarch or government.[19] On one occasion, however, Tyrrell refers to a monarch existing in the state of nature.[20] But most often he refers to the notion in its generally accepted sense as the natural condition of mankind before or outside civil society, a state into which man would again fall if civil government were dissolved. Like Pufendorf, Locke and Sidney, he believed this state to be social. When attacking Hobbes in the **Brief Disquisition**, for example, Tyrrell accused him of confusing "that first, and most natural amity, and sociableness of Persons of one and the same Family, as of Husband and Wife, Parents and Children, **Etc.** towards each other <with> that artificial Society, which proceeding wholly from Compacts, we call a Commonwealth."[21] The state of nature was characterized by family life on a grand scale. The institution of marriage was one of its corner-stones, a contractual relationship sanctioned and limited by the law of nature.[22] The relationship between parents and children was also of a contractualist kind, and so too was the relationship of "Masters of Families" to their servants and even their slaves.[23] These observations on mankind's natural state closely resemble Pufendorf's analysis of the mixed state of nature. And like Pufendorf's notions, Tyrrell's remarks depend for their coherence upon a prior conception of natural law and natural rights. Tyrrell, of course, recognized this and the first part of the **Brief Disquisition** followed Cumberland's attempts to establish the status of that law.

In a lengthy and difficult passage, based on the scientific ideas of his day, Tyrrell determined the first law of nature. God was the author of all "natural and necessary" processes, he asserted. Human ideas of natural and moral affairs arose naturally from sense experience. Thus God was the author of these ideas. Knowledge developed through the comparison and combination of these first ideas and it was God who encouraged men to compare and combine ideas. One of the most general ideas resulting from this activity of the human mind was that "a **whole** signifies the same with that of all the several Ideas of the particular parts put together." This idea leds the mind to the proposition "of the Identity of the whole, with all its parts" and to the further proposition "that the same Causes which preserve the whole, must also conserve all its constituent parts." These propositions, which Tyrrell regarded as "the more general Laws of Nature" in the sense of the laws governing the interrelationships of all natural things, when applied to moral affairs were supposedly reduceable to one basic dictate of the moral law:

> **The Endeavour, as much as we are able, of the common Good of the whole System of Rational Beings conduces, as far as lies in our Power, to the Good of all its several Parts or Members, in which our own Felicity is also contained, as part thereof; whereas the Acts opposite to this Endeavour, do bring along with them Effects quite opposite thereunto, and will certainly procure our own Ruin or Misery at last.**[24]

All other moral laws may be deduced from this, Tyrrell continued, "as their Foundation and Original, according to that respect or proportion they bear to the common Good, or happiest state of the whole aggregate Body of rational Beings."[25]

A moral imperative to seek the greatest happiness of the greatest number was certainly implied here. But Tyrrell's argument was not utilitarian. From considerations and arguments that recall Locke's epistemology, he proceeded to account for the obligation to obey the moral law by adopting arguments drawn from Pufendorf and the Christian natural law tradition. Such arguments could hardly have been further from Utilitarianism. Natural laws could only justifiably be considered laws when once we had a knowledge of God. Only then would the two conditions that Tyrrell believed necessary for some rule to acquire the status of a law be satisfied: the rule would have a known and authoritative source; and there would be known rewards and punishments attached to it. The **Brief Disquisition** was concerned to establish precisely these points about natural law and to draw certain implications from them.

Natural law defined and guaranteed man's natural rights. In the state of nature men had natural rights to self-preservation, to private property, and to self-government (although this last was explicitly restricted to the heads of families, to the heads of natural societies). A valid portrait of life in the state of nature, Tyrrell believed, must be evidenced by empirical observation and divine history. Since he understood the state of nature to have been an historical condition, his appeal to historical evidence is quite understandable. But the analysis of the state of nature was also an enterprise in moral philosophy. As such it is by no means obvious what relevance historical and empirical evidence might have for the validity of the speculations. Yet Tyrrell believed such evidence was essential. His understanding of philosophical activity, with a basic division between speculative and practical philosophy, helps explain why:

> tho I grant it is both lawful and usual for natural Philosophers, who not being able through the imbecility of our humane Faculties, to discover the true nature and essences of Bodies, or other Substances, do therefore take a liberty to feign or suppose such an Hypothesis, as they think will best suit with the nature of the things themselves, of which they intend to treat; and from thence to frame a body of natural Philosophy, or Physicks, as **Aristotle** of old, and Monsieur **Des Cartes**, in our age have performed: Yet can we not allow the same liberty in moral or practical Philosophy, as in speculative.[26]

One of the most important things that divine history and empirical evidence proved was that Hobbes' notion of the state of nature was wrong. Divine history showed that human life had from the start been organized in families, and that there had been an effective law governing human relations (as God's punishment of Cain indicated).[27] The evidence of contemporary travellors served to reinforce the conclusion that Hobbes' war of all against all was mistaken. For this evidence referred to peoples, especially in the Americas and the Carribean, living peacefully together without government.[28] Hobbes' speculations, then, were not only inappropriate as a part of moral philosophy, they were also historically and empirically wrong. But if life were genuinely social in the state of nature, from whence arose the necessity for constructing civil societies? And what was the difference between natural society, the state of nature and civil society? There was at least one fundamental difference between natural society and civil society: in the former there was no political authority although there was "Domestick Government."[29] We must clarify this distinction in a moment. But given that civil and natural society were significantly different, why did men leave the state of nature?

One ready to hand reason was that the separate families were forced to combine in defence against a common enemy, as Aristotle had suggested. Very occasionally Tyrrell did argue this, but more typically he dismissed the suggestion as "absolutely impossible" since no enemy society big enough, or powerful enough, could be supposed "in this early Age of the World" when governments were supposed to have been invented. The only explanation Tyrrell was prepared to accept, then, would have to be based on the principle that people would never "be brought to consent to put themselves under the absolute power of others, but for their own greater Good and Preservation," that they would never "part with, their Natural Liberty without advantaging themselves at all by the Change."[30] This rationality postulate was common to all the contractarian writers we have considered. It served them in their quest to explain why the dangerously powerful sovereign state needed to exist and it helped them in their attempts to harness that power in the interests of the governed. In Tyrrell's argument, the postulate provided the most general reason why civil society was formed. The Aristotelian explanation was rejected because it was too narrow and could not account for government arising in the circumstances described in Genesis - the circumstances, quite literally, of the earliest age of the world.

In filling in the reasons why the state of nature should have become so unattractive as to lead men to sacrifice their natural liberty and enter civil society, Tyrrell, like many before him, shed some of his sociability assumptions. The discussion continued in an historical vein. Biblical history provided the backcloth against which the dramatic origin of the state could be portrayed. And biblical history, interpreted by the light of reason, was the ultimate test for the validity of the account:

> the necessity as well as being of all Civil Government, proceeded from the Fall of **Adam**, since if that had not been, we had still liv'd as the Poets fancy Men did under the Golden Age, without any need of Kings or Common-wealths ... But after the Fall, the state of Mankind was altered, and Self-love, and the desire of Self-preservation grew so strong and exorbitant above all Natural Equity, that the inordinate passions of Men blinding their Reasons, they began to think they had a Right not only to the Necessaries of Life, but to whatever their unruly Appetites desired, or that they thought they could make themselves Masters of. To remedy which Inconveniences, I suppose the fathers and Masters of Families, and other Freemen (in whom alone then resided that little Government that then was in the World) were forced after some time to agree upon one or more Men into whose hands they might resign all their particular powers, and to make Laws for the due Governing and Restraining those disorderly Appetites and Passions, and also endowing them with a sufficient Authority to put them in Execution.[31]

It was because of the Fall, then, that civil government both had to be, and in fact was, instituted. Right reason, or the law of nature, taught men that it was best to establish a civil society. In particular, it was the abuse of natural rights to the necessities of life that led to the state of nature being superseded. Thus the definition and protection of property rights was turned into "one main end" of government.[32] The "Fathers and Masters of Families, and other Freemen" were the only parties to the contract. Indeed, as in Pufendorf, they were the only ones who could be parties since they alone possessed a right to self-government in the state of nature.[33] Here, perhaps more clearly than anywhere else in Tyrrell's writings, the social assumptions of his time led him to a contradictory position. In arguing against Filmer's characterization of the family, Tyrrell was at pains to prove a natural right of resistance for women against their husbands. This he did by reference to natural rights of freedom, self-government and equality, deducing from them the idea that marriage was contractual. But when he came to consider the formation of civil society, it appeared that husbands were naturally superior to their wives and children. The "Power of Fathers and Masters is Natural," he asserted. Women were "concluded by their Husbands" and were anyway "commonly unfit for civil business."[34] Children still living with their fathers were as servants.[35] Although, here again, when attacking Filmer's notion that the father had an absolute authority in the family, Tyrrell had argued that the relations of father to children and father to servants were contractual.[36] Consistency in these respects was quite obviously not at a premium.

But Tyrrell never doubted that the origin of civil society lay in an act of consent by the prospective members. He believed that the state of nature had been evidenced in history and it should then follow that he understood the social contract, the contract of civil society, as an historically verifiable event also. It appears that he did understand it in this way but he could not appeal directly to sacred history since it contained no unequivocal, explicit references to such contracts. Tyrrell turned this potentially embarrassing absence into an irrelevancy. His general claim was that the scriptures were not "written to show us the original either of Government, or Propriety."37 But even so, he felt able to argue, and he did so at great length, that biblical history was implicitly on his side.38 The considerable care he took to argue the point indicates how important such supposedly historical evidence from the bible was for him.39

Like sacred history, profane history was far from unequivocal about the contractual origin of commonwealths. Whilst acknowledging this, Tyrrell argued as before: where history was not explicit it still must be presumed to be on his side. Thus, for example, he set out to meet the anti-contractualist challenge for historical evidence of contracts by asserting that the origins of most kingdoms "like the head of **Nilus**, are hard to be traced up to their heads or Fountains, and no man can positively tell the manner of their beginning." But he nonetheless felt on safe enough historical ground to be able to answer the challenge with two examples: "the first was **Rome**, where all the People or Freemen consented to the election of **Romulus** ... and the second shall be that of **Venice**." And with these examples he believed he had successfully proved "some Governments to have had their beginning by the consent of the People."40

In similar fashion to a host of contract and consent theorists before him, Tyrrell dismissed the traditional distinction between governments begun by conquest and those begun by consent. The distinction, he argued, was born of a shallow understanding. Certainly, human history was full of conquests but these were not the origins of legitimate governments. Royalists who argued from the rights of conquest had missed the essential point. Conquering armies were made up of leaders and soldiers. Soldiers followed leaders for their own advantage and when the armies were successful the leaders "could have no farther Right over the men they brought with them than what sprung from their mutual Compacts and Consents." Conquest could only give rise to governments through the intervention of consent and contract. Governments begun by conquest, then, were simply a special case of governments begun by consent and only by the intervention of consent "were the **Goths**, **Vandals**, and **Saxon** Kingdoms erected by Generals."[41]

Tyrrell's examples of contracts from profane history clearly concern more a contract of government than a contract of society. The explanation is not difficult to find and sheds light on the character of his contract theory. In the first place, on his assumptions of a social state of nature, a contract of society is almost unnecessary. His problem here was the greater because he wished to deny that society was at all artificial. Second, his idea of a social contract was almost completely merged with the contract of government - the latter giving substance to the former. And finally, Tyrrell's concern throughout his general theory was to establish the reality of a government contract so that he could then locate it in English constitutional history and thus provide ammunition for defending first, opposition to Charles II and James II and ultimately, the legitimacy of the 1688 Revolution.

As to the first of these, Tyrrell had adopted social contract ideas as a way of undermining Filmerian patriarchalism but his insistence that the world must have been peopled as recounted in Old Testament history led him to portray the state of nature as a very social state. The pre-civil state differed from civil society in respect of the size of communities and their kind of government. Natural government existed in the family but was very different from political government. It was different because political power was "Artificial, as proceeding from compacts or the consents of diverse Heads of Families and other Free-men."[42] But the distinction was forced. There was a right of resistance in both sorts of government, guaranteed by the law of nature. A contract, then, did not establish any difference here. Indeed, contracts supposedly established the relationships in both domestic and political government. But a civil contract did appear necessary to Tyrrell to explain the bond that tied so many people together in civil societies. That bond could not be natural, springing from blood relationships after the initial contract of marriage, since civil societies were manifestly not single families, however extended. The only alternative, given a simple nature/art dichotomy, was that it must be artificial - the product of human design. The idea of an historical bond, a bond that was neither natural nor artificial, had not yet entered the mainstream of English or European consciousness.

But for all this, Tyrrell was clearly not entirely content with the rigid distinction between natural and artificial societies. His sociable state of nature, like Pufendorf's mixed state of nature, was sufficient to arouse some misgivings about the dichotomy and, indeed, he occasionally pursued the logic of its sociability. The difference between pre- and post-civil contract society was not so great, he argued at one point, "that there can be no passing from one to the other" almost imperceptibly.[43] The argument appears in Locke's **Two Treatises** and, like Locke, Tyrrell insisted that although such a change might be barely perceptible still a contract must be supposed to have been made. Without it, there appeared no way of explaining the bond holding people in civil society together, or of justifying the supposed limitations of political power.

His concern to define political power in terms of its rational origins in contract and consent, whilst distinguishing it from paternal power, encouraged the view that civil society was artificial. Hobbes had quite happily maintained this and so had Pufendorf, but Tyrrell would not. In the **Brief Disquisition**, he attacked Hobbes and attempted to restore civil society to a place amongst natural phenomena. Civil society, he argued, in similar fashion to Sidney, proceeded wholly "from the Rational Nature of Mankind." Since reason was a "natural Faculty," civil society itself was natural.[44] Tyrrell was clearly more avoiding the problem than solving it, but he did go on to explain why he was not prepared to accept that civil society was artificial. All political obligation proceeded from consent, he claimed. If that consent were viewed as something artificial, as "quite opposed to what is natural," then "it may become thereby less firm and durable." Hobbes had committed an error by failing to see that although "those words by which Compacts are expressed" arose "from the Arbitrary agreements of men," still the consent itself arose from natural reason. The compact was a "natural Consent, constituted by words, with some kind of Art" but this "doth not at all diminish its firmness or duration."[45]

In this way Tyrrell attacked Hobbes and insisted that civil society was a natural phenomenon. If it were not, he believed, political obligation would be too insecurely founded. He never doubted that consent was the only legitimate basis of civil order. In the prevailing circumstances of debate, it had to be if the resistance shown to Charles II and James II were to be proved to be legitimate. But Tyrrell's own foundation for political obligation turned out to be as precarious as the one he was rejecting. His final statement on the problem ended by locating the reason for continued consent to be governed in the gratitude of citizens for the civil order that government provided.[46] He insisted against royalist doubts that this foundation would not endanger a commonwealth. His argument drew upon the longstanding **monarchomachi** distinction between a people's right to resist and the individual's duty to obey.[47] But, as Tyrrell's justification of the 1688 Revolution will show, the appearance masked a revolutionary doctrine.

As a second explanation of the historical examples Tyrrell gives of the civil contract, I have suggested his merging of social and governmental contracts. That he did so would certainly seem to follow from the kind of state of nature he envisaged. Society was natural and had existed ever since the creation of Eve. It needed no contract to invent it. Both Pufendorf and Locke had portrayed life in the state of natural as social. Tyrrell had certainly read their works and his own views often seem to have been borrowed from them. Pufendorf, however, had rigidly distinguished between a social contract and a governmental contract, whilst Locke had talked of a civil contract and the trust of government. At times Tyrrell approached Pufendorf's view, but he never sustained it.[48] Occasionally, too, he employed the Lockian notion of a trust of government but only when explicitly quoting from **Two Treatises**.[49] Much more frequently there was just one contract in Tyrrell and that determined the form of government as well as the union of families.[50]

Tyrrell, then, did not share Pufendorf's concern to distinguish as clearly as possible the steps involved in the formation of civil society. His lack of interest in this, together with his general looseness in portraying the transition to civil society, might be further explained by looking at his particular focus of interest. On the one hand, he understood contract as an event and it was important for his argument that he could prove that some contracts had occurred in history. But the idea of contract was at least as important to him as a continuing process. In all his major works, except the reworking of the **Brief Disquisition**, Tyrrell was ultimately concerned to provide an interpretation of the English constitution. His general theory of the origin of society and government served as a foundation upon which to build what he believed was the proper view of the late seventeenth century constitution. Within that constitution he wanted to locate an unassailable right of resistance. Such a right of resistance would remove the stigma of rebellion from those whose activities culminated in the 1688 Revolution and the establishment of William and Mary on the English throne. The **Bibliotheca Politica** provides the clearest evidence of this intention. Tyrrell explained his purpose as follows:

> I think I can make it as clear as the Day, that <the nobility, gentry, clergy and people> have done nothing in joining in Arms with the Prince of **Orange**, but what is justifiable by the Principles of Self-preservation, the Fundamental Constitutions of the Government, and a just Zeal for their Religion and Civil Liberties, as they stand secured by our Laws.[51]

The "best method" he suggested for resolving this "Noble Controversie" about the justice and legality of 1688 involved examining the "Natural state of Mankind, after the Fall of **Adam**" and then considering the following questions:

First, If God has appointed any kind of Government by **Divine Institution** before another. **Secondly,** If he has not; how far Civil power may be lookt upon as from God, and in what sense, as deriv'd from the people. **Thirdly,** Whether Resistance by the Subjects, in some cases be incompatible and absolutely destructive to all Civil Government whatsoever. **Fourthly,** Whether such resistance be absolutely contrary to the doctrine of Christ contain'd in the Scriptures and that of the Primitive Church pursuant thereunto. **Fifthly,** Whether such Resistance be contrary to the Constitution of this Government, and the express Laws of the Land, **Sixthly,** Whether what has been done by the Prince of **Orange**, and those of the Nobility, Gentry, etc. in pursuance of these Principles, has been done according to the Law of Nature, the Scriptures, and the Ancient Constitutions of this Kingdom.[52]

Tyrrell's summary of the principal issues involved in the debates about 1688 emphasises the centrality of the idea of resistance. But the three standards of natural law, divine law (the scriptures) and constitutional law to which he appeals were not entirely separate sources for justifying actions. He acknowledged that the justification of resistance might be undertaken from the distinctive standpoints of the moralist, the divine and the constitutional lawyer but his interpretation of the English constitution was such that natural law, divine law and constitutional law were interwoven.[53]

Tyrrell's constitutional enquiries seem at first glance to have been conducted within the framework of the fairly longstanding ancient constitution debate. His works, especially the **Bibliotheca Politica** and **The General History of England** focus on the issues and key concepts of that debate.[54] But the concepts were all given somewhat different meanings. Fundamental law, fundamental rights, fundamental liberties, ancient constitution, common law, custom, all appear with monotonous regularity, but they are woven into a tapestry of moral theory far more explicity than in anything an

Atwood or a Petyt would have written. The justification for each was no longer drived from the supposed fact that they had always been, but rather that they were right, intrinsically good. Constitutionality, then, was no longer determined by precedent, rather by natural law.

But Tyrrell still presented his constitutional theory as historical. It was, after all, an interpretation of the ancient and continuing English constitution. Yet the method he pursued and the conclusions he reached bear the unmistakeable traces of social contract analysis. In the **General History of England**, for example, he presented an account of the origins of the English based on the book of Genesis. Having dismissed a number of popular myths, he continued:

> I shall ... now proceed to somewhat more Solid and Useful, and try if we can discover who were the first Inhabitants of this Island; but since the Scriptures, as well as Prophane Histories, are silent in this Point, it is impossible to tell the Name of the Man who brought the first Colony hither: Only this much seems probable, that **Europe** was Peopled by the Posterity of **Japhet** ⟨and⟩ this Island was first Inhabited (at least as to its Southern Parts) from the Continent of **Gaul**, as is delivered by **Bede** in his first Chapter as a current Tradition in his Time.[55]

The records of this time were extremely sparse and there were "no Authentick accounts left us of the **British Kings** that reigned in this Island till **Julius Caesar's** first Expedition hither."[56] But this was really no great handicap since Tyrrell's aim was to give the origin of the late seventeenth century constitution. That origin he located, as we have seen many of his contemporaries doing, at the time of the Saxon conquest. But because of the problem of conquest in constitutional controversy and in line with his own general theory of conquest, Tyrrell hastily added that the Saxon kings were not kings "by **Right of Conquest.**" Their soldiers and followers "set them up for what they were" and the ancient

Britains were either driven out of England or were "by Degrees **Incorporated** with the **Saxons**." Thus no Saxon subject had been conquered; instead, all had consented to be governed by their Saxon rulers.[57]

The association of this piece of supposed constitutional history with Tyrrell's understanding of social contract theory became clear when he turned to enquire into who these Saxons were. They were the posterity of Japhet, the son of Noah. In accounting for their manners and customs and in drawing implications for the character of the ancient English constitution, Tyrrell's report echoed the story of the repopulation of the world after the Flood under the conduct of the separate heads of the branches of Noah's household who eventually contracted amongst themselves to set up the first civil societies. The Saxons, it appeared, were a branch of the "**Getae or Goths**." These were the earliest populators of Scandinavia and Europe and could be traced back to Japhet.[58] Wherever they settled, the Goths contracted together to set up limited monarchies. Thus, when pressed to state what the earliest Saxon constitutions were like, Tyrrell argued that although Saxon records were very scarce it was perfectly appropriate to look at other Gothic constitutions described by Roman writers and simply draw a parallel. They were, after all, the same people with the same traditions, customs and manners. From these Roman accounts it appeared that the "Nations of the **Gothic Original**, were never Governed by **Absolute Monarchs**; but by **Kings** or Princes **limited** by the **Laws** and **Common-Councils** of their own Nations, as were all those that **descended** from this **Gothic Original**."[59]

The consequence of all this for England, Tyrrell insisted, was that its ancient Saxon constitution must have been a limited monarchy. The Saxons only came to seek new homes. Their armies were composed of volunteers. They were used to living in limited not absolute monarchies. Since they were free men when they came to England, then, their government in England must have been set up by compact after victory had been secured and the volunteer army dissolved. This must have been the case, Tyrrell argued, for "I can give no account, how these Princes should become **Kings** but by the **consent** or Election of their **Souldiers** or Followers." And this, he assured his readers, "is no **Romance** but true History."[60]

There were few records of the Saxon Heptarchy but there was evidence of a contract unifying all England. For this Tyrrell pointed to the **Mirror of Justices**.[61] The bargaining with the first prospective king of all England was, according to Tyrrell, the "original contract." That contract established fundamental laws (or "fundamental constitutions") which defined and protected certain fundamental liberties. These laws and constitutions were "fundamental" not because they had always existed but because they were the content and conclusion of the historically specified original contract.[62] They owed their existence to the express consent of the governed and they could only be legitimately modified with that consent. They were fundamental to the form of government decided upon at the contract and that form of government could be changed only through the consent of the majority of citizens. These fundamental laws, then, were basic constitutional laws and not natural laws. But Tyrrell's understanding of the notions of fundamental rights and constitutional law reveals that he saw the natural and the fundamental as so intertwined that the distinction effectively evaporated. Natural law was brought down to earth in the guise of the English constitution.

Thus his examination of Englishmen's fundamental rights portrayed them as both natural rights and the further particularization of those rights. They were natural rights in the sense that "the people in a limited Kingdom remain as to the defence of their Lives, Liberties, **Religion**, and Properties, always in the state of nature, in respect of their Prince as well as all the rest of Mankind."[63] But they were also the particularization of these natural rights with, accordingly, the possibility of legal defence and redress in the law courts of England. Thus when Freeman was pressed to say what Englishmen's "fundamental Rights and Liberties are," he replied that "they are only such as are contained in **Magna Carta** and the Petition of Right, and are no more than the immemorial Right and Liberties of this Kingdom." And these were specifically listed as legal measures designed for the defence of Englishmen's lives and liberties, their religion, their estates and their properties.[64] Englishmen's fundamental rights, then, were both rights at natural law and rights at English law. Since the function of English fundamental law was to define and protect fundamental rights, we might expect Tyrrell to argue that fundamental law was simply the particularization of natural law. J. W. Gough has shown that such arguments were implicit in some late seventeenth century discussions of fundamental law.[65] Tyrrell, however, seemed too aware of the differences between fundamental and natural law to bring them into this kind of union. On several occasions he noted how fundamental laws had legitimately changed over time. They could not then be the same as, equivalents of, the immutable laws of nature.[66] Instead, the English constitution, as an example of limited monarchy, was interpreted as comprising both natural and fundamental laws. Thus Tyrrell argued:

> It is already granted, that all those Laws in a limited Government, but those of Nature and right Reason are alterable, because the Government itself is so, and in respect of which alone they may be called Fundamental, or Foundations of the Government, but these being altered, it would cease to be the same kind of Government it was before.[67]

In this very simple way, then, Tyrrell constructed a bridge between considerations of morality and considerations of constitutional law and this bridge was characteristic of all integrated contract arguments.

But by acknowledging that fundamental law both could be and had been changed, Tyrrell opened to question the practical point of enquiries into the Saxon constitution. What relevance did the Saxon constitution have for men in seventeenth century England? What claim did any real or supposed Saxon law have to the obedience of Tyrrell and his contemporaries? Tyrrell suggested two reasons why the Saxon constitution was still binding on the present. The first was that the original contract had been renewed each time a new monarch took the coronation oath. Taking that oath thus became for Tyrrell, as in constitutional contractarian literature, a sort of contract in itself.[68] But this, Tyrrell felt, was an incomplete explanation both because some kings could not be shown to have taken any such oath and because the coronation oath on it's own (whereby a monarch undertook to rule according to the established law) could not account for the binding force of changes made within constitutional law. His solution was to add a second idea, a restricted idea of popular sovereignty. Thus, the consent of the governed was made the basis and binding force of the constitution. To his mind, the limited monarchy he supposed established by the Saxon contract was the only form of government that rational men would consent to. The basics of that constitution had been maintained in England right up to his day. Changes had certainly occurred. But he felt confident that he could show that monarchs in the late seventeenth century held their crowns "by, and under the same Title, and by vertue of the same original contract" as the first king of the Saxons who "took the Crown upon condition to maintain the Fundamental Laws, and constitutions of the Government."[69]

The Danish and Norman conquests were still obvious problems for this argument of legal continuity since Saxon times. If either conquest had fundamentally altered the constitution established by the Saxon contract, there would have been as little point in discussing that contract as Tyrrell admitted to be the case for government before then. Thus Tyrrell resorted to the same unhistorical arguments as many previous writers like Petyt, Atwood, Ferguson, Hunt and Cooke in order to prove that no conquests had occurred since Saxon times. He accepted that Cnute and William I "were victorious by their Arms" but insisted "yet was not this Nation subdued by either of them so entirely, as that its Submissions could properly be styled Conquests, but rather Acquisitions gained by those Princes upon certain

Compacts between them and the People of **England.**"⁷⁰ Cnute and William the Conqueror, then, were really kings by right of contract and not conquest. They made a bargain with the people of England and the most important part of it on their sides was that they promised to rule according to already established law.⁷¹ In the circumstances of the current constitutional controversies, once these points had been established then the contemporary relevance of Saxon law had been secured. The seventeenth century Civil Wars created no problem in this respect since although they were very widely condemned as a break in legal continuity, there had been a very conscious restoration following them - a restoration which tied together again the severed threads of continuity, threads which Tyrrell and the others believed stretched back at least to Saxon times.

So far I have examined the principal elements in Tyrrell's theories of government in general and the English constitution in particular. His political writings were certainly elaborate, but a fairly simple practical argument ran through them. His concern was to present an interpretation of the English constitution which would support a number of very pressing, practical recommendations. Englishmen had natural rights, part of which they gave up in order to reap the benefits of civil life. They agreed to a constitution which guaranteed the rights they retained. In return they owed allegiance to their government. The basic arrangements involved in all this had been worked out in Saxon times, but amended since. The violation of the Saxon constitution (established by contract and altered by consent) gave a constitutional right of resistance. This was the crux of Tyrrell's defence of the anti-royalist movement which forcefully manifested itself from the Exclusion Crisis to the 1688 Revolution. The whole argument was presented as based on English constitutional law. The **Patriarcha Non Monarcha**, for example, was written "in defence of the Government as it is establisht, and the just Rights and Liberties of all true English-men."⁷² The purpose of the detailed and wide-ranging **Bibliotheca Politica** is revealed in Freeman's summary of his principles:

> I thought I had sufficiently proved in our former Conversations, that taking up Arms in defence of our Religion and Civil Liberties, when no other Remedy could prevail, was not unlawful, according to our Constitution. Secondly, That there is such a thing as an **Original Contract** however ignorant you are pleased to make yourself of it. Thirdly, That by the **Abdication** or Forfeiture of King **James** (call it which you please) the Throne did really become vacant; and that it is legally filled by their present Majesties. That the Oath of Allegiance is of perpetual Obligation, I also grant; but it is still on condition, that the King shall likewise truly keep and perform that part of the Contract contain'd in his Coronation Oath, without going about to alter and invade our Religion and Civil Liberties by an armed Force and arbitrary Power ... These are indeed the Principles I have all along maintain'd, and I hope I shall never have occasion to be ashamed of them.[73]

But in turning his theories to justify the Revolution, Tyrrell met with two further problems. The one concerned the statute laws of Charles II outlawing armed resistance; the other concerned James II's son's title to the throne. In meeting these problems, Tyrrell was obliged to by-pass constitutional law as fundamental law and appeal to natural law. He could do this without admitting that he had changed the grounds of his defence because, on his interpretation of the English constitution, natural law was itself a part of constitutional law. In response to the first of these problems, for example, Tyrrell argued that despite Charles II's laws Englishmen "still have a good and sufficient Right left them of defending their Lives, Religion, and Liberties against the King ... in case of a general, and universal Breach and Invasion of the Fundamental Laws of the Kingdom, or Original Contract."[74] But his final statement on this problem shows how far outside positive law he was prepared to go in order to defend what he believed right. Yet, nevertheless, he still believed that his justification had to be, and was, according to

English constitutional law:

> I do not deny that ... our written Laws do no ways allow any Resistance, or Imprisonment of the King; but however, there are divers Actions, which, tho' not justifiable by the strict Letter of the Law, yet being for the publick Good, and Preservation of the Government, and original Constitution thereof and, in cases of extreme Necessity, when done indeed, ought to be justify'd and pardon'd by subsequent Parliaments.[75]

The constitutional grounds of resistance, it seems, were certainly beginning to crumble.

In response to the problem of James II's son, Tyrrell was even more explicit about forsaking the strict letter of constitutional law and appealing to a higher law. The problem arose because Tyrrell accepted that the monarchy was hereditary and that James may well have had a legitimate son just before the Revolution. Both points were fiercely contested at the time since an inescapable implication seemed to be that James's son had a constitutional right to succeed should James II, for whatever reason, be removed from the throne. Tyrrell accepted "that the legal and common course of Succession ought to be inviolately observed" but added the all-important proviso "when ever it may consist with the publick good and safety of the Kingdom." He then continued:

> I cannot believe, that the King himself much less any other, that only pretends as next Heir to him, can have such an absolute Right to a Kingdom, as that no considerations whatsoever can make him lose or forfeit the Right thereunto; <For> in the Right to a Kingdom, I take it to be a true Maxim, That the Representatives of a Nation (as the Convention was) ought to have more regard to the happiness and safety of the whole People, ... than to the Dignity or Authority of any particular Person whosoever ... when it is evident that the advancement of such a Person to the Throne, will

prove destructive to our Religion, Civil Liberties, and Properties.[76]

Thus in justifying William's and Mary's rights to the throne, Tyrrell by-passed strictly positive law and appealed to a higher law. Yet he still believed his justification was constitutional, for the higher law was a part of, and implicit within, the laws of the constitution.

This final point highlights the connection between Tyrrell's social contract analysis and his theory of the English constitution. I shall conclude my examination of the structure of his arguments with a number of remarks on that connection. Tyrrell's analysis of the general nature and extent of political authority took place within a rationalist framework. His arguments here had all the trappings of appeals to natural rights, natural law, state of nature, and social contract that were part of the political theory of rationalist constructivism. But Tyrrell refused to accept that there was anything hypothetical, speculative or abstract about his theory. At every turn he looked for empirical equivalents. Logical consistency and introspection were not enough, his theory had to accord with the evidence of history and contemporary societies. He was much more at home, it seems, with the common-sense empiricism of Locke (which he greatly admired) than with seventeenth century rationalism. His interest in origins was fundamentally an historical and not a philosophical one. Many of the peculiarities of his social contract theory spring from this. For example, the sometimes confusing and contradictory ways in which he used the notion of a state of nature become less confusing and more comprehensible if that notion were concerned with the state of affairs during the earliest age of the world rather than with a theoretical and hypothetical state from which to derive the nature and necessity of civil society. Similarly, Tyrrell's historical concern accounts for the otherwise extraordinary absence of any precise notion, or even determination to arrive at a precise notion, of social contract in his writings. As I have argued, Tyrrell's characterization of life in the state of nature was similar to Pufendorf's description of the "mixed state of nature." Yet for Tyrrell, a social state of nature seemed to imply that there was no problem in explaining how social life originated; whereas Pufendorf's main point was the quite different one of explaining that all forms of social life presupposed contracts between the parties involved. The crucial difference here was that Tyrrell and Pufendorf were asking themselves different questions. Tyrrell wanted to know what human life was like in the earliest times and the Bible provided the most important evidence for him here; Pufendorf wanted to characterize the kind of relationship between individuals that social life presupposed. Hence Pufendorf began his enquiry with the individual abstracted from social relations, and Tyrrell did not.

Tyrrell's social theory performs two functions in his political arguments. It served to combat the basic principles of Filmerian patriarchalism and it provided the general outline of a legitimate constitution. Since the English constitution was a legitimate constitution, the social theory outlined in general what a proper examination of English constitutional law and history provided in particular. His apparently rationalist social theory could do this because English constitutional history was written by Tyrrell in the light of that theory. Thus the critical points in the history - the origin of the Saxons, the original contract, the implicit reservations in English laws, the Danish and Norman contracts, the successive coronation oaths, and so on - were presented not simply as what was the case, or what may have been the case, but rather as what must have been the case. A theory of history similar to that of Atwood and the constitutional contractarians seems to be at work here. But it was employed to justify propositions about natural and divine law in the English constitution and about the origins and character of social life which were not only outside the terms of reference of constitutional contractarians but also explicitly rejected by them.[77]

It was to be a comparatively easy task for writers like Hume to show that the historical account of the origin of society and government presented by Tyrrell and other contractarians was wrong. As countless critics in the seventeenth century had already pointed out, there are hardly any contracts in history. Even at the time Tyrrell was writing, doubt was being cast on the validity of biblical history. And thus his crucial evidence from this source was losing its persuasiveness.[78] Yet for all his appeals to historical and empirical evidence, Tyrrell's theory was in form rationalist. As such it was open to still further lines of attack. Tyrrell himself was aware of two main difficulties: the artificiality of the social bond in contractualist thought; and the concomitant foundation of political obligation in the subjective will. Bernard de Mandeville, in the first decade of the eighteenth century, was soon to revolutionize the conception of social cohesion (at least implicitly) by introducing a middle term into the ancient dichotomy of nature and art. Society might no longer be viewed as either natural or artificial but it could be a sort of mixture: the result of human action but not of human design. The problem of political obligation could be reexamined along similar lines.[79] Yet in the meantime the ideas we have examined in Tyrrell claimed many adherents. They did, after all, and despite the problems they involved, serve a popular political purpose.

PART V

CHAPTER 11

CONCLUSION

In the preceding pages I have attempted to clarify the understandings of contract that appear in English political literature of the late seventeenth and early eighteenth centuries. I have dwelt on the various vocabularies associated with appeals to contract and in the process have pursued arguments which have long since lost any urgency or immediate interest. Many of the characters I have considered find no place in our conventional histories of political thought. In only the most specialised historical studies can their names be read. They are men who lost their public reputations almost as soon as they had made them. Theirs was that limited and momentary fame which accompanies prominence in practical political dispute and which fails to transcend it. Occasionally, but only when the need for clarification required it, I have moved away from English writers and considered Pufendorf or the arguments of sixteenth century Frenchmen. But my concern has always been with the contractualisms of late seventeenth century England. The short period that I have considered in some depth, the rehearsal of often exotic and obscure arguments, the appeal to writers long since forgotten, all these have issued in conclusions of considerable significance. Many commonly accepted generalizations both about the history of contract theory and about political ideas and groups in the late seventeenth century must be rejected or thoroughly modified.

It is simply wrong to suggest that there was **one**

CONCLUSION

contract theory which has appeared in a variety of more or less incomplete forms throughout history.[1] Contractualist political theory was not "universally associated with the rights of the individual person, with consent as the basis of government, and with democratic, republican, or constitutional institutions."[2] References to a "Social Compact" were not only concerned to "furnish either (A), a theory of political duty, or, (B), a theory of political origins."[3] Appeals to a "Social Contract" were not solely concerned with the "nature" rather than the "origin" of society.[4] The "state of nature" certainly was sometimes "meant to be taken as a historical fact."[5] English political theory after the Restoration was not neatly divided "between two main schools" of Anglican divine righters and Whig contractarians.[6] And Locke's politics, for all the myth-making there has been, were not representative of even those contemporaries who supported the same political causes as him.[7]

Broad and sweeping generalizations cannot begin to do justice to the evidence I have examined. Understandings of contract were simply far too various. I have suggested instead that we might better appreciate the meaning of contract in late seventeenth century English political argument if we notice that they fall into one or other of three categories. These categories I have called philosophical, constitutional and integrated contractarianism. The differences between these kinds of contractualism are most immediately apparent in terms of their distinctive vocabularies. In philosophical contract writing we constantly come across terms like natural rights, natural law, state of nature, and social contract. In constitutional contract literature we keep meeting terms like fundamental rights, fundamental law, fundamental liberties, fundamental contract, original contract and fundamental constitution. In integrated contract writings we find these two vocabularies related together in a particular way. The differences of vocabulary are indicative of other, and more significant differences, between the various contractualisms. The vocabularies were not always kept apart but the questions that elicited answers more frequently in one vocabulary rather than the others are sufficiently different to indicate that the understandings of contract cannot be reduced to one another. Furthermore, the different questions indicate very clearly that different evidence was being referred to. All this is most apparent in the distinction between philosophical and constitutional contractualisms. Philosophical contractarianism was concerned to answer questions like the following: why is civil society necessary, what is the essential nature of civil relations and what sort of government ought men to have? Constitutional contractarianism asked: how did this particular constitution originate, what kind of constitution is it, what specific rights and duties do its laws define and guarantee and what implications does all this have for current political practice? Philosophical contractarianism appealed primarily to reason. Constitutional contractarianism appealed to the evidence of history and law. Integrated contract literature seemed to pose the same questions as both philosophical and constitutional contractarianisms, and it appealed to the evidence of history, law and reason. The actual issues at stake in all three kinds of contractualism were frequently the same. But as between philosophical and constitutional contractualisms, those issues were transposed into different idioms and were accordingly treated differently. There was no logical connection between the questions asked in philosophical and constitutional contractualism. They were simply questions of different kinds. But in respect of these idioms and questions, the most difficult distinction to draw is that between constitutional and integrated contractualism. For both of these differed from philosophical contractarianism in that they were explicitly concerned to answer questions about the particular requirements of particular constitutions (here, most usually, the English constitution). But in constitutional contractarianism an attempt was made to portray positive laws as rational - though the emphasis was always on positive laws. In integrated contractarianism, on the other hand, the attempt was made to incorporate the rational into positive law - the emphasis was always on natural law as both an integral part of, and the source of, positive law.

CONCLUSION

The burden of my argument has been to insist that there was not a single contract theory to which various writers subscribed with greater or lesser degrees of completeness. Yet this fallacious view seems to have been held by almost all writers who have considered the history of contract theories. If we accept their view then we miss the crucial differences of levels of argument, types of question asked and kinds of evidence invoked by contractarian writers of the seventeenth and eighteenth centuries. Furthermore, we import into our accounts of contract theories entirely inappropriate criteria of criticism. For we may be tempted to criticize as incomplete works that could never have been intended to be complete according to our preconceived notion of what contract theory really was, or always should have been, about. Similarly, we may be tempted to exaggerate the historical importance of certain contractarian works which seem the more complete and to underestimate the importance of supposedly incomplete works. For example, in terms of the literature I have reviewed, it would seem, in part, for this reason that the importance of Locke's *Two Treatises* has been exaggerated whilst the writings of Atwood, Ferguson, Tyrrell and Sidney have been neglected. In short, if we adopt the kind of approach to the history of contractualist thought characteristic of the Gierke-Gough tradition we are certain to misunderstand the meaning of appeals to contract to both writers and audiences at any particular time.[8]

Some of the differences between the various kinds of contractualism that I have depicted have not, of course, entirely escaped the notice of historians of political thought. Gough himself pointed to differences between Locke's *Two Treatises* and the majority of Whig pro-Revolutionary tracts. But these he interpreted in terms of his mechanistic division of social contract theory into two parts - a contract of government and a contract of society.[9] Sir Leslie Stephen, however, came much closer to the point when he wrote of two different schools of contractarian thinkers: social contract/natural law theorists and writers of "a different school"

CONCLUSION

who believed the "compact" to have been an historical reality which "might vary indefinitely according to circumstances, and be the foundation as well of a democracy as of a despotism." This second type of contractualism, he asserted, was used "not to preserve the absolute character of certain laws, but to justify the most purely empirical methods."[10] Reviewing a broader and more European than English body of contractualist literature, Jürgen Dennert, too, has emphasised some fundamental differences between the contractualisms of a particularist, constitutional kind (like that of the sixteenth century **monarchomachi** and the rationalist, system-building of Hobbes and Rousseau.[11] With respect to similar evidence, G. del Vecchio has indicated many different interpretations of the meaning of contract within the modern tradition of contractarian writing.[12] And with respect to some of the evidence which has been directly my concern, Professor Pocock has noted that around 1688 the common law view of the ancient constitution turned into a conservative and legalistic version of contract theory.[13] But none of these writers have pursued their suggestions much further.

Although it has been my point to insist on the differences between the various kinds of contractualism, I have attempted to show that they did share certain very broad features in common. In particular, I have argued that the coherence and persuasiveness of each depended upon the widespread acceptance of rationalist constructivism. But even in the late seventeenth century (the "heyday" of contractarian thought)[14] some of the central notions of rationalist constructivism as well as notions more immediately related to the three types of contractarian argument were coming under attack. In 1705, Mandeville's **The Grumbling Hive** was published. Although the potentialities of the work were not realized until well into the eighteenth century, still Mandeville's argument implicitly attacked rationalist constructivism by denying that social and political institutions were solely the product of human design. Human institutions, it appeared, were the product of human action but not of human design. In making this claim, F.A. Hayek has argued, Mandeville" made Hume possible."[15] In terms of political explanation, there is evidence, too, of attention being directed away from the search for rational origins that was characteristic of rationalist constructivism. Sir William Petty's **Political Arithmetick** (1691) exemplifies one of the directions in which a new kind of explanation of political phenomena was sought. Petty declared that his new approach was "not yet very usual":

> for instead of using only comparative and superlative Words, and intellectual Arguments, I have taken the course (as a Specimen of the Political Arithmetick I have long aimed at) to express my self in Terms of **Number, Weight** or **Measure**; to use only Arguments of Sense, and to consider only such Causes, as have visible Foundations in Nature.[16]

In his **A Discourse Of the Contests and Dissensions Between the Nobles and the Commons in Athens and Rome** (1701), Jonathan Swift seemed to have been infected by a similar kind of scientific spirit when he declared that his task was the new one of a "pathology of politicks."[17] He was concerned, that is, with the relations of power within states and the causes of strength and weakness rather than with any search after origins. But Swift did not engage in the weighing and measuring characteristic of Petty's work. Both Petty and Swift do, however, exemplify the rise of a new focus of attention concerned neither with the rational nor the historical origins of states but rather with the relations of power and the balance of power within states.[18]

Of the three types of contractualist argument, it was constitutional contractarianism that came under the most severe and sustained attack as the period I have considered advanced. The Marquess of Halifax, for example, in his unpublished **Political Thoughts and Reflections** wittily criticised the notion of fundamentals.[19] Three of his remarks may serve to indicate how at least one of the constitutional contractarians' audience viewed their use of this central idea:

> Every Party, when they find a maxim for their

CONCLUSION

turn, they presently call it a **Fundamental**. They think they nail it with a peg of iron, whereas in truth they only tie it with a wisp of straw.

The word soundeth so well that the impropriety of it hath been the less observed. But as weighty as the word appeareth, no feather hath been more blown about in the world than this word **Fundamental**. ...

Fundamental is a word used by the laity, as the word sacred is by the clergy, to fix everything to themselves they have a mind to keep, that nobody else may touch it.[20]

Daniel Defoe, from within the ranks of Whig contractarians, attacked the constitutional contractarian appeal to the intentions and activities of their ancestors as well as the supposed excellence of the Saxon constitution. In **The True-Born Englishman** (1701), Defoe attacked the "Sham-whig" ideas of John Tutchin. Against glorifications of the purity and unbroken continuity of the English past, Defoe insisted:

... from a Mixture of all Kinds began,
That Het'rogeneous Thing, **An Englishman**:
In eager Rapes and furious Lust begot
Between a painted Briton and a Scot;
Whose gendering offspring quickly learnt to bow
And yoke their heifers to the Roman plough;
From whence a Mongrel half-bred Race there came,
With neither name nor Nation, speech or Fame.
In whose hot veins new Mixtures quickly ran,
Infused between a Saxon and a Dane,
While their rank Daughters, to their Parents just,
Received all Nations with promiscuous lust.
This nauseous Brood, directly did contain
The well extracted Blood of Englishmen.
...
Then let us boast of Ancestors no more,
Or Deeds of Heroes done in days of Yore,
In latent Records of the Ages past,
Behind the Rear of Time, in long Oblivion plac'd.
...
What is't to us, what Ancestors we had?

CONCLUSION

If Good, what better? or what worse, if Bad?

And in a similar vein to Defoe, Humphry Hody criticised the whole debate about the Norman Conquest as pointless since whatever had taken place some seven centuries earlier could make no significant difference to the present constitution.[21]

Many of the major elements in late seventeenth and early eighteenth century contractualist thought, then, were coming under scrutiny and attack from various quarters. What was being attacked and why it was relevant as criticism can only be fully appreciated when viewed against the evidence that I have examined. One obvious example is the sensitivity and vulnerability of contractualist thought to historical criticism. If contractualist thought is seen in terms of the Gierke-Gough story, royalist or Humean criticism that there are no contracts in history looks like either a wilful misrepresentation of contractarian rationalist argument or a classic case of missing the point (like Dr. Johnson and his stone). If, however, attention is paid to the arguments of constitutional contractarianism, historical criticism can be seen to be directly relevant. Integrated contract arguments were similarly vulnerable and social contract arguments were sensitive to historical criticism where their proponents believed that they should at least not run counter to the evidence of history even if historical evidence could in no way prove their validity.

My conclusions have been reached by looking at the evidence of contractualist ideas as uses of peculiar political vocabularies with distinctive associations answering different questions rather than as examples of some prestructured theory. My brief excursions back into late sixteenth century French political theory and Civil War controversies in England suggest that similar distinctions between constitutional law understandings of contract and philosophical understandings might be encountered there. In the eighteenth and nineteenth centuries, appeals to contract lost much of their purchase in political argument. But the story of how they did so, as well as of later revivals and reformulations, is long

CONCLUSION

and complicated. The ideas of contract that I have examined all changed their meanings as the eighteenth century proceeded. But to pursue and account for these changes would take me outside the scope of this book. I have already, on occasion, stepped beyond the task I described at the beginning as that of the historical under-labourer. I have presupposed some familiarity with the political history of England during the Restoration and Revolution periods and have concentrated my attention on the language of political discourse. How the ideas of contract I have outlined came to be as they were has been briefly touched upon. My point has been to emphasise how complex and various the understandings of contract have been in past political argument and to suggest that only by discarding conventional histories of contract theory can we begin to appreciate the meanings of appeals to contract in the history of political thought. But my study, too, has had its unintended consequences which border on the paradoxical. For in setting out to study the meaning of contract during the age of Locke, the evidence has revealed that Locke was the most untypical of all the writers of his time. He was certainly read but **Two Treatises** was rarely cited as an authority in political argument. Locke simply did not address himself to the constitutional questions which occupied the attention of so many of his contemporaries. In this respect, then, one pradoxical conclusion seems inescapable: if there ever was an age of Locke in the history of English political thought, it most certainly was not the age with which I have been concerned.

NOTES

CHAPTER 1

1. The issues involved here are discussed at length in the theoretical writings of Quentin Skinner and J.G.A. Pocock. I have found Skinner's argument in "Meaning and Understanding in the History of Ideas," **History and Theory**, 8 (1969), 3-53 and Pocock's **Politics, Language and Time** (London, 1972) especially helpful.
2. Gough, **The Social Contract** (2nd edn., Oxford, 1957), esp. 1-7.
3. Gierke, **Natural Law and the Theory of Society, 1500 to 1800**, ed. and trans. E. Barker, 2 vols. (Boston, 1934); D.G. Ritchie, **Darwin and Hegel** (London, 1893); F. Atger, **Essai sur l'histoire des doctrines du contrat social** (Nîmes, 1906); E. Barker, **Social Contract** (London, 1947), esp. v-lxi; Riley, "How Coherent is the Social Contract Tradition?," **Journal of the History of Ideas**, 34 (1973), 543-62 and "On Kant as the most Adequate of the Social Contract Theorists," **Political Theory**, 1 (1973), 450-71. For a more detailed criticism of these assumptions and organizing ideas, focussing upon Gierke, see: H. Höpfl and M.P. Thompson, "The History of Contract as a Motif in Political Thought," **American Historical Review**, 84 (1979), 919-44.
4. "Juristic sharpness" is Gierke's term in **The Development of Political Theory**, trans. B. Freyd (New York, 1939), 91. Gierke praises Althusius for the first, proper articulation of the model, whereas Gough prefers Salamonius and Riley prefers Kant. The idea of the demise of contractualist language in political theory was as premature as one might expect. Rawls, Nozick, Buchanan and Harold Wilson

have all shown that there is life in the language yet. For a critique of model-methodology, see: Skinner, "Meaning and Understanding," 3-53 and Pocock, "Languages and Their Implications," in **Politics, Language and Time**, 3-41.
5. Höpfl and Thompson, "The History of Contract," 919-28.
6. Skinner, "Meaning and Understanding," 11, 16-22 and "Motives, Intentions and the Interpretation of Texts," **New Literary History**, 3 (1972), 393-408.
7. Gough, **The Social Contract**, 126-46.
8. **Ibid.**, 126.
9. **Ibid.**, 145.
10. J.L. Duncan, "Juristic Theories of the British Revolution of 1688," **The Juridicial Review**, 44 (1932), 36.
11. O.W. Furley, "The Whig Exclusionists: Pamphlet Literature in the Exclusion Campaign, 1679-81," **Cambridge Historical Journal**, 13 (1957), 29. See also: J. Dunn, "The politics of Locke in England and America," in J.W. Yolton (ed.), **John Locke: Problems and Perspectives** (Cambridge, 1969), 57 and W.S. Hudson, "John Locke: Heir of Puritan Political Theorists," in G.L. Hunt (ed.), **Calvinism and the Political Order** (Philadelphia, 1965), 108. The singularity of Locke's contractualism is discussed in Chapter 7 below.
12. **Journal of the House of Lords (1688-89)**, 110.
13. Gough, **John Locke's Political Philosophy: Eight Studies** (Oxford, 1968), 121.
14. A single example of each may suffice. See respectively: S. Johnson, **Remarks Upon Dr. Sherlock's Book, Intituled The Case of Resistance** (London, 1689), preface, vi; R. Ferguson, **The Late Proceedings and Votes of the Parliament of Scotland** (Glasgow, 1689), 24; T.H., **Political Aphorisms** (London, 1690), 29; P. Allix, **An Examination of the Scruples of those who refuse to take the Oath of Allegiance** (London, 1689) in: **State Tracts**, I (London, 1705), 302; Sir R. Atkyns' speech to the Convention Lords reported in: **Historical Manuscripts Commission: 12th Report, Appendix Part VI.**

MSS. of the House of Lords, 1689-90 (London, 1889), 15.

15. See respectively: R. Ferguson, **A Brief Justification of the Prince of Orange's Descent into England** (London, 1689), 25; S. Johnson, **Remarks Upon Dr. Sherlock's Book, Intituled The Case of Resistance**, preface, x; G. Burnet, **An Enquiry into the Measures of Submission to the Supreme Authority** (London, 1689) in: **Harleian Miscellany**, 9 (London, 1808-11), 204; J. Savage, **The Ancient and Present State of Germany** (London, 1702), 36; W. Atwood, **The Fundamental Constitution of the English Government** (London, 1690), 9-10.

16. Respectively: Johnson, **Remarks Upon Dr. Sherlock's Book, Intituled The Case of Resistance**, preface, vi; R. Ferguson, **Whether the Preserving the Protestant Religion was the Motive unto, or the End that was designed in, the Late Revolution?** (London, 1695) in: **Somers Tracts**, 3 (London, 1748-52), 423; W. Atwood, **The Jacobite Principles Vindicated** (1691?) in: **Somers Tracts**, 10 (London, 1809-15), 526; T.H., **Political Aphorisms**, 16; Atwood, **The Fundamental Constitution**, 84; Anon., **An Entire Vindication of Dr. Sherlock** (London, 1691), 14; Anon., **A Political Conference between Aulicus, a Courtier; Demas, a Countryman; and Civicus, a Citizen** (London, 1689), 22-3.

17. P. Laslett, "Social Contract" in: P. Edwards (ed.), **Encyclopedia of Philosophy** (London, 1967).

18. Thus Laslett concludes that Hobbes was "the most rejected, and politically the least important, of all the absolutist writers" in the late seventeenth century. See, P. Laslett (ed.), **John Locke: Two Treatises of Government** (New York, 1965), Introduction, 80. For the immediate reception of Hobbes, see S. Mintz, **The Hunting of Leviathan** (Cambridge, 1969) and J. Bowle, **Hobbes and his Critics** (London, 1951).

19. For **de facto** arguments at the time of the 1688 Revolution, see Chapter 2 below and my "The Idea of Conquest in the Controversies over the 1688 Revolution," **Journal of the History of Ideas**, 38 (1977), 33-46. On Engagement Controversy appeals

NOTES

to Hobbes' authority, see G.W.S.V. Rumble's introduction to Anthony Ascham, **Of the Confusions and Revolutions of Governments** (New York, 1975) and Q. Skinner, "The Ideological Context of Hobbes' Political Thought," **Historical Journal**, 9 (1966), 286-317. The argument emphasising Hobbes' neglect and disreputability should not be pushed too far, however, since both Pufendorf and Spinoza amply testify to Hobbes' continuing, serious reputation as a political philosopher on the continent, whilst the very popularity of the derogatory label "Hobbist" in England indicates that Hobbes' name was far from ignored by opponents of absolutism.

20. Ferguson is discussed in detail in Chapter 5 below.
21. I have assumed all along a familiarity with the political history of the period and have concentrated attention instead on the character of political argument and political theory.
22. With due apologies to Locke, of course, in **An Essay concerning Human Understanding** (ed. and abridged by A.S. Pringle-Pattison), The Epistle to the Reader (Oxford, 1924), 7.

CHAPTER 2

1. Cf. H. Butterfield, **The Whig Interpretation of History** (Harmondsworth, 1973) and **The Englishman and His History** (Cambridge, 1944).
2. See respectively: M. Ashley, **The Glorious Revolution of 1688** (London, 1968), 266-67; D. Bahlman, **The Moral Revolution of 1688** (New Haven, 1957); J.H. Plumb, **The Growth of Political Stability in England 1675-1725** (Harmondsworth, 1969); and D. Abel, "Liberty v. Authority in Stuart England," **The Contemporary Review**, 937 (Jan., 1944).
3. T.B. Macaulay, **The History of England from the Accession of James II** (London, 1906), II, 210.
4. For these classes, see J.R. Western, **Monarchy and Revolution: The English State in the 1680s** (London, 1972), 33. Western writes: "The Corporation

NOTES

Act of 1661 obliged municipal officers to take an oath affirming 'that it is not lawful upon any pretence whatsoever to take arms against the king; and that I do abhor that traitorious position of taking arms by his authority against his person, or against those that are commissioned by him.'... This oath was successively imposed on militia officers, the clergy, schoolmasters and university teachers." This was just one of the very positive oaths of allegiance which I take to identify fairly clearly the layers of society which constituted the politically relevant classes.

5. "'The Violent Party': the Guildhall Revolutionaries and the Growth of Opposition to James II," **Guildhall Miscellany**, 3 (1970), 121.

6. See respectively: Western, op.cit.; W.H. Greenleaf, **Order, Empiricism and Politics** (London, 1964), 14-94; G.L. Cherry, "The Legal and Philosophical Position of the Jacobites, 1688-9," in G.M. Straka (ed.), **The Revolution of 1688: Whig Triumph or Palace Revolution?** (Boston, 1968), 59-67; G. Schochet, **Patriarchalism and Political Thought** (Oxford, 1975); and G.M. Straka, "The Final Phase of Divine Right Theory in England," in Straka (ed.), op.cit., 86-96.

7. J.P. Kenyon, **Revolution Principles** (Cambridge, 1977), chs. 1-5.

8. See also my "The Idea of Conquest in Controversies over the 1688 Revolution," **Journal of the History of Ideas**, 38, (1977), esp. 34-6.

9. See E. Bohun, **The History of the Desertion** (n.p., 1689), in **State Tracts**, I, 38.

10. See the refutation of this standpoint in S. Johnson, **The Argument Proving, That the Abrogation of King James by the People of England from the Regal Throne, and the Promotion of the Prince of Orange ... was according to the Constitution of the English Government** (London, 1692), passim.

11. E.g.: W. Lloyd, **A Discourse of God's ways of Disposing of Kingdoms. Part I** (London, 1691), partially reprinted in Straka (ed.), op.cit., 25-8; G. Burnet, **Pastoral Letter** (London, 1689), passim; C. Blount, **King William and Queen Mary**

NOTES

Conquerors (London, 1693), passim; Anon., **A Vindication of the Divines of the Church, Who have Sworn Allegiance to K. William and Q. Mary** (London, 1689), 7; W. Sherlock, **A Vindication of the Case of Allegiance due to Soveraign Powers** (London, 1691), 12-13. For the extent and ramifications of these ideas, see my "The Idea of Conquest in Controversies over the 1688 Revolution," 33-46 and "On Dating Chapter XVI of Locke's **Second Treatise**," **The Locke Newsletter** (Summer, 1976), 95-100. Cf. M. Goldie, "Edmund Bohun and **Jus Gentium** in the Revolution debate, 1689-1693," **Historical Journal**, 20 (1977), 569-86.

12. E.g. J. Collier, **The Desertion Discuss'd** (London, 1689), in **State Tracts**, I, 111.
13. E.g. Anon., **A Letter to a Bishop concerning the present Settlement** (n.p., n.d.) in **Somers Tracts** (Scott edn.), IX, 381.
14. G. Burnet, **A Sermon Preached in the Chappel of St. James's ... the 23rd of December, 1688** (London, 1689), passim.
15. E.g. S. Johnson, **Remarks Upon Dr. Sherlock's Book, Intituled, The Case of Allegiance** (London, 1691), Preface, vi.
16. E.g. C. Lawton, **The Jacobite Principles Vindicated** (n.p., 1691?), in **Somers Tracts** (Scott edn.), X, passim.
17. E.g. W. Sherlock, **A Letter to a Member of the Convention** (London, 1688), 1.
18. Ibid., 1-2. Sherlock lists a number of current proposals.
19. E.g. Anon., **Reflections upon the present State of the Nation** (n.p., 1689) in **Somers Tracts** (Scott edn.), X, 203.
20. E.g. Anon., **Some Short Considerations relating to the settling of the Government, humbly offered to the Lords and Commons of England** (n.p., 1689) in **Somers Tracts** (Scott edn.), X, passim; W. Sherlock, **A Letter to a Member of the Convention**, 2.
21. E.g. Anon., **Now is the Time: A Scheme for a Commonwealth** (London, 1688/9) in Straka (ed.), op.cit., 20-24.

NOTES

22. Mullett, "Religion, Politics and Oaths in the Glorious Revolution," **Review of Politics**, X (Oct., 1948), passim.
23. See, for example, P. Hazard, **The European Mind 1680-1715**. Trans. J.L. May (Harmondsworth, 1964); Sir G.N. Clark, "The Augustan Age," in F.J.C. Hearneshaw (ed.), **The Social and Political Ideas of Some English Thinkers of the Augustan Age** (London, 1928); and S.L. Bethell, **The Cultural Revolution of the Seventeenth Century** (London, 1963).
24. See Western, op.cit., esp. 156-238, for a sophisticated account of the role of religion in late seventeenth century English politics.
25. Seller, **The History of Passive Obedience since the Reformation** (Amsterdam, 1989), preface.
26. See fn. 4 above.
27. Sir R. Atkyns, **Parliamentary and Political Tracts** (London, 1734), 189.
28. Atwood, **The Fundamental Constitution**, preface, xxxii.
29. Anon., **The Case of the Oath Stated** (n.p., n.d.) in **State Tracts**, I, 342-3.
30. Anon., **Reflections upon our late and present Proceedings in England** (n.p., 1688/9) in **Somers Tracts** (Scott ed.), X, 179.
31. Cf. C.F.Mullett, "A Case of Allegiance: William Sherlock and the Revolution of 1688," **Huntington Library Quarterly**, x (1946-7), passim.
32. **The Case of Allegiance Due to Soveraign Powers, Stated and Resolved. According to Scripture and Reason, And the Principles of the Church of England, With a more particular Respect to the Oath, lately enjoyned, of Allegiance to Their Present Majesties** (London, 1691), preface.
33. See G. Every, **The High Church Party 1688-1718** (London, 1956), 64.
34. Loc. cit., 1-2.
35. Ibid., 3.
36. Ibid., 5.
37. Ibid., 14.
38. Collier, **Dr. Sherlock's Case of Allegiance Considered. With some Remarks upon his Vindication** (London, 1691), 1.

39. Ibid., 74.
40. E.g. R. Downes, **An Examination of the Arguments Drawn from Scripture and Reason, In Dr. Sherlock's Case of Allegiance, And his Vindication of it** (London, 1691), 14-15; Anon., **Historio-Theologicus** (London, 1715), preface, 3, where Hobbes appears as the intellectual forbear of all those who changed allegiance after 1688.
41. Johnson, **Dr. Sherlock's Two Kings of Brainford Brought upon the Stage** (London, 1690), 4.
42. Johnson, **The Second Part of Dr. Sherlock's Two Kings of Brainford** (London), 1690), 3.
43. Jenkin, **The Title of an usurper After a Thorough Settlement Examined, In answer to Dr. Sherlock's Case of Allegiance** (London, 1690), 32.
44. Straka (ed.), **op. cit.**, 87.
45. Defoe, too, may be added to the list, see his **Reflections Upon the Late Great Revolution** (London, 1689), 1.
46. Johnson, **Remarks upon Dr. Sherlock's Book, Intituled, The Case of Allegiance**, preface, iii.
47. **Loc. cit.**, 34.
48. The story seems to be Macaulay's and has generally been accepted ever since. But see M. Goldie, "Charles Blount's Intention in Writing 'King William and Queen Mary Conquerors' (1693)," **Notes and Queries** (December, 1978), 527-32.
49. **Loc. cit.**, 3.
50. A. Grey (ed.), **Debates in the House of Commons 1667-1694** (London, 1763), X, 297-8.
51. W. Cobbett (ed.), **Cobbett's Parliamentary History of England** (London, 1806-12), V, 756.
52. A. Grey (ed.), **op. cit.**, X, 297. See my "The Idea of Conquest" **op. cit.** passim: and Goldie, "Edmund Bohun and **Jus Gentium** in the Revolution Debate 1689-93," **Historical Journal**, 20 (1977), 584.
53. But see Ch. 7 below for a discussion of the peculiarities of Locke's notion of consent.
54. **Loc. cit.**, 12-3. Skinner, "The Ideological Context of Hobbes' Political Thought," **Historical Journal**, 9 (1966), 286-317.
55. **Loc. cit.**, 13.

56. Q. Skinner, "History and Ideology in the English Revolution," **Historical Journal**, 8 (1965), esp. 171-8. See also Ch. 3 below.
57. **An Enquiry into the Measures of Submission to The Supreme Authority** (London, 1689), 9-10. This pamphlet ran to at least six editions within a year.
58. Ibid., 10-11. "1. All general words how large soever, are still supposed to have a tacit exception and reserve in them, if the matter seems to require it ... 2. When there seems to be a contradiction between two articles in the constitution, we ought to examine which of the two is evident, and the most important ... and then we must give such an accommodating sense to that which seems to contradict it, that so we may reconcile those together, ... since the chief design of our whole law ... is to secure and maintain our liberty ... therefore the other article against resistance ought to be so softened, as that it does not destroy us. 3. ... the not resisting the King, can only be applied to the executive power, that so upon no pretense of ill administration in the execution of the laws, it should be lawful to resist him: but this cannot with any reason be extended to an invasion of the legislative power, or to a total subversion of the government ... 4. ... The <word> King ... imports a prince clothed by law ... but if he goes to subvert the whole foundation of the government ... he annuls his own powers and then ceases to be King."
59. Ibid., 10.
60. Johnson, **Dr. Sherlock's Two Kings of Brainford**, 4, 18.
61. Ibid., 21.
62. Johnson, **Remarks Upon Dr. Sherlock's Book, Intituled, The Case of Allegiance**, 19.
63. Ibid., 1-2.
64. E.g. Wilson, **God, the King and the Countrey**, 11, 34.
65. E.g. Collier's refutation of this argument in **Animadversions upon the modern Explication of 11. Hen. 7. Cap. 1: Or a King de Facto** (London, 1689). D. Whitby, **Obedience due to the present King,**

notwithstanding our Oaths to the former (London, 1689), passim.

66. E.g. Anon., **Four Questions Debated** (London, 1689), passim; Anon., **Their Present Majesties Government Proved to be Thoroughly Settled, and That we may Submit to it, without Asserting the Principles of Mr. Hobbs** (London, 1691), 9.

67. E.g. Johnson, **An Argument Proving**, preface, 3; Anon., **Some Short Considerations relating to the settling of the Government** (London, 1689), in **Somers Tracts** (Scott edn.), X, passim.

68. See above p.12.

69. Allix, **An Examination of the Scruples of those who refuse to take Oath of Allegiance** (London, 1689) in **State Tracts**, I, 302.

70. **A Collection of the Parliamentary Debates in England, from the Year M,DC,LXVII To the present Time** (London, 1741), II, 248-9.

71. Ibid., 244.

72. Ibid., 204.

73. **Historical Manuscripts Commission, 12th Report, Appendix Part VI, MSS of the House of Lords 1689-90** (London, 1889), 15.

74. Ibid., 15-16.

75. Anon., **Good Advice before it be too late: Being a Breviate for the Convention** (n.p., 1688/9). Reprinted in Straka (ed.), **op. cit.**, 21. Sir J. Montgomery, **Great Britain's just Complaint for her late Measures, present Sufferings, and the future Miseries she is exposed to** (London, 1692) in **Somers Tracts** (Scott edn.)., X, 468. For Ferguson's ideas, see Ch. 5 below. **God, the King and the Countrey**, 11. Anon., **The Dear Bargain; or, a true Representation of the State of the English Nation under the Dutch** (n.p., 1690) in **Somers Tracts** (Scott edn.), X, 377.

76. J. Collier, **The Desertion Discuss'd**, 110.

77. Collier, **Vindiciae Juris Regii** (London, 1689), 42-3.

78. Cf. S. Kliger, **The Goths in England** (Cambridge, Mass., 1952); E. Hoelzle, **Die Idee einer altgermanischen Freiheit vor Montesquieu** (Berlin, 1925); and Ch. 3 below.

NOTES

79. Ferguson, **A Brief Justification of the Prince of Orange's Descent into England**, 5-6. Cf.: Junius Brutus, **Vindiciae Contra Tyrannos** (1597) in J.H. Franklin (ed.), **Constitutionalism and Resistance in the Sixteenth Century: Three Treatises by Hotman, Beza, & Mornay** (New York, 1969), 196-7; T. Beza, **Du droit des magistrats sur leur subiets** (1574) translated in Franklin (ed.), **op. cit.**, 123-4; Anon., **Discours des Jugemens de Dieu contre les Tyrans** (n.p., n.d.) in S. Goulart (ed.), **Mémoires de l'Estat de France sous Charles IX** (2nd edn., Heidelbourg, 1578), II, 554ff. See also: R. Parsons, **A Conference about the next Succession to the Crown of Ingland** (London, 1593), 1; G. Buchanan, **De Jure Regni apud Scotos** (1579-80), ss. xi-xii. Indeed, as J.W. Allen suggests, all right was looked upon as divine in origin in the sixteenth century (**Political Thought in the Sixteenth Century**, 121-4). For the transmission of French ideas into English political thought of the late-sixteenth and seventeenth centuries, see J.H.M. Salmon, **The French Religious Wars in English Political Thought** (Oxford, 1959), passim.
80. Anon., **Some Remarks upon Government, And particularly upon the Establishment of the English Monarchy, Relating to the present Juncture** (n.p., 1689), 6-7. Anon., **A Political Conference between Aulicus etc.**, 22-3. For how widespread this was, and the varied implications drawn from it, see Schochet, **Patriarchalism in Political Thought**, esp. Chs. X, XI. See also: J. Locke, **Two Treatises**, II, ss. 105, 110.
81. This may well reflect the authority of Pufendorf as well as the accumulated sources of contractualist argument from the late-sixteenth century onwards. Both methodological and moral individualism were very much the exception in the literature reviewed here. See Ch. 6 below for Pufendorf.
82. Lawton, **The Jacobite Principles Vindicated**, 526.
83. Lawton, **Loc. cit.**, in **Somers Tracts** (Scott edn.), IX, 370.
84. Jenkin, **The Title of an Usurper**, 57, 59.

NOTES

85. Loc. cit., "Dialogue the Ninth," Preface. The three sections were the third dialogue (moralist), the fourth (divine), and the ninth onwards (lawyer).
86. Locke, **Two Treatises**, II, ss. 97-99. Tyrrell quotes directly from Locke's **Second Treatise** in the third dialogue. See the **Bibliotheca Politica**, "Dialogue the Third,", 155-6, 173.
87. Locke, **Two Treatises**. Ed. P. Laslett (New York, 1965), 171. The seriousness of Locke's stated intention has been questioned recently. See Charles D. Tarlton, "'The rulers now on earth': Locke's **Two treatises** and the Revolution of 1688," **Historical Journal**, 28 (1985), 279-98. For a rejoinder, see my forthcoming "Significant Silences in Locke's **Two treatises of government**."
88. See my "The Reception of Locke's **Two Treatises of Government** 1690-1705," **Political Studies**, 24 (1976), 184-91 and "Reception and Influence: A Reply to Nelson on Locke's **Two Treatises**," **Political Studies**, 28 (1980), 100-108. See also Kenyon, **Revolution Principles**, 5-20; and J.H. Franklin, **John Locke and the Theory of Sovereignty** (Cambridge, 1978), 87-126. Cf. J.C.D. Clark, **English Society 1688-1832** (Cambridge, 1985), 45-50.
89. R. Ashcraft and M.M. Goldsmith, "Locke, Revolution Principles, and the Formation of Whig Ideology," **Historical Journal**, 26 (1983), 773-800.
90. A point emphasised by Laslett in Locke, **Two Treatises**, ed. Laslett, 88-91.
91. Gough, **The Social Contract**, 135. Cf. Sir E. Barker, **Social Contract** (Oxford, 1947), xv-xvi.
92. See Locke's comments in J. Axtell (ed.), **Locke's Educational Writings** (Cambridge, 1968), 400.
93. Slaughter, "'Abdicate' and 'Contract' in the Glorious Revolution," **Historical Journal**, 24 (1981), 323-37 (here, 333). The debate continues, though without critical examination of what "Lockean" and "Hobbesian" might mean. See J. Miller, "The Glorious Revolution: 'contract' and 'abdication' reconsidered," **Historical Journal**, 25 (1982), 541-55 and T.P. Slaughter, "'Abdicate' and 'contract' restored," **Historical Journal**, 28 (1985), 399-403.

NOTES

94. Locke, **Two Treatises**, ed. Laslett, 126-28. Hobbes, **Leviathan**, ed. M. Oakeshott (Oxford, 1946), Ch. 18. Hence the very idea of talking of Hobbesian and Lockean contracts of government seems eccentric.
95. Slaughter, "'Abdicate' and 'Contract'," 325.

CHAPTER 3

1. See Höpfl and Thompson, "The History of Contract as a Motif in Political Thought," 929-33.
2. For the German Empire see, for example, the **Tübinger Vertrag** of 1514 in W. Näf (ed.), **Herrschaftsverträge des Spätmittelalters**. Quellen zur neueren Geschichte, 17 (Bern u. Frankfurt am Main, 1975) and F.L. Carsten, **Princes and Parliaments in Germany. From the 15th to the 18th Century** (Oxford, 1959); for the rest of Europe see: G. Griffiths, **Representative Government in Western Europe in the Sixteenth Century: Commentary and Documents for the Study of Comparative Constitutional History** (Oxford, 1968), 7, 71, 265-6, 302, 348-9, 429, 431, 461-2, 456, 493, 494, 495, 499, 502, 511-2, 518; L. Anquez, **Histoire des assemblées politiques réformées de France, 1573-1622** (Paris, 1859); J.F. Maclean, "Samuel Rutherford: The Law and the King," in G.L. Hunt (ed.), **Calvinism and the Political Order** (Philadelphia, 1965), 69-72.
3. See J.H. Elliott, **The Revolt of the Catalans** (Cambridge, 1963), esp. ch.1; and R.E. Giesey, **If Not, Not: the Oath of the Aragonese and the Legendary Laws of the Sobarbe** (Princeton, 1968), passim.
4. See Höpfl and Thompson, op. cit., 930.
5. Atwood, **The Fundamental Constitution of the English Government**, 32. What follows is the briefest of summaries. Full references are given in the next and subsequent chapters.
6. Ibid., 84.
7. Ibid., 59. A very similar point had been made by Innocent Gentillet, one of the earliest theorists of fundamental law. See: **Briève remonstrance à la**

NOTES

noblesse de France sur le faict de la déclaration de Mgr. le duc d'Alençon (n.p., 1576), 13-14.
8. Atwood, **The Fundamental Constitution of the English Government**, 79.
9. Ibid., 78.
10. See F.W. Maitland's Introduction to W.J. Whittaker (ed.), **The Mirror of Justices**. Seldon Society (London, 1895); H. Butterfield, **The Englishman and his History** (New York, 1970 edn.), 29-30.
11. Loc. cit., 6.
12. Atwood, **Wonderful Predictions of Nostredamus** (London, 1689), preface, n.p.; Tyrrell, **Bibliotheca Politica**, Advertisements to Dialogues 2, 9, 10; Pufendorf, **De Officio Hominis et Civis** (Lund, 1673), II, 8, 2.
13. Atkyns, **Parliamentary and Political Tracts**, 61: D. Defoe, **The Original Power of the Collective Body of the People of England, Examined and Asserted** (London, 1702), 16-19.
14. See Ch. 7 below. But see the argument of J. Richards, L. Mulligan and J.K. Graham, "'Property' and 'People': Political Usages of Locke and Some Contemporaries," **Journal of the History of Ideas**, 42 (1980), 29-51. For a brief account of changes in understandings of the term 'people' in political discussion see C.S. Emden, **The People and the Constitution** (Oxford, 1962 edn.), esp., Appendix I.
15. Pocock, **The Ancient Constitution and the Feudal Law** (Cambridge, 1957); see also Hoelzle, **Die Idee einer altgermanischen Freiheit vor Montesquieu** (Berlin, 1925); and S.L. Kliger, **The Goths in England** (Cambridge, Mass., 1952). The latter, however, must be read with caution since it contains some astonishing errors of fact (see fn. 4, Ch.10 below); it also appears to exaggerate the extent and significance of Gothicism during the seventeenth century (see Pocock, op. cit., 56-8).
16. This was the view of James Tyrrell. See Chs. 8 and 10 below.
17. Pocock, op. cit., 57-8.

NOTES

18. Brady, **An Introduction to the Old English History** (London, 1684), The Epistle to the Candid Reader, 3-4.
19. **Ibid.**, passim.
20. Petyt, **Inner Temple <IT> Ms 512 'H'** fols. 10, 22, 28-9, 97, 155; **IT Ms. 'P'**, fols. 72-3, 88-90; **IT Ms. 'U'**, fols. 8-9, 9-21, 65-67, 261-62.
21. For the broad context here, see Western, **Monarchy and Revolution**, esp. 5-45.
22. Petyt, **IT Ms. 512 'M'**, fol. 22. Draft copy of **The Rights of the Commons of England reasserted against Dr. Brady**. See also **IT MS. 512 'U'**, fol. 304.
23. **Ibid.**, fols. 304-5.
24. As suggested in: C.C. Western, "Legal Sovereignty in the Brady Controversy." **Historical Journal**, 15 (1972), 417.
25. Petyt, **IT MS. 512 'M'**, fol. 22.
26. Cf. Western, "Legal Sovereignty," 417ff. Western's criticisms of Pocock are thus wide of the mark.
27. In **The Ancient Right of the Commons of England Asserted** (London, 1680), 59-60, Petyt argued that in the earliest times English kings were popularly elected. He also accepted that the Saxons imported an ancient German form of government into England (Preface, 6). But he did not go much further than this along contemporary constitutional contractarian lines. In his manuscripts however, his emphasis on Germanic/Gothic origins became stronger (e.g. **IT MS. 512 'U'**, fol. 253) throughout the period and he can be found underlining that the English monarch's prerogatives were "setled upon Them by Original Grants from the People" (**IT MS. 512 'U'**, fol. 66) and that William I "had taken the Soveraignty upon Compact with the English and that solemnly ratified and confirmed by his sacred Coronation oath." (**IT MS. 512 'H'**, fol. 12.)
28. At least one contractarian writer in the early 1680s, Thomas Hunt, did suggest that the original contract dated from the Norman Conquest. He was, however, severely criticized by William Atwood for doing so. See Atwood, **Lord Hollis His Remains** (London, 1682), 271-30.

NOTES

29. Atwood, **Jus Anglorum ab Antiquo** (London, 1681), Preface, n.p.
30. Noted by T. Hunt, **Mr. Hunt's Postscript for Rectifying Some Mistakes in some of the Inferior Clergy, Mischievous to our Government and Religion.** (London, 1682), 6. P. Laslett (ed.), **Patriarcha** (Oxford, 1949), 23-40
31. Cf. Pocock, op. cit., 217-8.
32. **Ibid.**, 217-228.
33. See, e.g., Laslett (ed.), **Patriarcha**, 275-313.
34. As noted in Ch. 2., M. Goldie's analysis of 237 pamphlets contributing to the allegiance controversy 1689-1693 shows that half appealed to notions of contract. See Goldie, "The Revolution of 1689 and the Structure of Political Argument," **Bulletin of Research in the Humanities**, 83 (1980), 490.
35. See p.12 above.
36. Hayek, "Kinds of Rationalism," in **Philosophy, Politics and Economics** (London, 1967), 85ff.
37. See Schochet, **Patriarchalism and Political Thought**, 192-224; Clark, **English Society 1688-1832**, Ch. 3; J.A.W. Gunn, **Beyond Liberty and Property** (Kingston, 1983), 120-193.
38. Brady, **A True and Exact History of the Succession** (London, 1681), 1-2; Seller, **The History of Passive Obedience**, Preface; Anon., **The Royal Apology: or, An Answer to the Rebels Plea** (London, 1684), passim.
39. Craig, **The Right of Succession to the Kingdom of England.** Ed. J.G. (London, 1703), Preface; Anon., **The Jesuit's Memorial** (London, 1640), passim; Anon., **The Character of a Rebellion** (London, 1681), 4.
40. Anon., **The Royal Apology**, To The Reader, n.p.
41. E.g., A. Sidney, **The Works**, ed. J. Robertson (London, 1772), 5; J. Welwood, **A Vindication of the Present Great Revolution in England** (London, 1689), 2; Anon., **The Supremacy Debated: Or, The Authority of Parliament (formerly owned by the Romanish Clergy) the Supremest Power** (n.p., n.d.) in State Tracts I, 231.
42. Hunt, **Mr. Hunt's Postscript**, 1-5.

NOTES

43. Burnet, **An Answer to a Paper Printed with Allowance, Entitled, A New Test of the Church of England's Loyalty**, in **A Collection of Eighteen Papers, Relating to the Affairs of Church & State, During the Reign of King James the Second** (London, 1689), 55.
44. Loc. cit., 3.
45. Burnet, **History of His Own Time** (London, 1823 edn.) IV, 37-8.
46. Long, **The Historian Unmask'd; Or Some Reflections On the late History of Passive Obedience** (London, 1689), 7-9.
47. Hickes, **An Apology for the New Separation** (London, 1691), Preface.
48. Collier, **Animadversions upon the modern Explication of 11 Hen. 7 Cap. 1. Or a King de Facto** (London, 1689), 1.
49. Kettlewell, **Christianity a Doctrine of the Cross: or, Passive Obedience, under any Pretended Invasion of Legal Rights and Liberties** (London, 1691), 80.
50. See respectively: C. Leslie, **The New Association of those Called Moderate-Church-Men, with the Modern-Whigs and Fanaticks** (London, 1702), 10; Sir G. Mackenzie, **A Vindication of the Government in Scotland, During the Reign of King Charles II** (London, 1691) in The Works (Edinburgh, 1716-22), II, 346; Anon., **The Character of a Rebellion, And what England May expect from one** (London, 1681), 4; and Seller, op. cit., Preface.
51. Brady, **An Inquiry Into the Remarkable Instances of History, and Parliament Records, used by the Author of the Unreasonableness of a new Separation on Account of the Oaths; Whether they are faithfully cited and applied** (London, 1690), 20.
52. Jenkin, **The Title of an Usurper**, 32.
53. Collier, **Dr. Sherlock's Case of Allegiance Considered** (London, 1691), 10; Burnet, **An Enquiry into the Measures of Submission to the Supreme Authority**, 9-10; Anon., **The Case of Allegiance Consider'd** (London, 1689), 6-7; Atwood, **The Fundamental Constitution**, 2-3; S. Johnson, **Remarks Upon Dr. Sherlock's Book** (London, 1689), 19.

NOTES

54. The point has been denied by J.C. Corson, "Resistance No Rebellion," **Juridical Review** (Sept., 1930), 245-6. Corson claims Pollock's authority for this point.
55. **Loc. cit.**, 317.
56. For complications in the views of Tyrrell and Sidney, see below chs. 9 and 10.
57. Johnson, **Remarks Upon Dr. Sherlock's Book, Intituled, The Case of Resistance**, 19.
58. Ferguson, **A Sober Enquiry into the Nature, Measure and Principle of Moral Virtue, Its distinction from Gospel-Holiness** (London, 1673), 77.

CHAPTER 4

1. Ashley, **The Glorious Revolution of 1688** (London, 1968 edn.), 145; Gough, **Fundamental Law in English Constitutional History** (Oxford, 1955), 163; Greenleaf, **Order, Empiricism and Politics** (London, 1964), 142, 187, 194, 280; Goldie, "The Revolution of 1689," 508; Pocock, **Virtue, Commerce, and History** (Cambridge, 1985), 224; Robbins (ed.), **Two English Republican Tracts** (Cambridge, 1969), 18; Franklin, **John Locke and the Theory of Sovereignty**, 105.
2. Laslett (ed.), **John Locke: Two Treatises of Government**, 90 fn. 32; Schochet, **Patriarchalism and Political Thought**, 213.
3. See, for example: Brady, **An Introduction to the Old English History** (London, 1684), 165; and James Anderson, **An Historical Essay** (Edinburgh, 1705), passim.
4. Petyt, **The Pillars of Parliament Struck at by the Hands of A Cambridge Doctor, Or a Short View of some of his Erroneous Positions, Destructive to the Ancient Laws and Government of England** (London, 1681), 9. In IT. MS. 538. Vol. 16.fol. 324ff; Cooke, **Argumentum Anti-Normannicum** (London, 1682), lxix; Neville, **Plato Redivivus** in C. Robbins (ed.), **op.cit.**, 120.

NOTES

5. In 1681 even James Tyrrell was writing to Petyt as his superior in historical learning. **IT. MS. 538. Vol. 17**, fol. 302: letter dated Oxford, Jan. 12, 1681.
6. These were: **Jani Anglorum Facies Nova** (London, 1680); **Jus Anglorum ab Antiquo** (London, 1681); **Lord Hollis His Remains** (London, 1682); and **Reflections Upon Antidotum Britannicum, and Mr. Hunt's late Book and Postscript** (London, 1682).
7. Loc. cit., 4.
8. **Lord Hollis His Remains**, 230.
9. **Jus Anglorum ab Antiquo**, 117.
10. Ibid., Preface.
11. Ibid., Preface.
12. **Lord Hollis His Remains**, 266. And in the Preface to **Jus Anglorum ab Antiquo** he argues: "I know that it has been whisper'd about, as if I would have this Government to be new modelled, which I utterly abhor."
13. **Lord Hollis His Remains**, 271.
14. **Jus Anglorum ab Antiquo**, Additions, 37.
15. **The Fundamental Constitution of the English Government**, 2.
16. **The Fundamental Constitution**, 3.
17. **Lord Hollis His Remains**, 293; **The History, and Reasons, of the Dependency of Ireland upon the Imperial Crown of the Kingdom of England** (London, 1698), 211; and **The Superiority and Direct Dominion of ... England over ... Scotland** (London, 1704), 392.
18. **The Fundamental Constitution**, 2-3.
19. **The Superiority and Direct Dominion**, 487, 391.
20. **The Fundamental Constitution**, Preface, xxii, xxi.
21. **Lord Hollis His Remains**, 271.
22. **The Fundamental Constitution**, 4.
23. See below, Ch. 8 and my "A Note on 'Reason' and 'History'," 491-500.
24. **The Fundamental Constitution**, 9-10.
25. Mornay, **Vindiciae contra tyrannos**, trans. H.J. Laski (London, 1924), 134.
26. **The Superiority and Direct Dominion**, 377-8.
27. **The Superiority and Direct Dominion**, 377-8; and **The Fundamental Constitution**, 30.

NOTES

28. **The Fundamental Constitution**, 2.
29. **Ibid.**, Preface, xxxii-xxxiii.
30. **Ibid.**, 59. Atwood was quoting Robert Sheringham (1602-1678). Very similar sentiments, however, can be found amongst the earliest French speculators about fundamental law. Innocent Gentillet, for example, in the **Brièvé remonstrance à la noblesse de France** (1576) argues "quand l'on abbat les **lois fondamentales** d'un royaume, le roy, et la royauté qui sont basties dessus tombent quand et quand ... les **lois fondamentales** d'un royaume ne se peuvent jamais abolir, que le royaume ne tombe bien tost après." Quoted in A. Lemaire, **Les lois fondamentales de la monarchie française d'après les théoriciens de l'Ancien Régime** (Paris, 1907), 107-8.
31. **The Fundamental Constitution**, 50.
32. "I. The two great Charges against the Company are the seizing of Ships and Goods of **Interlopers**, and condemning them as forfeited. II. The passing Sentences of Death, and executing Men, by the Governor of St. **Helena**, in a Method not wholly agreeable to the Laws of **England**; or else the procuring a Commission from the King, for trying and executing Men there, by Martial Law." **An Apology for the East-India Company** (London, 1690), 4, 31.
33. **The Fundamental Constitution**, 78.
34. **Ibid.**, 81.
35. **Superiority and Direct Dominion**, 524.
36. B. Behrens, "The Whig Theory of the Constitution in the Reign of Charles II," **Cambridge Historical Journal**, V, (1941).
37. **The Fundamental Constitution**, 27.
38. **Ibid.**, 26, 61, 65, 54.
39. **Ibid.**, 78-9.
40. On this aspect of modern rationalism see: M. Oakeshott, **Rationalism in Politics** (London, 1967 edn.), title essay; and F.A. Hayek, "Kinds of Rationalism," in **Philosophy, Politics and Economics** (London, 1967), Ch. 5.
41. **The Fundamental Constitution**, 12. Exactly the same passage occurs in Atwood's Preface to his **Won-**

derful Predictions of Nostredamus, Grebner, David Pareus, and Antonius Torquatus (London, 1689).

42. On the notion of fundamental law in early seventeenth century England, see J.D. Eusden, **Puritans, Lawyers and Politics in Early Seventeenth Century England** (New Haven, 1958); Gough, **Fundamental Law in English Constitutional History**; and Sir C.K. Allen, **Law in the Making** (7th edn., Oxford, 1964), Ch. VI.

43. **The Fundamental Constitution**, Preface, xxxii, iii-iv: "We **may resist** when the **Original Contract is Notoriously broken**, and we **must not** resist when the Original Contract is **notoriously** broken; are **contrary** and contradictory Propositions one of which I grant to be true; But we **must** resist in no case, and we **may** resist in any case, when **every Man pleases** ... are not **Contraries**, but **Extreams**; and tis odds but the Truth lies in the middle, that we may resist in some case, which cries aloud, and justly stirs up a Nation, as with the **Voice of God**."

44. Ibid., v: Beza, for example, argues with respect to private persons who have once consented to be governed: "Ie dy que sans extraordinaire vocation de Dieu, à laquelle ie ne touche point, il n'est licite à aucun particulier d'opposer force à la force du Tyran de son autorite privee," private persons may only suffer and pray to God for relief even when a ruler has turned into a tyrant. **Du Droit des Magistrats sur leur subiets** (1574) in S. Goulart (ed.), **Mémoires de l'Estat de France sous Charles IX** (2nd edn., Heidelbourg, 1578), 491-2.

45. Ibid., v-vi: In Beza this argument entitles the Estates to resist (**op. cit.**, 496). In the **Vindiciae contra tyrannos** (1579), the argument entitles "the authorities that have the power of the people in them, or ... the greater part of these authorities ⟨to⟩ use force against a prince who commands unholy action." See the translation of the **Vindiciae** in J.H. Franklin (ed.), **Constitutionalism and Resistance in the Sixteenth Century** (New York, 1969), 154. Here too, private persons "have no right whatsoever to take up arms on their own

NOTES

        initiative unless they have clearly received an extraordinary calling." (Ibid., 158).
46. **The Fundamental Constitution**, 34, 36, 33.
47. Ibid., 84.
48. Ibid., 72.
49. Ibid., 100; **The Superiority and Direct Dominion**, 389.
50. Although, of course, Tyrrell and several others suspected it right from the beginning. For Locke's reception see my "The Reception of Locke's **Two Treatises of Government 1690-1705**," **Political Studies**, (June, 1976).
51. **The Fundamental Constitution**, 101.
52. Ibid., 101-2.
53. Cf. the brief survey of Pufendorf's contract theory in J.W. Gough, **The Social Contract**, 121-124.
54. **The Fundamental Constitution**, 102. See also, **Wonderful Predictions**, Preface.
55. **The Fundamental Constitution**, 85.
56. In his **Reflections upon a Treasonable Opinion, Industriously promoted, Against Signing the National Association** (London, 1696), Atwood asserted that "the King for the time being, is the only **Rightful King**." His denial of the validity of the common distinction between **de jure** and **de facto** kings in fact follows from his constitutional theory only when seen in the light of his peculiar understanding of what had supposedly happened in 1688. Yet Atwood was here claiming the universal inapplicability of such a distinction. Here we see a first glimpse of what was to become a major problem for Whig constitutional historians and lawyers in the first decade of the eighteenth century. Whig theorists were asserting that only kings by contract and consent were rightful kings. From this it followed that non-contract kings (e.g., by conquest), although **de facto** monarchs, were not rightful kings. In the post-1688 period, however, many persistently argued that William and Mary were only **de facto** monarchs whilst James II remained king **de jure**. To combat these claims, several Whigs compromised their insistence that

legitimacy could only derive from contract by either admitting that allegiance was due whenever protection was effective or by reinterpreting conquest so that it inevitably involved consent (cf. the 'Sherlock controversy' outlined in Ch.2 above). From these revisions, it followed that an effective king, or a king **de facto**, because he was effective was also **de jure**. The Whig concern with legitimate government once again turned from a concern with explicit origins to a concern with the continuing purposes of government. But in this transition, benevolent conquerors became legitimized and the Whigs could argue, as Sir John Willes and William Higden did, that William I, though in fact a conqueror, had been king **de jure** because of the effective protection he gave to his subjects. The Norman Conquest thus became an event acceptable to Whig historians, whereas in the 1680s it solely featured in Tory histories of a Bradyite kind. See Skinner, "History and Ideology in the English Revolution," **Historical Journal**, 8, (1965), esp. 171-8.

57. References to, and quotations from, all these writers begin to appear in Atwood's works only after 1689.
58. **The Fundamental Constitution**, 3-4.
59. **Wonderful Predictions**, Preface.
60. Behrens, **op. cit.**, 50-53.
61. **Reflections upon a Treasonable Opinion**, The Epistle Dedicatory. The treasonable opinion referred to in the title was that the English constitution did not require taking additional oaths of allegiance to William and expressly disavowing allegiance to the Pretender; **The Superiority and Direct Dominion**, 111, 559.
62. **The Fundamental Constitution**, 95.
63. **The Superiority and Direct Dominion**, 20.
64. **The History and Reasons, of the Dependency of Ireland upon the Imperial Crown of the Kingdom of England** (London, 1698), 195: "on consent depends the obligation of all humane Laws: insomuch that without it, by the unanimous Opinions of all Jurists no sanctions are of any force."

NOTES

65. Ibid., 5.
66. **The Scotch Patriot Unmask'd**, 35.
67. **The Fundamental Constitution**, Preface, vii; **The Superiority and Direct Dominion**, 386.
68. Ibid., 569. Here Atwood argued: "As I remember, that great Man **Grotius**, in his Treatise of the Truth of the Christian Religion, uses it as an undeniable argument of the **Divine Providence**, and interposition in Humane Affairs; that whatever form of Government, has obtained in any Nation, is preserved, notwithstanding all the Plots and Machinations of Men to the contrary." That this did not mean that Atwood understood Grotius to be arguing that any enduring form of government was legitimate in God's eyes is apparent from Atwood's translation into verse of Grotius' text. The relevant stanza argues not only that men can impose other forms of government than those based on popular consent on their fellow citizens but also that Providence is most in play in the foundation of states (i.e., at the original contract). The stanza reads:
XI. <That the universe is governed by God> prov'd from the preservation of Governments.
The special Influ'ence of a Pow'r above,
Kingdoms and Common-wealths continued, prove.
A form of Government that first prevail'd,
Has not through many tracts of ages fail'd.
For this we might all Histories apply,
Where a Republick, where a Monarchy,
All the contrivances and Plots of Men,
If they unsettle, bring the same agen;
So that against a long fixt Pow'r to fight,
Seems ev'n the Providence of Heaven to slight.
Tho Human Wisdom might preserve it long,
Yet the subjected Rabble are so strong,
Such the Vicisitudes of human things,
That none could fix them but the King of Kings.
But then this Providence chiefly appears,
When the Foundations of a **State** he tears;
This **Cyrus, Alexander, Caesar** too,
Tartarian Cingi, and **Namcaa** shew.
These Men in things where Prudence has a share,

By far beyond its force successful are;
Nay, the uncertainty of things below,
Unto their prosp'rous Fortunes seem to bow;
When like Events to the same constant end
As 'twere by a Conspiracy do tend,
They argue a direction from on high:
Sometimes a lucky size turns on the Die;
But if the same an hundred times you fling,
'Tis evident it from some Art must spring.
Grotius his Arguments for the Truth of the Christian Religion (London, 1686), 10-11.

69. The purpose of Grotius' original work was essentially to prove this. This was, of course, the age when Relevation was itself for the first time being opened to rational criticism. See P. Hazard, **The European Mind 1680-1715** (harmondsworth, 1964) Pt. 2, Ch. 3.

70. The maxim appears particularly appropriate to contractualist theories which dwelt on historical origins rather than rational origins; theories, that is, which underlined the historicity of rational origins rather than formalizing arguments from consent in terms of contracts. Thus the arguments of Locke, Pufendorf, Sidney and Tyrrell could not tolerate such a maxim. But nor did all constitutional contractarians consistently subscribe to the maxim. What mattered was which aspect of their arguments they were emphasising; whether they were primarily concerned with historical origins or with principles of legitimacy. It should be noted that this dualism appeared very early in arguments which appealed to fundamental laws and which tended to interpret them as constructed at the historical origin of a particular state which might be seen as an original contract. Such arguments might embody maxims directly contrary to Atwood's. Thus, for example, Beza argues in one of the earliest contractualist-fundamental law treatises that the absence of a legitimate title "at the beginning of a usurpation may subsequently be repaired. He who began as a tyrant may become a legitimate and inviolable magistrate through that free and lawful consent by which

NOTES

legitimate rulers are created." (**Du Droit des Magistrats**, trans. and ed. J.H. Franklin, **op.cit.**, 107.) Such arguments might, of course, be accommodated to Atwood's maxim by insisting that an act of consent made a bad title good and that this act had nothing to do with the simple passage of time. Atwood, however, did not confront this issue nor did he consider the associated argument, common enough amongst his contemporaries, that a "quiet settlement" and the absence of opposition to a ruler was tantamount to a tacit consent.

71. See my "A Note on 'Reason' and 'History'," passim.

CHAPTER 5

1. See Macaulay, **op.cit.**, II, 634ff.
2. Anon., **Robert against Ferguson: or a New Dialogue between Robert an Old Independent Whig, and Ferguson a New Tory Jacobite** (London, 1704), Preface, n.p.
3. **The History of the Revolution** (n.p., 1706), 6; **A Letter to Mr. Secretary Trenchard, Discovering a Conspiracy against the Laws and ancient Constitution of England** (London, 1694), 33. Macaulay, **op.cit.**, II, Chs. XV and XVI shows how widespread Protestant Jacobitism was in the early 1690s.
4. Jones, **The First Whigs** (Durham, 1962), 15. Bastide, **John Locke: ses théories politiques et leur influence en Angleterre** (Paris, 1907), 82.
5. Burnet, **History of My Own Time**, ed. O. Airy (London, 1897-1900), II, 357. Macaulay, **The History of England**, II, 635. Ferguson, **Robert Ferguson the Plotter** (Edinburgh, 1887), passim. Cf. K.H.D. Haley, **The First Earl of Shaftesbury** (Oxford, 1968), 719.
6. Oldmixon, **The History of England during the Reigns of King William and Queen Mary, Queen Anne, King George I** (London, 1735), 99-100, 133, 325-7.
7. R. Ashcraft, "Revolutionary Politics and Locke's **Two Treatises of Government**," **Political Theory**, 8 (1980), 456-8.

NOTES

8. The defence of a threatened Protestantism was the single, ostensibly consistent thread running through all Ferguson's writings.
9. **No Protestant Plot** (London, 1681), 37.
10. Anon., **A Word of Advice to the Author of that Scurrilous and Seditious Libel entitled No Protestant Plot** (London, 1681), 2.
11. Anon., **Mr. Ferguson's Lamentation For the Destruction of the Association and the Good Old Cause** (London, 1683), 11, 13. K.H.D. Haley, **op. cit.**, 717; Ashcraft, "Revolutionary Politics and Locke's Two Treatises," 456-8.
12. Under a new title of **The Design of Enslaving England Discovered In the Incroachments upon the Powers and Priviledges of Parliament by K. Charles II** (London, 1689).
13. Ibid., 44.
14. Ibid., 43.
15. Ibid., 38.
16. **A Brief Justification of the Prince of Orange's Descent into England And of the Kingdoms Late Recourse to Arms** (London, 1689), 26, 44.
17. Ibid., 18, 25.
18. **The Second Part of No Protestant Plot** (London, 1682), 1.
19. Ibid., 1-2.
20. **A Brief Justification of the Prince of Orange's Descent**, 5.
21. Ibid. No-one had a right "to enlarge and extend the power of those whom they constitute Rulers, beyond the Limits and Boundaries, unto which God hath staked and confined Magistrates, in the Charters of Nature and Revelation."
22. Ibid., 6-7.
23. See: J.H. Franklin (ed.), **op. cit.**, 146-7.
24. **A Brief Justification of the Prince of Orange's Descent**, 1.
25. Ibid., 7.
26. Ibid., 7-8.
27. Ibid., 11.
28. Ibid., 12.
29. As, for example, over Charles II's statutes against resistance and the Norman Conquest as a

NOTES

        break in the legal continuity of the ancient constitution.

30. **A Brief Justification of the Prince of Orange's Descent**, 29. Ferguson, of course, was insisting that Harold was not the legal king.
31. **The Second Part of No Protestant Plot**, 20. The example being considered here was trial by jury. **A Brief Justification of the Prince of Orange's Descent**, 13: "The several Charters, especially that stiled the **Great Charter**, in and by which our Rights stand secured, sworn, and entailed unto us and to our Posterity, were not the Grants and Concessions of our Princes, but Recognitions of what we had reserved unto our selves in the Original Institution of our Government, and of what had always appertained unto us by Common Law, and Immemorial Customs." **The Second Part of No Protestant Plot**, 21.
32. **The Design of Enslaving England**, 20: "Thus wisely did our Ancestors provide that the K. and His People should have frequent need of one another, and by having frequent opportunities of mutually relieving one anothers wants, be sure ever to preserve a dutiful affection in the Subject, and a fatherly tenderness in the Prince."
33. **A Brief Justification of the Prince of Orange's Descent**, 14-15.
34. Ibid., 17.
35. **The Design of Enslaving England**, 1.
36. **A Brief Justification of the Prince of Orange's Descent**, 24. Ferguson's statements here seem to be a very clear summary, and thus further evidence for, C.C. Weston's thesis about the role of the House of Lords in the constitutional theory of mixed monarchy during the late seventeenth century. (**English Constitutional Theory and the House of Lords 1556-1832** <London, 1965>, Ch. 3.).
37. Ibid., 31, 29.
38. Ibid., 13-14.
39. Ibid., 25.
40. Ibid., 19-20: These were noted as dispensing with the oath of supremacy and thereby opening the door to papal domination; overthrowing "the whole

Legislative part of the Government;" subverting "the very Fundamental Constitutions of the Realm; and reducing the courts to "Ministers of his Will, Pleasure, and unruly Lusts."

41. **The Late Proceedings and Votes of the Parliament of Scotland** (Glasgow, 1689), 6.
42. **A Representation of the Threatning Dangers, Impending Over Protestants in Great Brittain** (n.p., 1687), 30, 31.
43. **A Brief Justification of the Prince of Orange's Descent,** 9.
44. Ibid., 20-21, 18, 32, 36, 24, 9.
45. A warrant was issued for his arrest on this charge (C.S.P.D., 1690-1692).
46. **Whether the Preserving the Protestant Religion was the Motive unto, or the End that was designed in, the late Revolution?** (London, 1695), in **Somers Tracts,** III, 423.
47. **The History of the Revolution,** 6.
48. **A Letter to Mr. Secretary Trenchard,** 33.
49. **Whether the Preserving the Protestant Religion,** 439.
50. **The History of the Revolution,** iv, 31; "I know it hath been industriously urged by several Catholicks as improbable that King **William** should be of their Church, because he communicated with the Church of **England**. To this I answer, that Dispensations have been allowed to inferior Catholicks, much more then to Kings and Princes, to disguise themselves under any Shape whatever necessary to carry on their Designs."
51. See Macaulay, op. cit., Chs. XV and XVI.
52. **Whether the Preserving the Protestant Religion,** 422.
53. Ibid., 422-3.
54. **A Letter to Mr. Secretary Trenchard,** 5.
55. **Whether the Parliament be not in Law dissolved by the Death of the Princess of Orange?** (London, 1695), 7, 11-12.
56. Ibid., 14.
57. **Whether the Preserving the Protestant Religion,** 423.

NOTES

58. **Whether the Parliament be not in Law dissolved,** 17-18.
59. **A Letter to Mr. Secretary Trenchard,** 5; **Whether the Parliament be not in Law dissolved,** 16.
60. **A Letter to Mr. Secretary Trenchard,** 4.
61. Ibid., 4-5.
62. Ibid., 5: King William "may be sure, that they who could extort and wrest from the **Constitution**, which gave no such Allowance, and much less Authority, a Power and Right to dethrone K. James ... will be ready and forward enough when the Humor and Caprice takes them, to treat him in case of Miscarriages after the same rate."
63. Ibid., 6.
64. **Whether the Preserving the Protestant Religion,** 417.
65. **A Letter to Mr. Secretary Trenchard,** 34. Ferguson was here quoting from Burnet's **An Enquiry into the Measures of Submission to The Supreme Authority** (London, 1689), a Williamite tract, and characteristically prided himself on turning the opposition against itself.
66. **A Brief Justification of the Prince of Orange's Descent,** 7-8.
67. Lemaire, **Les lois fondamentales de la monarchie française d'après les théoriciens de l'Ancien Régime** (Paris, 1907), iii.
68. Ibid., iv, 82-89.
69. **Francogallia,** eds. R.E. Giesey and J.H.M. Salmon (Cambridge, 1972), 459. French kings were not set up free from all laws "sed eos certis legibus et pactionibus obligatos esse." (458).
70. Loc. cit., I, 2.
71. See **Francogallia** (eds. Giesey and Salmon), Introduction, 113ff. See also, for example, A. d'Aubigné, **Du Devoir mutuel des Roys et des Subjects** (1621) in **Oeuvres** (Paris, 1969), 467; where d'Aubigné recommends his reader "un livre intitulé **la France Gaule** d'Hottoman, ⟨et⟩ un autre qui a pour titre **Deffence contre les Tyrans** que nous avons longtemps attribué au mesme autheur."
72. Lemaire, **op. cit.,** 106.
73. Franklin (ed.), **op. cit.,** 122.

NOTES

74. In S. Goulart (ed.), **op. cit.**, II, 522.
75. See: Lawton, **The Jacobite Principles Vindicated** (1691?) in **Somers Tracts** (Scott edn.), X, 526; and his **A Letter formerly sent to Dr. Tillotson, and for Want of an Answer made publick** (1690?) in **Somers Tracts** (Scott edn.), IX, 370; also, Jenkin, **The Title of an Usurper** (London, 1690), 57.

CHAPTER 6

1. J. Axtell (ed.), **Locke's Educational Writings**, 400.
2. **Ibid.**, 400-401.
3. See above, Ch. 3.
4. See below, Chs. 8, 9 and 10.
5. Cf. G. del Vecchio, "Über die verschiedenen Bedeutungen der Lehre vom Gesellschaftsvertrag," in U. Klug (ed.), **Philosophie und Recht**) (Wiesbaden, 1960), 20-27.
6. Locke, **Some Thoughts Concerning Education** (London, 1693), in Axtell (ed.), **op. cit.**, 294-5.
7. Tooke (ed.), **The Whole Duty of Man According to the Law of Nature** (London, 1691), To the Reader, n.p.
8. Atwood, **The Fundamental Constitution**, 30, 87.
9. Textor, **loc. cit.**, ed. L. von Bar (Washington, 1916), II, 9.
10. A.P. d'Entrèves, **Natural Law** (London, 1951), Ch. 3.
11. **Loc. cit.**, eds. C.H. and W.A. Oldfather (Oxford and London, 1934), II, x.
12. **Loc. cit.**, ed. W.A. Oldfather (Oxford and London, 1931), II, xxviii.
13. Krieger, **The Politics of Discretion: Pufendorf and the Acceptance of Natural Law** (Chicago, 1965), 102.
14. Minogue (ed.), T. Hobbes, **Leviathan** (London, 1973), Introduction, vii-viii.
15. Von Leyden, **Seventeenth Century Metaphysics** (London, 1968), 65-68.
16. **Elementorum**, II, xxx.

17. Cf. Gierke, **Natural Law and the Theory of Society 1500-1800**. Trans. E. Barker (Cambridge, 1958 edn.), 142-4, 314-5, 337; Krieger, **op. cit.**, 105; 6, 284. When a community resists, the sovereign has ceased to exist and it is no longer a "governed community."
18. **Elementorum**, II, xxviii.
19. As, for example in his **An Introduction to the History of the Principal Kingdoms of Europe**. Trans. J. Crull (5th edn., London, 1702).
20. **Elementorum**, II, Bk. II, Axiom I, s. 1, 209.
21. **Ibid.**, II, Bk. II, Obs. III, ss. 1-2, 233-4.
22. **Ibid.**, II, Bk. II, Obs. III, s. 3, 234.
23. **Ibid.**, II, Bk. II, Obs. III, s. 4, 235.
24. **Ibid.**, II, Bk. II, Obs. III, s. 6, 237.
25. **Ibid.**, 238.
26. **Ibid.**, II, Bk. II, Obs. IV, s. 3, 241.
27. **Leviathan**, ed. Oakeshott, 85.
28. Quoted in Krieger, **op. cit.**, 94.
29. **De Officio Hominis et Civis**. Trans. F.G. Moore (Oxford and London, 1926), II, I, 3, 13.
30. **Ibid.**, II, I, 6, 1-2.
31. **Ibid.**, II, I, 8, 1.
32. **Ibid.**, II, I, 9, 1.
33. **Ibid.**, II, I, 9, 3.
34. See below, Ch. 7 and my "Hume's Critique of Locke and the 'Original Contract'." **Il Pensiero Politico**, 10 (1977), 189-201.
35. **De Officio**, II, I, 3, 10.
36. Krieger, **op. cit.**, 107-8.
37. **Ibid.**, 112.
38. **Ibid.**, 112-117.
39. **De Officio**, II, II, 5, 1.
40. **Ibid.**, II, II, 5, 2.
41. **Ibid.**, II, II, 5, 4: "The man who becomes a citizen suffers a loss of natural liberty, and subjects himself to an authority which includes the right of life and death - an authority at whose command one must do many things from which one would otherwise shrink, and must leave undone many things which one greatly desired to do. And then many actions must be referred to the good of

NOTES

the society, which often conflicts with the good of individuals."
42. **Ibid.**, II, II, 5, 8.
43. **Ibid.**, II, II, 5, 6-7.
44. **Ibid.**, II, II, 5, 9.
45. **Ibid.**, II, II, I, 9: "in the natural state each man is protected by his own powers only, in the community by those of all. In the former no one has a certain reward for his industry; in the latter all have it. In the one there is the rule of passion, war, fear, poverty, ugliness, solitude, barbarism, ignorance, savagery; in the other the rule of reason, peace, security, riches, beauty, society, refinement, knowledge, good will." To make security sufficiently pressing a need, Pufendorf painted his state of nature in very Hobbesian colours.
46. Krieger, **op. cit.**, 120-121.
47. **De Officio**, II, II, 6, 7-9.
48. **Ibid.**, II, II, 6, 10.
49. See Gough, **The Social Contract**, 178-9, for a brief account of Fichte.
50. **De Officio**, II, II, 10, 1.
51. See above, Ch. 2.
52. **De Officio**, II, II, 6, 13.
53. **Ibid.**, II, II, 8, 2.
54. **Elementorum**, II, Bk. II. Obs. V, s. 3, 275.
55. **Ibid.**, s. 4, 277-8.
56. **Ibid.**, s. 8, 281.
57. **Ibid.**, 281-2.
58. **Ibid.**, s. 15, 286.
59. **De Officio**, II, II, 6, 14.
60. **Ibid.**, II, II, 9, 1-2.
61. **Elementorum**, II, Bk. II, Obs. V. ss. 11-12, 284; Ibid., s. 18, 288-9.
62. **Ibid.**, s. 18, 288-9.
63. **Ibid.**, II, Bk. II, Obs. V, s. 19, 291.
64. **Ibid.**, ss. 20-21, 291-2.
65. **De Officio**, II, II, 11, 3.
66. **Ibid.**, II, II, 9, 6.
67. **De Jure Naturae et Gentium**, II, VII, 8, 5; **Elementorum**, II, Bk. II, Obs. V, s. 17, 287.
68. **Elementorum**, II, Bk. II, Obs. V, s. 17, 288.

NOTES

69. *Ibid.*, s. 22, 292-3.
70. *Ibid.*, s. 23, 293-4; **De Jure Naturae et Gentium**, II, VII, 8, 5.
71. **Elementorum**, II, xxviii-xxx.
72. See above, Ch. 2.
73. Locke did recommend Paxton's work (see Axtell (ed.), **op. cit.**, 400-401). Cf. Greenleaf, **op. cit.**, 176.
74. **Loc. cit.**, The Preface Introductory, no page numbers.

CHAPTER 7

1. See respectively: **History of English Thought in the Eighteenth Century** (London, 1962 edn.), II, 114-121; R.I. Aaron, **John Locke** (3rd. edn., Oxford, 1972), 270; M. Seliger, **The Liberal Politics of John Locke** (London, 1967), 45; W. Kendall, **John Locke and the Doctrine of Majority Rule** (2nd edn., Urbana, 1959); C.B. Macpherson, **The Political Theory of Possessive Individualism** (London, 1962 edn.), Ch. V; L. Strauss, **Natural Right and History** (Chicago, 1965 edn.), Ch. V.
2. See respectively: R. Polin, **La politique morale de John Locke** (Paris, 1960) 1; J. Dunn, "The politics of Locke in England and America in the eighteenth century," in J.W. Yolton (ed.), **John Locke: Problems and Perspectives** (Cambridge, 1969), 57; W.S. Hudson, "John Locke: Heir of Puritan Political Theorists," in G.L. Hunt (ed.), **Calvinism and the Political Order** (Philadelphia, 1965), 108.
3. T. Redpath, "John Locke and the Rhetoric of the Second Treatise," in H.S. Davies and G. Watson (eds.), **The English Mind** (Cambridge, 1964), 78.
4. P. Laslett, "The English Revolution and Locke's 'Two Treatises of Government'," **Cambridge Historical Journal**, 12 (1956), 40-55. Ashcraft has recently suggested a slightly later date and has radicalized Locke the more for it. See Ashcraft, "Revolutionary Politics," **Political Theory**, 4 (1980), 429-86.

NOTES

5. See my "On Dating Chapter XVI of Locke's Second Treatise," **Locke Newsletter**, (Summer, 1976), 95-100.
6. De Beer, "Locke and English liberalism: the **Second Treatise of Government** in its contemporary setting," in Yolton (ed.), **op. cit.**, 36.
7. J. le Clerc, **Bibliothèque universelle et historique** (Amsterdam, 1686ff.), Octobre, 1690, 573.
8. **Two Treatises**, II, s. 1.
9. Aaron, **op. cit.**, 270.
10. Filmer, **Patriarcha and Other Political Works** (ed. P. Laslett), 239.
11. Mark Goldie has recently broadened the context of Locke's attack in a direction even further away from Hobbes and towards Filmer and other Anglican ideologists. See Goldie, "John Locke and Anglican Royalism," **Political Studies**, 31 (1983), 61-85.
12. Noted in Hunt, **Mr. Hunt's Postscript** (London, 1682), 6.
13. Certainly Sidney, Tyrrell and Hunt were concerned to refute Filmer. See Furley, "The Whig Exclusionists: Pamphlet Literature in the Exclusion Campaign, 1679-81," 19-36; Schochet, **Patriarchalism and Political Thought**, 192-204.
14. The title of Filmer's work runs **Patriarcha: or, the Natural Power of the Kings of England Asserted.**
15. In the preface to **Two Treatises**, Locke informed his readers that the lost part of the manuscript amounted to "more than all the rest."
16. **Two Treatises**, Preface, 171.
17. **Patriarcha**, Chs. 21-32. See also: **The Freeholder's Grand Inquest; The Anarchy of a Limited or Mixed Monarchy;** and **Directions For Obedience to Government in Dangerous or Doubtful Times.** It seems from this evidence that Laslett's contention that since Locke was never very interested in the detailed constitutional debates of his day it is unlikely that the missing part of **Two Treatises** was concerned with them, is itself unlikely. There certainly are grounds for assuming that Locke was not as interested in the particular laws and customs of the English constitution as he was in many

NOTES

other things. But these grounds are not sufficient for the further assumption that the lost part of the **Treatises**, following the plan Locke suggested in his preface, would not have involved an examination of English constitutional affairs. (Cf. Laslett's introduction to his edition of **Two Treatises**, 89-91).

18. **Two Treatises**, Preface. Tarlton has recently doubted the seriousness of Locke's intention in this respect. C. Tarlton, "'The rulers now on earth': Locke's **Two Treatises** and the Revolution of 1688," **Historical Journal**, 28 (1985), 279-98.
19. See respectively: Sir F. Pollock, "Locke's Theory of the State," **Proceedings of the British Academy** (1903-4), 241; W. Kendall, **op. cit.**, 75; M. Seliger, **op. cit.**, 83; J. Dunn, **The Political Thought of John Locke** (Cambridge, 1969), 97; P. Laslett (ed.), **op. cit.**, 82, 111-2; S.P. Lamprecht, **The Moral and Political Philosophy of John Locke** (New York, 1918), 130, 138, 140; and R.H. Cox, **Locke on War and Peace** (Oxford, 1960), 104.
20. See respectively W. von Leyden, "John Locke and Natural Law," **Philosophy** (Jan., 1956), 25; G. Schochet, "The Family and the Origins of the State in Locke's Political Philosophy," in Yolton (ed.), **op. cit.**, 88.
21. Cox, **op. cit.**, 72-3; Strauss, **op. cit.**, 224-5; Macpherson, **op. cit.**, 241.
22. Both of the first two views are suggested by H. Aarsleff, "The State of Nature and the Nature of Man," in Yolton (ed.), **op. cit.**, 101-2. For the third, see Dunn, **op. cit.**, 97-8.
23. **Two Treatises**, II, s. 77.
24. **Ibid.**, II, s. 14.
25. **Ibid.**, I, s. 58. Sir L. Stephen, **op. cit.**, II, Ch. X, s. 9, suggested that Locke understood the state of nature as a golden age.
26. **Two Treatises**, II, s. 111.
27. **Ibid.**, II, s. 15.
28. **Ibid.**, II, s. 171.
29. **Ibid.**, II, ss. 14, 15.
30. **Ibid.**, II, ss. 101, 102, 103, 108.
31. **Ibid.**, II, s. 103.

NOTES

32. **Ibid.**, II, s. 112.
33. **Ibid.**, II, ss. 105, 106.
34. **Ibid.**, II, ss. 74, 75, 76, 107.
35. **An Essay Concerning Human Understanding**. Ed. A.S. Pringle-Pattison (Oxford, 1964 reprint), Bk. IV, Ch. X.
36. Dunn, **op. cit.**, 97.
37. Cf. Schochet, **op. cit.**, 259ff.
38. Laslett, **Two Treatises**, Introduction, 99.
39. **Ibid.**, 98.
40. **Ibid.**, 95-7.
41. **Ibid.**, 99.
42. Polin, **loc. cit.**, 2-3.
43. **Ibid.**, 1-2.
44. See above, Ch. 6.
45. **Lovelace MS., f. 5.**, fols. 76-8.
46. **Ibid.**, fols. 81-3.
47. Axtell (ed.), **op. cit.**, 395-6.
48. **Loc. cit.**, Bk. IV, Ch. III, s. 18.
49. **Two Treatises**, II, s. 4.
50. **Ibid.**, II, s. 6.
51. **Loc. cit.**, Pt. I, Ch. III, s. 1.
52. **Ibid.**, Greetings to the Reader, v-vi.
53. **Two Treatises**, II, s. 12.
54. Dunn, **op. cit.**, Ch. 14.
55. D. Hume, **A Treatise of Human Nature**. Ed. L.A. Selby-Bigge (Oxford, 1951 reprint), Bk. III, Pt. II, esp. s. viii.
56. See J. Dunn, "Consent in the Political Theory of John Locke," reprinted in G. Schochet (ed.), **Life, Liberty and Property: Essays on Locke's Political Ideas** (Belmont, 1971), 129-61.
57. J. Plamenatz, **Man and Society** (London, 1963 edn.), I, Ch. 6, s. III.
58. Dated 15 July, 1979; also quoted in Dunn, "Consent," in Schochet (ed.), **op. cit.**, 132.
59. **Loc. cit.**, 183.
60. Sidney, **Discourses Concerning Government**, 467; Paxton, **Civil Polity**, 173-5.
61. **Two Treatises**, II, s. 122. Locke's italics.
62. **Ibid.**, II, s. 119.
63. Cf. C. B. Macpherson, "The Social Bearing of Locke's Political Theory," in Schochet (ed.), **op.**

cit., 60-85. On oath-taking see Western, **op. cit.**, 32ff. and D. Ogg, **England in the Reigns of James II and William III** (Oxford, 1969 edn.), 230.

64. **Loc. cit.** Ed. J.C. Meredith (Oxford, 1957 reprint), 192.
65. Locke, **Some Thoughts Concerning Education**, ss. 188, 189.
66. L. Cooper (ed.), **The Rhetoric of Aristotle** (New York, 1932), 1-16.
67. D. Hume, "Of the Original Contract," in C.W. Hendel (ed.), **David Hume's Political Essays** (New York, 1953), 43.
68. See C. Leslie, **The New Association, Part II** (London, 1702-3); and Anon., **An Essay upon Government** (London, 1705), as well as, C. Leslie, **The Rehearsal of Observator** (London, 1705), Nos. 36, 37, 38, 49, 53, 55, 58, 59, 60.
69. Hoadly, **The Original and Institution of Civil Government, discuss'd** (London, 1710), 4-5.
70. **Loc. cit.** (Amsterdam, 1686ff.), Octobre 1690, Avril 1691.
71. **Loc. cit.** (Rotterdam, 1687ff.), Juin 1691.
72. "The politics of Locke," in Yolton (ed.), **op. cit.**, 56-7.
73. See the letters of W. Molyneux to Locke (July/August 1692) in J. Locke, **Works** (London, 1823), Vol. IX, 291-2; and J. Tyrrell to Locke (30th August, 1690), **Lovelace MS. Locke c. 22.**, fol. 119.
74. **Loc. cit.** (ed. T. H.). See R. Ashcraft and M.M. Goldsmith, "Locke, Revolution Principles, and the Formation of Whig Ideology," **Historical Journal**, 26 (1983), 773-800.
75. Atwood, **Loc. cit.**, 100.
76. Bayle, **Lettres de Mr. Bayle** (Amsterdam, 1729), II, 535-6. Letter dated 24 Septembre 1693.
77. Tindal, **An Essay Concerning Obedience to the Supreme Powers, and the Duty of Subjects in all Revolutions** (London, 1694) in **State Tracts**, II, 452.
78. Molyneux, **The Case of Ireland's being bound by Acts of Parliament in England** (Dublin, 1725), 18, 101-4. The first edn. appeared in 1698.

NOTES

79. Clement, **An Answer to Mr. Molyneux** (n. p., 1698), 30-1. For a similar criticism see Cary, **A Vindication of the Parliament of England** (London, 1698), 103.
80. Leslie, **Considerations of Importance to Ireland** (London, 1698), 3-4.
81. J. Somers, **Jura Populi Anglicani** (London, 1701), 30.
82. Dunn, "The politics of Locke", 57.
83. Atwood, **The Fundamental Constitution**, 101-2.
84. **A Collection of the Parliamentary Debates in England, from the Year M, DC, LXVIII. To the PresentTime** (n. p., 1741), II, 249.
85. Atwood, op. cit., Appendix, 4.
86. For a contrary judgment, see Schochet, **Patriarchalism and Political Thought**, 220-4; and J.A.W. Gunn, **Beyond Liberty and Property** (Kingston and Montreal, 1983), 132-36.
87. W. Moyle, **The Whole Works** (London, 1727), 57-8.
88. Loc. cit., Vol. III, No. 100, 31 March, 1705.
89. Ibid., Vol. II, No. 47, 15 September, 1703.
90. Leslie, op. cit., 3. (See fn. 80).
91. Leslie, **The New Association, Part II. A Supplement**, 4.
92. Leslie, **Cassandra. Num. I** (London, 1704), 4.
93. Leslie, **Rehearsal**, No. 36, March 31 - April 7, 1705.
94. Ibid., No. 37, April 7-14, 1705.
95. Ibid., Nos. 38, 55, 56, 58, 59, 60, 61, 66 (1705).
96. A fairly good indication of Locke's popular image can be gained from John Dennis' preface to his **Liberty Asserted** (London, 1704): "the Design of this Tragedy is to make Men in Love with Liberty, by shewing them that nothing can be more according to Nature, and by shewing this not by such forcible and extraordinary Arguments as require more than ordinary Penetration to be understood, for that has been already done so incomparably by Mr. **Lock** that nothing need or can be added to it; but by something so plain that ev'ry Understanding is capable of it, and that is, by the most Tender of Sentiments which Nature has implanted in the Minds of Men, and that is, Love of their Children." The

NOTES

Critical Works of John Dennis, Ed. E.N. Hooker (Baltimore, 1939-43), I, 321. Quoted in H.-J. Müllenbrock, **Whigs kontra Tories** (Heidelberg, 1974), 65. For the above discussion, see my "The Reception of Locke's **Two Treatises of Government** 1690-1705," Political Studies 24 (1976), 184-91. For a contrary position, see J. Nelson, "Unlocking Locke's Legacy: A Comment," Political Studies, 26 (1978), 101-8. For my reply, see "Reception and Influence," Political Studies, 28 (1980), 100-8.

CHAPTER 8

1. Sidney, **Discourses Concerning Government**, 436.
2. Somers, **Jura Populi Anglicani**, 31.
3. Collier, **Dr. Sherlock's Case of Allegiance Considered**, 96.
4. J. Tutchin, **The Observator**, Num. 99, 3 April, 1703.
5. **Loc. cit.**, Preface, n.p.
6. Brady, **The Great Point of Succession Discussed** (London, 1681), 25-6.
7. The group arrested for presenting a petition to the Commons appealing for the voting of supplies to enable the king to assist his allies in the conflict with France. The arrests were made under an Act of 1661 against "tumultuous petitioning."
8. **Loc. cit.**, 31.
9. Anon., **The Proceedings of the Present Parliament Justified by the Opinion of the most Judicious and Learned Hugo Grotius** (n.p., n.d.), in State Tracts, I, 178.
10. **Loc. cit.**, 119, 189. Even though the obligation to obey natural law itself rested on God's command.
11. **Loc. cit.**, 119; and **Two Treatises**, II, s. 135.
12. See Ch. 3 above.
13. **Loc. cit.**, 3.
14. **Loc. cit.** in State Tracts, I, 284.
15. Wilson, **God, the King, and the Countrey**, 10.
16. **Loc. cit.**, 23.
17. Wilson, op. cit., 1.

NOTES

18. H. Finch, Lord Nottingham, **Lord Nottingham's 'Manual of Chancery Practice' and 'Prolegomena of Chancery and Equity'**. Ed. D. Yale (Cambridge, 1965), 189. Nottingham was here quoting from Lord Chief Justice Hobart.
19. Atkyns, **An Enquiry into the Jurisdiction of the Chancery in Causes of Equity** (London, 1695), 17.
20. **Op. cit.**, 200.
21. See, for example, Allix, **Reflections Upon the Opinions of Some Modern Divines, Concerning the Nature of Government in General and that of England in Particular** (London, 1689), 3; Sidney, op. cit., 16-17; Leslie, **The Case of the Regale and of the Pontificat Stated** (London, 1700), 214-8, for a report of several views incorporating this notion.
22. See R.W. Frantz, **The English Travellor and the Movement of Ideas 1660-1732** (Lincoln, Nebraska, 1967 reprint), esp. Ch. V.
23. See, for example, Pufendorf, **An Introduction to the History of the Principal Kingdoms of Europe**, 1ff.
24. See Ch. 10 below.
25. See Wilson, **op. cit.**, 1.
26. Sidney, **op. cit.**, 23-4.
27. Tyrrell, **Bibliotheca Politica. Dialogue the Third**. Advertisement to the Reader.
28. Somers, **A Brief History of the Succession**, 265. Somers was rehearsing divine right arguments in order to refute them.
29. Filmer, **Patriarcha**, Chs. IV-XII.

CHAPTER 9

1. See respectively: G.P. Gooch, **English Democratic Ideas in the Seventeenth Century** (Cambridge, 1927), 282; M. Ashley, **England in the Seventeenth Century 1603-1714** (Harmondsworth, 1961), 152; G. Schochet, **Patriarchalism and Political Thought**, 4; C. Robbins, **The Eighteenth Century Commonwealthman** (Cambridge, Mass., 1959), Ch. 2; B. Haydon, "Algernon Sidney 1623-1683," **Archaeologia Can-**

tiana, LXXVI (1961), 110; G.H. Sabine, **A History of Political Theory** (3rd. edn., London, 1954), 514; G. Van Santvoord, **Life of Algernon Sidney** (New York, 1851), 333; A.C. Ewald, **The Life and Times of the Hon. Algernon Sidney 1622-1683** (London, 1873), II, 330.
2. For the growth of Sidney's reputation, see B. Worden, "The Commonwealth Kidney of Algernon Sidney," **Journal of British Studies**, 24 (1985), 1-40.
3. Axtell (ed.), **The Educational Writings of John Locke**, 400.
4. **The Arraignment, Trail, and Condemnation of Algernon Sidney**, in J. Robertson (ed.), **The Works of Algernon Sidney** (London, 1772), 57-8.
5. **Paper Delivered to the Sheriffs upon the Scaffold on Tower-Hill** (1683), in **Works**, 37-8. Henceforth: **Paper**.
6. **Ibid.**, 38.
7. **Discourses Concerning Government** (1698), in **Works**, 1. Henceforth: **Discourses**.
8. **Ibid.**, 440; **Paper**, 38.
9. **Discourses**, 3.
10. **Ibid.**, 449.
11. **Ibid.**, 14.
12. **Ibid.**, 11; cf. Schochet's discussion of Sidney's patriarchalist arguments, **op. cit.**, esp., 200-1.
13. **Discourses**, 23-4; Atwood, **Jus Anglorum ab Antiquo**, Preface, n.p.; Locke, **Two Treatises**, II, s. 103.
14. **Discourses**, 59-60.
15. **Ibid.**, 75.
16. **Ibid.**, 21, 77.
17. **Ibid.**, 13.
18. **Ibid.**, 389.
19. **Ibid.**, 13-14.
20. **Ibid.**, 256.
21. **Ibid.**, 269.
22. **Ibid.**, 17.
23. **Ibid.**, 29.
24. **Ibid.**, 71.
25. **Ibid.**, 25-6. There was nothing obscure or difficult in contractualist argument, Sidney felt sure. (Cf. J. Dennis, quoted in fn. 96 of Ch. 7). Hence his belief that the opposition were being

NOTES

deliberately perverse and obscurantist.
26. See my "A Note on 'Reason' and 'History'," 499-500.
27. **Discourses**, 79-81.
28. **Ibid.**, 444.
29. **Ibid.**, 318.
30. **Ibid.**, 98. Worden, **op. cit.**, 16, comes to the same conclusion.
31. **Ibid.**, 190.
32. See above, Ch. 8.
33. As discussed for example, in F. Kern, **Kingship and Law in the Middle Ages** (Oxford, 1956), Pt. II.
34. **Discourses**, 366.
35. **Ibid.**, 166.
36. **Ibid.**, 265.
37. **Ibid.**, 151.
38. Z.S. Fink, **The Classical Republicans** (Evanston, 1945).
39. **Discourses**, 462.
40. **Ibid.**, 160.
41. **Ibid.**, 443.
42. **Ibid.**, 86.
43. **Ibid.**, 3.
44. **Ibid.**, 10, 386.
45. **Ibid.**, 481-2.
46. **Ibid.**, 281.
47. **Ibid.**, 405.
48. **Ibid.**, 188.
49. **Ibid.**, 288.
50. **Ibid.**, 347.
51. **Ibid.**, 82-3.
52. **Ibid.**, 346.
53. **Ibid.**, 409-10.
54. **Ibid.**, 327-9.
55. **Ibid.**, 405.
56. **Ibid.**, 342.
57. **Ibid.**, 459.
58. **Ibid.**, 457.
59. **Ibid.**, 479. The argument is Machiavelli's. See Worden, **op. cit.**, 18.
60. **Ibid.**, 187.
61. **Ibid.**, 191.
62. **Ibid.**, 451-2.

63. **Ibid.**, 496.
64. **Ibid.**, 312.
65. **Ibid.**, 403.
66. **Discourses**, 420-1.
67. **Ibid.**, 321.
68. **Ibid.**, 421-2.
69. **Ibid.**, 422.
70. **Ibid.**, 451-2.
71. **Ibid.**, 451-2.
72. **Ibid.**, 436.
73. **Ibid.**, 417.
74. **Ibid.**, 415.
75. **Ibid.**, 361.
76. **Ibid.**, 345.
77. **Ibid.**, 339.
78. **Ibid.**, 91.
79. **Ibid.**, 420.
80. **Ibid.**, 457.
81. **Ibid.**, 491.
82. **Ibid.**, 496.
83. **Ibid.**, 408.
84. **Ibid.**, 463.
85. **Ibid.**, 464.
86. **Ibid.**, 465.
87. **Ibid.**, 501.
88. **Ibid.**, 163-4: "man being a rational creature, nothing can be universally natural to him, that is not rational. But ... liberty without restraint being inconsistent with any government, and the good which man naturally desires for himself, children, and friends, we find no place in the world where the inhabitants do not enter into some kind of society or government to restrain it ... The truth is, man is hereunto led by reason, which is his nature. Every one sees they cannot well live asunder, nor many together, without some rule to which all must submit. This submission is a restraint of liberty, but could be of no effect as to the good intended, unless it were general; nor general, unless it were natural. When all are born to the same freedom, some will not resign that which is their own, unless others do the like. This general consent of all to resign such a part

NOTES

of their liberty, as seems to be for the good of all, is the voice of nature, and the act of men, according to natural reason seeking their own good ... But as a few or many may join together, and frame smaller or greater societies, so those societies may institute such an order or form of government as best pleases themselves; and if the ends of government are obtained, they all equally follow the voice of nature in constituting them."

89. Gooch, **op. cit.**, 285; Greenleaf, **op. cit.**, 189. See, also, Kenyon, **Revolution Principles**, 19 and Dickinson, **Liberty and Property**, 64-5, 72-3.
90. **Discourses**, 34-4, for the full context.
91. **Ibid.**, 403.
92. **Ibid.**, 23-4.
93. **Ibid.**, 169.
94. **Ibid.**, 138.
95. **Ibid.**, 463.
96. **Ibid.**, 144.
97. **Ibid.**, 144-5.
98. **Ibid.**, 406.
99. **Ibid.**, 304-5: "The bestial barbarity in which many nations, especially of Africa, America, and Asia, now live, shews what human nature is, if it be not improved by art and discipline; and if the first errors, committed through ignorance, might not be corrected, all would be obliged to continue in them; and for anything I know, we must return to the religion, manners, and policy, that were found in our country at Caesar's landing. To affirm this is no less than to destroy all that is commendable in the world, and to render the understanding given to men utterly useless. But if it be lawful for us, by the use of that understanding, to build houses, ships, and forts, better than our ancestors, to make such arms as are most fit for our defence, and to invent printing, with an infinite number of other arts beneficial to mankind, why have we not the same right in matters of government, upon which all others do almost absolutely depend?"
100. **Ibid.**, 184.

NOTES

101. This very general notion of history has claimed enormous support since the Renaissance though understandings of precisely what was meant have varied considerably. A very clear, early statement of it is to be found in Pier Paolo Vergerio's discussion of the ideal curriculum in his early fifteenth century treatise **De ingenius moribus et liberalibus studiis adolescentiae**: "We come now to the consideration of the various subjects which ought to be included under the name of liberal studies. Among these I accord the first place to history on the grounds both of its attractiveness and its utility, qualities which appeal equally to the scholar and the statesman ... History, then, gives us the concrete examples of the principles inculcated by philosophy. The one shows what men should do, the other what men have said and done in the past and what practical lessons men may draw therefrom for the present day." Quoted in M. P. Gilmore, **Humanists and Jurists** (Cambridge, Mass., 1963), 20.
102. The point has subsequently been made by Worden, **op. cit.**, 16.

CHAPTER 10

1. For Tyrrell's life see **D.N.B.** and J.W. Gough, "James Tyrrell, Whig Historian and Friend of John Locke," **Historical Journal**, 19 (1976), 581-610.
2. J.W. Gough, **op. cit.**, 584-5.
3. Sir R. Filmer, **Patriarcha**, ed. E. Bohun (London, 1685); Introduction; Hunt, **Mr. Hunt's Postscript**, 81; Locke, **Two Treatises**, I, s. 124.
4. S. Kliger, **op. cit.**, 171-2, somewhat inexplicably thinks the **Bibliotheca Politica** contains a dialogue between F. who "stands for an understanding Freeholder and J. ... a Justice of Peace." Tyrrell, however, expressly states on the first page of the first dialogue that the discussion was between "Mr. FREEMAN, a Gentleman; and Mr. MEANWELL a Civil Lawyer." There is, perhaps, a connec-

tion between Professor Kliger's confusion on this point and the fact that I am unable to locate any of his supposed quotations from Tyrrell in any of the editions of the **Bibliotheca Politica**.

5. Loc. cit., 419; see also the June 1692 issue of **The Gentleman's Journal**.
6. S. Warren, **Law Student** (2nd edn., London, 1845), 260. Quoted in **Allibone's Dictionary of British and American Authors** (London, 1871).
7. See C. Robbins, **The Eighteenth Century Commonwealthman**, 76-8.
8. See the December 1692 issues of both journals.
9. Noted in Motteux, **The Gentleman's Journal** (Nov., 1692).
10. Douglas, **English Scholars 1660-1730** (2nd edn., London, 1951), 134; Atwood, **The Superiority and Direct Dominion**, 13; Toland in J. Milton, **A Complete Collection**, ed. Toland (London, 1698), I, 44; Hearne, **A Vindication of those who take the Oath of Allegiance** (London, 1731), 79-80. Originally published in 1700.
11. Quoted in **Allibone's Dictionary**. See also Gough, "James Tyrrell," 605.
12. Gough, "James Tyrrell," 584.
13. Pocock, **The Ancient Constitution and the Feudal Law**, 188.
14. P. Abrams (ed.), **John Locke: Two Tracts on Government** (Cambridge, 1967), Introduction; and Gough, "James Tyrrell", 582.
15. Quoted by Tyrrell in his **Patriarcha Non Monarcha** (London, 1681), 2. Henceforth cited as **P.N.M.**
16. See, for example, Schochet, **Patriarchalism and Political Thought**, 18-53.
17. **Bibliotheca Politica** (London, 1694), 10. All quotes are from this collected edition, unless otherwise stated.
18. **P.N.M.**, 13; **Bibliotheca Politica**, 59.
19. **P.N.M.**, 78.
20. Ibid., 232.
21. Loc. cit., 265.
22. **P.N.M.**, 14.
23. Ibid., 16-17; 102-3.
24. Loc. cit., xxvii-xxviii.

NOTES

25. Ibid., xxviii.
26. Ibid., 353-4.
27. Ibid., 356-7.
28. Ibid., Epistle Dedicatory.
29. **P.N.M.**, 74.
30. **Bibliotheca Politica**, 12.
31. Ibid., 10-11.
32. **P.N.M.**, 116. The pagination of the 1681 edition is confused with two consecutive sections numbered 97 to 136.
33. Ibid., 91.
34. **Bibliotheca Politica**, 63.
35. **P.N.M.**, 83-4.
36. Ibid., 9-17; 102-114.
37. **Bibliotheca Politica**, 104.
38. **P.N.M.**, 105ff.
39. Ibid., 82-3.
40. Ibid., 84-5.
41. Ibid., 85.
42. **Bibliotheca Politica**, 63.
43. **Bibliotheca Politica**, 778. Cf. Locke, **Two Treatises**, II, S. 107.
44. Loc. cit., 347; cf. Sidney's arguments discussed in Ch. 9 above.
45. Ibid., 348-9.
46. **Bibliotheca Politica**, 946-7.
47. Ibid., 58: "I utterly deny that these Principles I have here laid down, do at all countenance Rebellion, ... since I grant no particular Subject can contradict or resist the Supreme Power of the Lawful Magistrate (however unjustly exercised) by force, without disturbing or at least endangering the quiet and happiness of the whole Community, and perhaps the dissolution of the Government it self, which is against the duty, not only of a good Subject, but also of an honest Moral Man, who will not disturb the public tranquillity for his own private security or revenge."
48. **P.N.M.**, 132-3: "at the first institution of the Government, the first Compact was, That the agreement of the major part should conclude the whole Assembly; and whoever either then would not, or now refuses to be so concluded, is still in the

NOTES

> state of Nature, in respect of all the rest, and is not to be lookt upon as a member of that Commonwealth, but as an Enemy, and a Covenant-breaker." The implied second contract never comes.

49. E.g. **Bibliotheca Politica**, 154.
50. **P.N.M.**, 91-2.
51. **Bibliotheca Politica**, 4.
52. **Ibid.**, 10.
53. **Ibid.**, Preface to Dialogue the Ninth.
54. Dickinson, **Liberty and Property**, 64-5; Kenyon, **Revolution Principles**, 19.
55. **Loc. cit.**, I, Bk. I, 4.
56. **Ibid.**, 6.
57. **Bibliotheca Politica**, 358.
58. **The General History of England**, 1, Bk. III, 121.
59. **Bibliotheca Politica**, 356.
60. **Ibid.**, 357, 352.
61. **The General History of England**, 1, Preface, xlix.
62. **P.N.M.**, 136.
63. **Bibliotheca Politica**, 670.
64. **Ibid.**, 666.
65. Gough, **Fundamental Law in English Constitutional History**, 153-6.
66. **P.N.M.**, 229-30.
67. **Ibid.**, 219-20.
68. **Bibliotheca Politica**, 814.
69. **Ibid.**, 70.
70. **The General History of England**, 1, Epistle Dedicatory, iii.
71. **Ibid.**, iii-iv.
72. **P.N.M.**, Preface to the Reader.
73. **Bibliotheca Politica** (1727 edn.), 739.
74. **Bibliotheca Politica**, 616-7.
75. **Ibid.** (1727 edn.), 731.
76. **Ibid.**, 879.
77. See Chs. 3, 4 and 5 above.
78. See my "Hume's Critique and the 'Original Contract'," 189-201 and Hazard, **The European Mind 1680-1715**, Pt. II, Ch. 3.
79. See Hayek, "The Results of Human Action but not of Human Design," in **Studies in Philosophy, Politics and Economics**, 96-105.

NOTES

CHAPTER 11

1. Gough, **The Social Contract**, Ch. I.
2. Laslett, "Social Contract," in Edwards (ed.), **Encyclopedia of Philosophy.**
3. R.W. Lee, **The Social Compact** (Oxford, 1898), 1.
4. W. Kendall, "Social Contract," in **International Encyclopedia of the Social Sciences** (ed. D.L. Sills).
5. See H. Arendt, **On Revolution** (London, 1963), 10.
6. Gough, **op. cit.**, 126.
7. E.g. Duncan, "Juristic Theories of the British Revolution of 1688," 36; Furley, "The Whig Exclusionists,", 29.
8. For a more detailed critique of this tradition see Höpfl and Thompson, "The History of Contract," 919-44.
9. Gough, **op. cit.**, 135.
10. Stephen, **History of English Thought in the Eighteenth Century**, II, Ch. X, s. 5.
11. Dennert (ed.), **Beza, Brutus, Hotman**, Introduction, XLVff.
12. Vecchio, "Über die verschiedenen Bedeutungen der Lehre vom Gesellschaftsvertrag," in U. Klug (ed.), **Philosophie und Recht**, passim.
13. Pocock, **The Ancient Constitution and the Feudal Law**, 231.
14. Gough, **op. cit.**, 1.
15. Hayek, **Dr. Bernard Mandeville: British Academy Lecture on a Master Mind** (London, 1966), 139.
16. Petty, **Several Essays in Political Arithmetick** (London, 1699), Preface to **Political Arithmetick.**
17. **Loc. cit.**, 48.
18. See Sir G.N. Clark, "The Augustan Age," in F.J. Hearneshaw (ed.), **The Social and Political Ideas of Some English Thinkers of the Augustan Age 1650-1750** (London, 1928), passim. Pope's oft quoted lines: "For Forms of Government let fools contest;/Whate'er is best administer'd is best:" might also serve to indicate a change in the

NOTES

       direction of attention in political enquiry (**An Essay on Man** <London, 1744>, Epistle III, lines 303-4). Pocock, too, in much of his most recent work has shown that the kind of enquiries in which Lockian contractarian answers were of relevance were on the periphery of political discussion in eighteenth century England.

19. Unpublished during our period, that is. They were first published in 1750.
20. **Loc. cit.**, ed. J.P. Kenyon (Harmondsworth, 1969), 193, 198.
21. Hody, **A History of English Councils** (London, 1701), Preface. Such a view of course, might well be licensed by the kind of progress argument we have met in Sidney.

INDEX

Aaron, R.I., 152
Abdication, 20,33
Allix, P., 33, 54, 61, 72
Althusius, J., 130, 141, 144
Ashley, M., 75
Atger, F., 9
Atkyns, Sir R., 35, 54, 61, 192
Atwood, W., 28, 49-54, 59, 61, 63, 74, 75-103, 104, 107, 114, 117, 124, 127, 132, 177, 180, 181, 228, 243, 247, 252, 257

Basnage, H., 131, 176-7
Bastide, C., 105
Bayle, P., 131, 177
Beddard, R.A., 19
Behrens, B., 89, 98-9
Bellarmine, R., 69
Beza, T., 92, 125, 211, 212
Blount, C., 29
Bohun, E., 28, 29, 30, 120, 153, 226
Bradbury, Mr Justice G., 36
Brady, Dr R., 55, 58-63, 65-6, 69-70, 72-3, 75, 76, 77, 79, 82, 120, 127, 188-9
Buchanan, G., 48, 211

Burnet, G., 28, 29, 31, 32, 70-1, 106, 14

Cary, J., 178
Charles II, 98, 104, 106, 109, 238, 240, 249
Cherry, G.L., 19
Church of England, 18, 19, 22, 23, 41, 66, 70-1, 169
Civil Wars, 14, 28, 69, 107-8, 143, 144, 248, 261
Clarendon, 2nd earl of, 3
Clement, S., 178
Cnute, 247-8
Coke, Sir E., 33, 53, 91, 127, 192, 210
Collier, J., 14, 27, 38, 72, 153, 185
Commonwealthman, 107-9
Conquest
  1688 as, 21, 29-30
  Norman, 51, 53, 55-6, 57, 60, 62, 77, 79, 80, 85, 100, 114, 193, 213, 214, 217, 228, 247-8, 252, 261
Consent, 13, 30, 64, 82-6 95, 96, 100, 112-3, 139, 144, 167, 170-3, 200-2, 207-8 220, 234, 236, 237, 239-40, 244-5, 247

INDEX

Constitution
  ancient, 33, 46, 49-56,
    57-67, 77-80, 83,
    97, 109, 114, 116,
    122, 125, 155, 181,
    187, 193, 213, 216,
    224, 227, 242,
    243-8, 258
  fundamental, 52-5, 81-2,
    87-8, 94, 97, 116-7
  Gothic, 56-7, 193, 216,
    244
Contract
  constitutional, 13, 41,
    46, 47, 48-125, 185-
    96, 203, 255
  covenant, 41, 44
  double, 94, 95, 141-3,
    147
  governmental, 9, 34,
    43, 193, 238, 240,
    257
  integrated, 46, 47, 184,
    185-253, 255, 261
  marriage, 40
  mutual, 13, 203, 237
  original, 12, 13, 21,
    33-8, 41, 46, 51
    53, 54, 57, 59-61,
    66-7, 71-2, 93, 97,
    98, 100, 107, 109,
    114, 116, 117, 120,
    121, 122, 127, 159,
    160, 193, 203, 205,
    245, 247, 249, 252
  philosophical, 46, 47,
    126-84, 185-96, 255
  political, 13, 48
  rectoral, 13
  Saxon, 50, 54, 63, 247
  scriptural, 41
  secular, 19

  social, 7-8, 9, 11, 17,
    43, 46, 74, 127,
    130-49, 151, 187,
    189, 193, 236, 238,
    240, 251, 255, 257,
    261
Convention Parliament, the
  12, 20, 32-3, 34-7,
  41, 93, 120, 123,
  147, 250
Cooke, E., 49, 59, 61, 76,
  247
Coronation oaths, 21,
  85-6, 247, 249, 252
Corporation Act (1661), 24
Craig, Sir T., 69
Cromwell, O., 28, 70
Cumberland, R., 227-8, 231

De Beer, E.S., 151
Defoe, D., 54, 190, 260-1
De la Crose, J.C., 131,
  177
Del Vecchio, G., 258
Dennert, J., 258
Desertion, 20
Dissolution, 33, 94, 95,
  172, 180
Divine right, doctrines of
  11, 14, 19, 20, 27,
  28, 38, 39, 64-6,
  69, 71, 90, 96, 97,
  101-2, 109, 122,
  182, 195-6, 255
Dolben, Sir W., 36
Douglas, D.C., 228
Du Haillon, B., 124
Dunn, J., 11, 160, 169,
  177, 179
Du Tillet, J., 124

Edward I, 53, 56

315

INDEX

Engagement Controversy, 14, 30
Exclusion Crisis, 16, 55-6, 58, 59, 64-6, 107, 109, 151, 153, 195, 226, 229, 248
Eyres, Sir G., 28

Ferguson, J., 106
Ferguson, R., 14, 37, 39, 49, 74, 103, 104-25, 247, 257
Fichte, J.G., 142
Filmer, Sir R., 39, 59, 64-6, 94, 96-7, 148, 152-4, 167, 181, 183, 187-8, 196, 197-9, 204, 205, 214, 222, 226, 229-30, 236
Fortescue, J., 78
Franklin, J.H., 11, 75

Gentillet, I., 87
Gierke, O., 9, 257, 261
Goldie, M., 75
Gooch, G.P., 221-2, 225
Gothicism, 38, 50, 55, 56-7, 1, 193, 216, 244
Gough, J.W., 8, 9, 10, 11, 13, 42, 75, 246, 257, 261
Greenleaf, W.H., 19, 75, 222, 225
Grotius, H., 36, 41, 130, 132, 134, 137, 144, 146, 154, 176, 182

Halifax, marquess of, 259-60
Harrington, J., 219
Hayek, F.A., 68, 99, 258-9

Hearne, T., 228
Henry I, 56
Henry III, 56, 77, 80, 82
Henry VII, 33
Hickes, G., 72
Hoadly, B., 176, 181
Hobart, C.J., 91, 192
Hobbes, T., 7, 14, 44, 45, 47, 70, 74, 130, 132, 134, 136, 137, 140, 145, 146, 152, 153, 154, 227-8, 231, 233-4, 239-40, 258
Hobbist, 14, 27
Hody, H., 261
Holt Sir, J., 36, 181
Hooker, R., 24, 35, 59, 61, 82, 126, 147, 157, 174, 176, 197
Horn, A., 53
Hotman, F., 124
Hume, D., 138-9, 170-1, 252-3, 258-9
Hunt, T., 61, 70, 204, 226, 247
Hunton, T., 49

Jacobites, 14, 16, 19, 20, 37, 38, 67, 69, 71, 104, 105, 118-20, 122, 125, 179
James I, 35
James II, 12, 15, 18-22, 25, 27-9, 32, 33, 35, 40, 43-4, 66, 67, 80, 88, 93, 95-6, 104-6, 109, 112, 116-21, 147, 226, 238, 240, 250
Jeffreys, Sir G., 197
Jenkin, R., 27, 40, 73, 125

INDEX

Johnson, S., 27, 28, 32, 73
Jones, J.R., 105-6
Jones, Sir W., 108

Kant, I., 175
Kenyon, J.P., 11, 19
Kettlewell, J., 72
Kingship
  de facto and de jure, 21, 26, 27-8, 32-3, 96, 123
Krieger, L., 133

Laslett, Pl, 75, 151, 161-2, 163, 164, 166, 167, 168-9, 170
Law
  common, 36, 55-6, 91, 107, 119-20, 191-2
  divine, 25, 50, 72, 88
  see also natural
  fundamental, 12, 21, 33, 41, 46, 49-52, 81, 86-90, 95, 97, 99, 114, 116-7, 124-5, 127, 145, 186-7, 215-6, 242-3, 245
  human, 24
  of nations, 25
  natural, 25, 30-2, 41, 46, 50, 72, 74, 76, 80-1, 87-9, 94-5, 96-7, 107, 112, 117, 121, 123, 127, 132-49, 167, 168-9, 170, 180-1, 185-96, 215-6, 217, 227-8, 231-3, 245-6, 256
  positive, 25-6, 31-2, 46, 72, 76, 88, 109, 113, 189, 190-6, 209-13, 249-50, 256

  statute, 24, 25, 207, 116, 119-20
Lawton, C., 14, 40, 125
Le Clerc, J., 176
Lee, Sir T., 34
Leslie, C., 153, 178-9, 182-3
Levinz, Sir C., 36
Leyden, W. von, 133
Lloyd, W., 28, 29
Locke, J., 7, 11-2, 16, 30, 38-9, 41-2, 44 45, 47, 54, 74, 76 94, 96, 97, 126-9 130, 131, 132, 135 138, 147-9, 150-84 190, 197, 200, 202 204, 222, 226-9, 231-2, 239, 240-1, 251, 255, 257, 262
Long, T., 71

Macaulay, T.B., 18, 106
Magna Carta, 62, 114, 120 121, 193, 217-8, 24
Maitland, F.W., 53
Mandeville, B. de, 253, 258-9
Manningham, T., 228
Mariana, J., 69
Maynard, Sir J., 181
Militia Act (1661-2), 24, 31, 91
Milton, J., 49, 154
Minogue, K.R., 133
Mirror of Justices, 53-4, 61, 63, 84-5, 98, 127, 245
Models, historical, 9-11, 15-6
Molina, L., 69
Molyneux, W., 81, 178-9, 182

INDEX

Monmouth, J., duke of, 16, 66, 104, 107
Montagu, Sir E., 36
Montgomery, Sir J., 37
Mornay, P.D.,
  Vindiciae, 48, 84, 92, 112, 124, 211, 212
Motteux, P., 177, 227, 228
Moyle, W., 182
Mullett, C.F., 22

Nevill, Sir E., 36
Neville, H., 76
Nottingham, 2nd earl of, 192

Oldmixon, J., 106
Overall, J., 25, 26

Parsons, R., 48-9, 69-70, 211
Pasquier, E., 124
Passive obedience, 18, 19, 23-4, 25, 70-1, 122, 145-6, 169
Patriarchalism, 19, 38, 39, 64-6, 69, 96, 120, 158-9, 178, 182, 229, 238, 252
  see also Filmer
Paxton, P., 126, 147, 148, 172, 174, 177, 197
Pembroke, earl of, 34
Petty, Sir W., 259
Petyt, W., 36, 49, 59-61, 63, 75, 76, 77, 79, 127, 226, 228-9, 243, 247
Pocock, J.G.A., 9, 55-7, 75, 229, 258

Polin, R., 160-1, 163-4, 168-9, 170
Pollexfen, Sir H., 181
Providence, 19, 21, 26-8
Pufendorf, S., 7, 41-3, 54, 74, 76, 94-5, 96, 97, 126-7, 130, 131-49, 150, 156-7, 161, 164, 166-9, 173-4, 176-7, 179, 180, 183, 197, 199-200, 202, 220, 231-2, 239, 240-1, 252, 254

Rationalism, 22, 67-9, 83-4, 90-2, 98-103, 130-1, 133-49, 158-61, 200-1, 206-8, 216-7, 221-5, 238-40, 251-3, 258-9
Rebellion, 21, 82-3, 89-90, 96, 212-3, 241
Resistance, right of, 9, 23, 32, 38, 40, 66-7, 71, 78, 90, 92-6, 109, 110, 113-4, 121-2, 145-6, 147, 169, 178, 195, 202, 208-9, 213, 236, 238, 240, 241-2, 248-51
Revolution of 1688, 14, 16, 18-47, 58, 71-2, 80, 88, 90, 95, 97, 104, 109, 110, 116-20, 122-3, 143, 151, 170, 174, 226, 238, 240-1, 248
Revolution Settlement, 20, 27, 32, 71, 125
Richard I, 60
Richard II, 228

318

INDEX

Riley, P., 9
Ritchie, D.G., 9
Robbins, C., 75
Rousseau, J.-J., 8, 258

Sacheverell, W., 181
Salus populi, 52, 87-92, 95, 98-9, 103, 120, 122, 144-5, 190, 192, 216, 218
Saxons, 36, 50-4, 216-9, 243-5, 246-7
  see also Constitution: ancient
Schochet, G.J., 19, 75
Seller, A., 23-4, 69
Shaftesbury, 1st earl of, 151
Sharp, J., 28
Sheringham, R., 87
Sherlock, W., 25-9, 30, 32, 83, 146
Sidney, A., 39, 42, 43, 70, 73, 76, 126, 127, 143, 147-8, 153-4, 157, 172, 174, 176-7, 179, 182-3, 185, 194, 196, 197-225, 226, 231, 239, 257
Skinner, Q., 9, 30
Slaughter, T.P., 44-5
Somers, J., lord, 70, 181, 185, 188-9
Spelman, Sir H., 55
Spinoza, B. 130
Stephen, Sir L., 257-8
Stillingfleet, E., 72
Straka, G.M., 19, 27
Swift, J., 259

Tenison, T., 28
Textor, J.W., 132

Tillotson, J., 28
Toland, J., 228
Tooke, A., 131
Tories, 14, 20, 64-5, 67, 69, 71, 79, 105, 119, 122, 179, 227
Turner, F., 34
Tutchin, J., 182, 260
Tyrrell, Sir J., 39, 40-2, 43, 54, 61, 73, 76, 96-7, 127, 143, 147-8, 153-4, 157, 176-9, 181, 187-8, 194, 196, 202, 204, 225, 226-53, 257
Tyrrell, Sir T., 226

Western, C.C., 60
Western, J.R. 19
Whigs, 11, 14, 20, 39, 67, 71-2, 75, 78, 98, 105-7, 118-9, 121-2, 125, 152, 176, 182-3, 206, 227, 255, 257
Whitelocke Sir W., 36
William I, 55-6, 62, 77, 85, 114, 247-8
  see also Conquest: Norman
William III, 14, 21, 33, 37, 42, 71, 105, 107, 112, 118, 119, 122, 125, 155
  and Mary, 21, 25-33, 35, 37, 71, 79, 80, 89, 93, 104, 117, 119, 155, 170, 179, 241, 251
Williamites, 18, 19, 20, 28, 38
Wilson, T., 30, 37, 190-1
Wooley, R., 177, 228

For Product Safety Concerns and Information please contact our EU
representative GPSR@taylorandfrancis.com
Taylor & Francis Verlag GmbH, Kaufingerstraße 24, 80331 München, Germany

www.ingramcontent.com/pod-product-compliance
Lightning Source LLC
Chambersburg PA
CBHW071802300426
44116CB00009B/1176